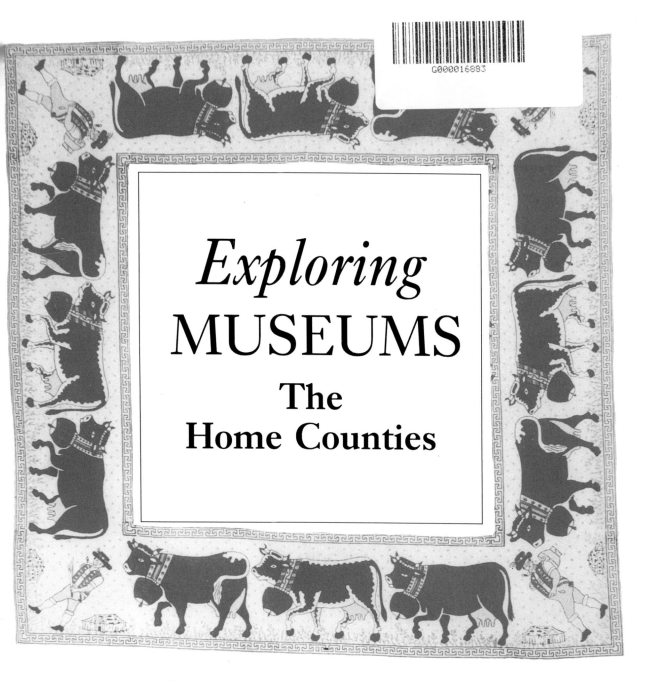

Exploring MUSEUMS

The Home Counties

Half title page

Detail from a Swiss cotton handkerchief, one of the European peasant art exhibits. Haslemere Educational Museum, Haslemere.

Cover

Clockwise: Ceramic model of the 1890s Dunlop Racing Team with their Ariel Quintuplet – Mark Hall Cycle Museum and Gardens, Harlow; Korean mask – Pitt Rivers Museum, Oxford; Detail from a painting of a Dodo *by John Savery, c.1650 – The University Museum, Oxford; Sharnbrook village fire engine – Bedford Museum, Bedford; Tin-glazed earthenware plate with double portrait of King William III and Queen Mary, c.1678–94 – Maidstone Museum and Art Gallery, Maidstone; Detail from the unfinished painting,* Christ Preaching at Cookham Regatta *by Stanley Spencer – Stanley Spencer Gallery, Cookham-on-Thames; Huntley and Palmer 'sundial' buscuit tin – Reading Museum and Art Gallery, Reading; Meissen porcelain Harlequin and Family, c.1740 – The Cecil Higgins Art Gallery and Museum, Bedford.*
Centre: Martinware stoneware bowl, 1887 – Hollytrees Museum, Colchester.

MUSEUMS & GALLERIES COMMISSION

A MUSEUMS ASSOCIATION GUIDE

Exploring MUSEUMS

The Home Counties

Nell Hoare, Karen Hull and Geoffrey Marsh

LONDON: HMSO

© Crown Copyright 1990
First published 1990
ISBN 0 11 290471 8

British Library Cataloguing in
Publication Data
A CIP catalogue record for this book is
available from the British Library

HMSO publications are available from:

HMSO Publications Centre
(Mail and telephone orders only)
PO Box 276, London, SW8 5DT
Telephone orders 071–873 9090
General enquiries 071–873 0011
(queuing system in operation for both numbers)

HMSO Bookshops
49 High Holborn, London, WC1V 6HB 071–873 0011 (Counter service only)
258 Broad Street, Birmingham, B1 2HE 021–643 3740
Southey House, 33 Wine Street, Bristol, BS1 2BQ (0272) 264306
9–21 Princess Street, Manchester, M60 8AS 061–834 7201
80 Chichester Street, Belfast, BT1 4JY (0232) 238451
71 Lothian Road, Edinburgh, EH3 9AZ 031–228 4181

HMSO's Accredited Agents
(see Yellow Pages)

and through good booksellers

CONTENTS

OTHER VOLUMES IN THE SERIES

BUCKINGHAM PALACE

I hope that through this series of Regional Guides "Exploring Museums", you will derive great enjoyment from the fascinating world of museums and galleries; there are some two and a half thousand of them offering an immense variety and range of experiences so there is something for everyone. It is so exciting to feel the sense of exploring new areas in the world of museums and galleries. Make the most of what is on offer.

Sarah

EDITOR'S NOTE

This volume is one of a series of eleven regional guides to museums in the British Isles. The term 'museum' is often applied to a wide variety of collections and buildings: most of the places selected for description in the *Exploring Museums* guides, however, comply as far as possible with the Museums Association's definition of a museum as 'an institution that collects, documents, preserves, exhibits and interprets material evidence and associated information for the public benefit'.

Given the sheer quantity of museums in the British Isles, the guides describe only a selection, concentrating on those places that authors considered most worthy of a visit, either because of the quality of their collections and displays, or because of the interesting or unusual nature of what they have on view. Museums in each area not described in full are listed at the back of the guides, with brief details of their collections; please note that some of these are only open by appointment. The lists include new museums that are scheduled to open in the near future.

The principal aim of this series is to describe, through words and pictures, the types of things that visitors can expect to see and do at various museums. Authors have tried to put themselves in the shoes of a general museum visitor, and present a personal rather than an official view in their descriptions. It should be noted that specific items they describe may not be on show when you visit: most museums now change their displays fairly often, and if you want to see something in particular you should check beforehand with the museum concerned. Most of the illustrations have been selected by the authors, and highlight lesser-known objects and museum activities, as well as exhibits for which particular museums are renowned. Basic information about access and facilities has been kept to a minimum, as opening times or bus routes, for example, are frequently subject to change; please check with museums before visiting for precise details of opening times, holiday closures, admission prices, and how to get there, and for information on special events and activities.

Krystyna Matyjaszkiewicz
Series Editor

The views expressed in this guide are those of the author and not necessarily those of the Museums Association.

FOREWORD

President of the Museums Association
Patrick Boylan
and the Chairman of the Museums & Galleries Commission
Brian Morris

The first volumes of Exploring Museums were published in Museums Year, which marked the centenary of the Museums Association. When the Association's first conference was held in York in 1889, there were already several hundred museums in Britain. Now there are some 2,300, and new ones are opening every month. They vary enormously in size and scope, from the large all-purpose museum to the small collection in a converted house. Many of the smaller museums are less well known than they should be, and it is these particularly that the books in this series seek to highlight.

Never before have museums in general been as popular as they are today. In 1989 alone they received between them something like 100 million visits (which is more than any sport or other leisure activity). They are especially attractive to young people, to the curious of all ages and to the lovers of beautiful, unusual and exciting things. There are indeed museums for every taste and interest, for every day and in every area. We are sure that these books will help many more people to discover the museums of Britain, to learn from them and to enjoy them.

INTRODUCTION

The museums and galleries of the eight counties that surround London offer the adventurous visitor a wealth of fascinating collections, with many pleasant surprises. Everyone will find something to interest and entertain them. There are no golden rules as to what a visitor may expect to discover in any one place, and half the pleasure of exploring the area is coming across some unusual collection: Tunbridge ware at *Tunbridge Wells* is logical enough, but why anthropology at **Saffron Walden** or carriages at **Maidstone**?

The towns and villages of the Home Counties do not yield their treasures as easily as they might. The area has always looked to London for its main provision of museums and galleries, so there are few of the large, prominently-sited municipal museums that you find in most towns in the North or Midlands. Many of the region's museums are the creation of enthusiastic individuals or societies, and this factor accounts for much of their rich variety and special character. The museums are often housed in historic buildings, tucked away in parks or side streets, and although this adds to their charm it requires the visitor to have that extra bit of determination to seek them out. In addition, tourism over the last decade has generally had a lower priority here than elsewhere in Britain. There are relatively few of the new independent-style museums, and sign-posting of many facilities could do with upgrading. But visitors willing to go off the beaten track will be well rewarded. Even the ardent enthusiast may be surprised at some of the lesser-known attractions highlighted by this guide.

The range of museums in south-east England reflects the general economic and social history of the region. The lack of major industries until the present century means that there are few sites dealing with industrial history. The new museum of aviation and motor racing at **Brooklands**, Surrey, will be a notable exception. Most of the area's railway network has remained in use so there are few preserved steam railways. Conversely, the region's strategic significance has resulted in many museums dealing with aspects of Britain's defence. These complement the enormous range of defensive fortifications, dating from the Roman period to the 20th century, that are scattered across the South East. The army garrisons around Aldershot have resulted in a particular concentration of military museums along the Surrey/Hampshire border (for Hampshire see *Exploring Museums: Southern England*), but other strategic locations, such as the Royal dockyard at **Chatham**, have their own history to tell. It is difficult to imagine today how undeveloped much of the area remained until the economic and housing boom of the 1920s and 1930s. Huge areas that are now suburban and commuter-belt housing were countryside within living memory. Up until the Second World

War, county towns such as **Maidstone, Aylesbury** and **Reading** remained the focus of local aspirations. County-based natural history and archaeological societies were often vital in establishing collections that have developed into major museums. In other counties, such as Hertfordshire and Essex, historic towns attracted attention with the result that **St Albans** and **Colchester** now house the major museums in these areas.

The most important concentration of museums is in **Oxford**, where the University has attracted a wealth of important collections and objects since the 17th century. The **Ashmolean**, the first public museum in Britain, is of international standing and houses a stupendous choice of riches ranging from paintings to archaeological discoveries from around the world. Visitors should also explore the smaller collections in the city, which include gems like the **Christ Church Picture Gallery**. Many of the museums originated as, and often still remain, teaching collections. Displays can therefore be rather traditional; but the lack of modern exhibition techniques is often made up for by the sheer range and quality of material on show. Nowhere is this more apparent than in the **Pitt Rivers Museum**, where anthropological material from across the globe is displayed much as it would have been a century ago. But what material! Products of over 100 different cultures vie for attention and remind us of the uniformity that the 20th century has imposed on much of the world.

Many other towns have gained from the generous benefaction of collections, some of national importance such as the Rothschilds' bird collection at **Tring** and the Shuttleworth aircraft collection at **Old Warden**. Such gifts don't just belong to the past: 1989 saw the public opening of Lord Harris's fascinating clock collection at *Belmont House*, near Faversham in Kent, and other schemes are currently being developed. Nor should one forget the steady stream of individual donations, from priceless paintings to commonplace objects, that year by year help to enrich the collections and public enjoyment of every museum. Although the escalating price of many items makes the development of collections increasingly difficult, many museums and individuals continue to make important acquisitions before wider interest has developed and prices rise. In the magnificent setting of **Finchcocks House**, Kent, the Burnetts display their remarkable collection of early pianos, most in working condition. Assembled in less than thirty years through intuition and enthusiasm, it would be virtually impossible to create a similar collection today. Every visitor to Finchcocks, as with so many other museums in the area, is grateful for the foresight of the founders. Elsewhere, there is gratitude also for the dedication of succeeding guardians who have ensured the continued survival of particular collections, such as the remarkable one of General Powell-Cotton at **Birchington**, which offers a unique insight into the world of the Edwardian big game hunter and explorer. Numerous similar collections have been destroyed over the years or broken up by sale through auction houses.

Country estates proliferated in the counties surrounding London, ranging from Royal palaces to stately homes and small rural villas. Many have been destroyed or converted to institutional use, but a large number are now open to the public, in the care of the National Trust or private owners. Furnished with collections of paintings and decorative art, they provide a superb complement to many museums. Those included in this guide contain museums in their own right.

The heritage of the Home Counties is a rich one and we hope that this guide will encourage many more to discover it. Even if you feel drawn to the 'safe bets' in London, why not combine a trip to the capital with a visit to a related museum beyond (transport allowing!): the National Maritime Museum, Greenwich, could be twinned with a tour of **The Historic Dockyard, Chatham**; or, if the RAF Museum at Hendon is more to your taste, why not combine it with a trip to the Battle of Britain display at *Hawkinge* airfield, near Folkestone? And if you're inspired by Lord Leighton's studio and town house in Kensington, the rural retreat of his contemporary G. F. Watts at **Compton**, Surrey, will provide a fascinating contrast.

The museum world is rarely static and there is a continuous stream of new ideas, only a few of which will probably reach fruition. At Sutton Place, near Guildford, plans are underway to create an international art study centre, while at Cressing Temple, Essex County Council have recently purchased two medieval barns to house a study centre and museum about the region's architectural heritage. Elsewhere important collections remain hidden to all but the most determined enthusiast. One can only hope that collections such as the extraordinary group of Victorian paintings at *Royal Holloway and Bedford New College, Egham*, will be listed as fully open to the public in subsequent editions of this guide.

Nell Hoare, Karen Hull and Geoffrey Marsh

ACKNOWLEDGEMENTS

The Museums Association is grateful to the museums described for generously lending photographs and agreeing to their reproduction herein.

Further acknowledgement is due to the following:

pp. 5–6 and fire engine on Cover (Bedford Museum), photos © North Bedfordshire Borough Council; p. 13 and p. 14, left (Chalfont St Giles), photos by R.W.J. Mallows, Watford; pp. 15–16 (Historic Dockyard, Chatham), photos by Barry Duffield; p. 35 (Eton), photo Courtauld Institute of Art; p. 38 (Goudhurst), photo by Andrew Sydenham; p. 40 (Guildford Museum), postage stamp case reproduced courtesy of Guildford Muniment Room; pp. 42–43 and cyclists group on Cover (Harlow), photos by G.W.C. Taylor, Harlow; p. 45 (Haslemere), detail of schoolchildren taken from a photograph by Neil Hardy, Farnham Castle Newspapers Ltd; pp. 48–50 (Hertford), photos © Hertfordshire Archaeological Trust; pp. 58–59 and plate on Cover (Maidstone Museum and Art Gallery), photos by Ronald White, Maidstone; p. 61 (Tyrwhitt-Drake), detail of museum exterior from a photograph by Sloman and Pettit, Maidstone; p. 62 (Newbury), tin-glazed charger on loan to Newbury District Museum from Mr N. Murray-Bogg; pp. 63–65 (The Shuttleworth Collection), photos © Air Portraits; pp. 71–73 and Colour plate 4 (Christ Church), photos reproduced courtesy of the Governing Body, Christ Church, Oxford; p. 90 (Slough), photo of Ellimans Embrocation advertisement by Mr. Stanley; pp. 94–96 (Tring), photos supplied by and reproduced courtesy of The Natural History Museum.

Key to Symbols Used

F Free admission

£ Admission charge

V Voluntary donation requested

▣ Restaurant/cafeteria on premises

P Car Park on premises

♿ Good access and facilities for disabled

♿ Difficult/limited access and facilities for disabled and infirm

> **W** Unstepped access via main or side door, wheelchair spaces, and adapted toilet
>
> **T** Adapted toilet
>
> **X** Flat or one-step access
>
> **A** Access with 2–5 steps, or split level exhibition space
>
> **S** Many unavoidable steps and/ or other obstacles for wheelchair users and the infirm
>
> **G** Provision made for guide dogs
>
> (based on disabled access code devised by ARTSLINE (01 388 2227), the free telephone information service on the arts in Greater London for people with disabilities)

♔ Group visits

♛ School group visits

◎ Workshops/holiday events/ guided tours/talks – 'phone for details

Museums shown in **bold** type in the text are described in full elsewhere in the volume; those shown in *italic* type are briefly described in the list of museums and collections at the back.

AYLESBURY

Buckinghamshire County Museum

Church Street, Aylesbury, Buckinghamshire HP20 2QP (0296) 88849 (address for enquiries: *Buckinghamshire County Museum Service, Tring Road, Halton, Aylesbury, Buckinghamshire HP22 5PJ (0296) 696012)* Undergoing major refurbishment until 1992–93; only 2 galleries (accessible from churchyard) open – closed Sundays, **F** ♿ 🏛 & ♿ must book (limited access to collections during closure).

Works outing charabanc, 1921

Buckinghamshire County Museum has fine collections that include paintings, drawings, ceramics, textiles, costume, and items relating to the geology, archaeology and natural history of the whole county. Most of these collections are in store at present as the museum building, parts of which date back to the 15th century, is undergoing complete renovation. Two large galleries remain open: the Special Exhibitions Gallery, where exhibitions that draw on the museum collections are included in the varied programme of temporary exhibitions, and the Aylesbury Gallery, which tells the story of the town.

Appropriately enough, the first things the visitor encounters in the Aylesbury Gallery are three Aylesbury ducks. These were first mentioned as a distinct breed in 1750, and have pure white plumage, orange legs and feet, and a pinkish beak. Aylesbury ducks were reared by cottagers and there were also breeding stocks on farms around Aylesbury. The earliest written reference to the town is in 571, when Cuthwulf fought against the Britons at Biedcanford and captured four towns that included Aylesbury. From 971–1204 Aylesbury was a Royal Manor, and one of only fifty mints in the country was established here in 978. Centuries later, during the Civil War, Aylesbury became a Parliamentary gar-

rison. The Royalists were defeated here and this was marked by the publication of a pamphlet describing the defeat, entitled 'Good and joyful newes out of Buckinghamshire . . .'.

John Wilkes (1725–97), MP for the town in 1757 and 1761, and High Sheriff of the County in 1754, was brought up and lived in Aylesbury. He was a popular hero as a defender of liberty, having been expelled from the House of Commons for publishing a

denouncement of a speech from the throne, accusing Lord Bute's government of a return to despotic rule.

One of the first industries to be established in Aylesbury was a silk mill in 1830. The mill was in part of a workhouse on the Oxford Road, and the museum has examples of silk produced there. It began with forty hand looms and eventually boasted an additional seventy steam looms. The production of milk products became im-

Working model of a manual fire engine

Roof finial from the Railway Hotel, 1898

BANBURY

Banbury Museum

*8 Horsefair, Banbury, Oxfordshire
OX16 0AA   (0295) 259855*
Closed Sundays, and on Mondays
October to March. 🅵 ▣
♿ W: entrance from rear of
museum.

This museum overlooks Banbury
Cross and tells the story of Banburyshire, an area about twenty miles across
that appears on no map but has a
distinct character of its own. Part of the
museum building used to be the
boardroom of the Poor Law Guardians. Downstairs is the shop, coffee
bar and temporary exhibition gallery
(new exhibitions are shown every two
months). At the time of writing there is
also the reconstructed studio of photographer G.A. Beales, as it was around
1905–10. Some 1500 glass plate negatives from Beales' survive in the
museum's collections and may be
viewed on microfiche. By 1915 the
studio had new owners and was renamed Blinkhorns; you can still see

Reconstructed photographer's studio

Blinkhorns photographic shop a few
doors from the museum.

Upstairs is a reconstruction of Rath-
bone's butchers shop, which was
founded in 1856 and in 1879, appro-

portant in the town, and there are
examples of packaging from the
Dominion Dairy Co. Ltd and the
Anglo-Swiss Condensed Milk Co. (later called Nestlé). Another local firm
featured in the displays is Hazell, Wat-
son and Viney, a printing and publishing company. The firm employed
many local people and had an important social role to play in the town, with
its own fire brigade, band, and many
amenities for its employees. (Unre-
lated, but among exhibits elsewhere in
the gallery, is a delightful working
model of a manual fire engine.)

Aylesbury's markets are first recorded in the Domesday survey in
1086. These early markets were probably held in the church precinct: the
Market Square was not developed until
the Middle Ages. The charter of 1554
confirmed Aylesbury's right to hold a
weekly market for horses, pigs, poultry
and grain, and two annual fairs. Displays show the development of the
market and of the town's shops. There
were several local banks based in the
town, the earliest established in 1795.
As a major market centre, Aylesbury
also had many inns and taverns: in
1876, we learn, the town had sixty
pubs, twenty-eight beerhouses and one
off-licence. In common with many
towns Aylesbury also had several
breweries in the 19th century, of which
the Aylesbury Brewery Company became the most important. (NH)

A fantasy painting of Banbury Cross by J. Hutchins, c. 1850

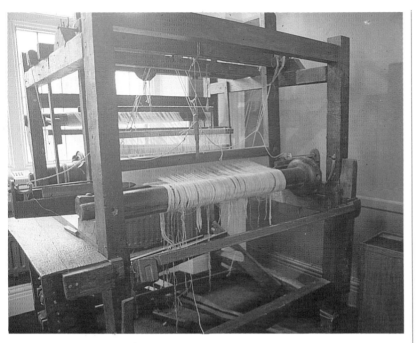

Shutford plush loom

BASILDON

National Motor Boat Museum

Wat Tyler Country Park, Wat Tyler Way, Pitsea, Basildon, Essex SS16 4UW   (0268) 550077
Open daily. 🇫 🇪 🇵 ♿

The National Motor Boat Museum is one of a number of attractions within the Wat Tyler Country Park – 120 acres of marshland just outside Basildon. It is the first museum in the world devoted to the specific theme of motorboats, and traces their history and evolution in the fields of leisure, water sports, and as work boats and military craft. Exhibits include a range of boats dating from 1909 to the present day, and various engines and accessories; there are also videos of boats in action.

The museum itself, opened in 1986, is housed in a huge converted Ministry of Defence warehouse, now enlivened by an impressive mural painted on the exterior. The concrete roads, flat horizons and MOD building may seem a bit bleak, but this only serves to highlight the startling brightness, sleek lines and gleaming paintwork of the exhibits inside. On entering the museum, the visitor is faced with a sea of vessels and raised walkways, which give a sense of great space. Exhibits are arranged in chronological sequence to show how hull design evolved.

The first exhibit, 'Defender II', a 21ft racing motorboat of 1909, is the museum's earliest vessel. The boats that follow illustrate the transformation of hull design from 'displacement craft' – those that sit in the water – to 'hydroplanes', which skim across the surface of the water. The museum has several racing hydroplanes from the 1920s and a rare example of a Ventnor 'three-pointer' from the 1930s. The Ventnor was of pivotal importance in hull design as it replaced the traditional 'stepped' hull with two lateral outer ridges or 'sponsons'; with the 'transom' at the rear, the boat thus made contact with the water at three points, hence

priately enough, moved to Butchers Row. Cattle are important in the life and economy of Banburyshire: this is one of the most fertile regions in Europe, and the areas of heavier clay pasture are where dairy farming is concentrated.

Banbury began as a Saxon Manor. In the 12th century the Bishop of Lincoln built a castle here, and laid out the market place between the church and river. Banbury was at the crossroads of ancient routes between southern England and the Midlands, so the Bishop sited the market place at Banbury to ensure that he could reap the maximum reward in tolls and rents!

Banbury has been a major centre of cloth making since the Middle Ages. By 1700 some mills specialised in particular cloths, such as linen and silk. The main specialism, though, was plush – the velvety material that was formerly used to cover cinema and theatre seats; red plush was a particular favourite of the Victorians. At its peak Banbury made 70% of all English plush, and the museum has an original

plush loom. Shutford West was the last of Banbury's mills to close, in 1948.

Another flourishing local industry was brewing. In the 19th century the canal and railway helped to widen the market for local brews, but today only one, Hook Norton, is still made in Banbury.

The museum offers one of the best views of the Banbury Cross, and recalls the famous rhyme: 'Ride a cock-horse to Banbury Cross/To see a fine lady on a white horse/With rings on her fingers and bells on her toes/She will have music wherever she goes.' Rather disappointingly, the rhyme has nothing to do with the Banbury Cross you see. Although the origin of the rhyme is unknown, it predates the present cross, which was erected in 1859 to commemorate the wedding (in 1858) of Queen Victoria's eldest daughter to Prince Frederick of Prussia. Medieval Banbury had three crosses, the High or Bread Cross being the most imposing. The puritans of the 16th century disliked religious images, so by 1621 they had destroyed all three. (NH)

'Defender II', the museum's oldest boat, pictured 1909 – the year she was built

the name 'three-pointer'. The early Ventnor on display was once owned by Donald Campbell. A post-war Ventnor, 'Rooster', continues the evolution. Built of aluminium, this boat is a 'three-point prop-rider' – the third point on which the boat glides is the propeller shaft not the transom. Due to the boat's design, 'Rooster' achieved speeds of up to 90 mph. In 1982 the world water speed record for a diesel engined boat was captured by another three-point prop-rider, 'Miss Britain IV'. Visitors to the museum can see both the boat and a video showing it breaking the record on Coniston Water. A large boot-shaped object next to 'Miss Britain IV' is a prototype safety cell, designed by Chris Hodges, to protect the drivers of these awesomely fast power boats.

The museum's Hall of Speed also contains two offshore powerboats, 'Surfury' and 'Apache'. The huge 'Surfury' won the Cowes to Torquay Race in 1967, while 'Apache's' racing career lasted a full ten years and included victory in the world's longest ever powerboat race, the London to Monte Carlo held in 1972.

An upper walkway gives an overview of the displays and allows visitors to see down into the boats. The museum also has a range of historic outboard and inboard engines on display. Even if you're not mechanically minded, these objects are amazing to look at. A beautiful copper and green Ailsa Craig Engine, made in 1902, is the oldest in the museum's collection.

The walkway leads through to the second part of the museum, where workboats and naval craft are arranged in a quayside setting. They include a 1930s Thames pleasure launch and the Captain's barge from the last HMS 'Ark Royal'. Also in this part of the museum is the conservation workshop, where visitors can watch boats and engines being restored. By arrangement, visitors may consult the museum's extensive reference library, which contains books, magazines, plans, photographs and other archival material relating to motorboats over the past century.

Another museum currently under development in Wat Tyler Country Park is the *Basildon Heritage Centre*, the first phase of which is scheduled to open in 1991. When completed this museum will contain rural life displays illustrating domestic and working life in and around Basildon since the time of Wat Tyler, who led the Peasants' Revolt in 1381 (the Park is dedicated to the people of Essex and Kent who took part in the Revolt). The museum's indoor displays will be complemented by a range of historic buildings, rescued from around the county, which will be re-erected nearby. Amongst the buildings already relocated to the Park are 17th century timber-framed cottages from Stansted and Raleigh, and a 16th century barn from Billericay. Reflecting Basildon's history as a New Town, the museum will also feature displays relating to the second half of the 20th century. And there will be a study room where local history researchers will be able to consult local records, photographs and other archival material. (KH)

Cosworth-Hodges Tunnel Hull racing catamaran, which set British world records in 1978

BEDFORD

Bedford Museum

Castle Lane, Bedford, Bedfordshire
MK40 3XD   (0234) 53323
Closed Sunday mornings and all
day Monday (except Bank Holiday
Monday afternoons). **F**
& **W**: lift to first floor by
arrangement.
⋔ & **⋔** book in advance.

Bedford Museum is the museum for
North Bedfordshire. Its collections
illustrate the geology, archaeology,
natural and social history of the region.
The museum (housed in what was
once the Higgins Castle Brewery) is
entered through gracious wrought iron
gates and across a paved courtyard.
The building served as a clothing factory and GPO sorting office before its
conversion to a museum began in
1979. Opened in 1981, Bedford
Museum is the fruit of a collection
begun in 1884 when Charles Prichard,
a local solicitor, gave his collection of
fossils and minerals to his old school,
the Bedford Modern School. The
Borough took over responsibility for
the growing museum collection in
1959. These origins are illustrated in a
display about the old School Museum
on the first floor: a wonderful cabinet
of curiosities ranging from beetles,
shells, parasol handles and the head of
Old Billy (the longest-lived horse,
which made an entry in the *Guinness
Book of Records*) to a collection of
ethnographic and Egyptian items
brought back by globe-trotting Old
Boys of the Bedford Modern School.
The building's conversion combines
old and new materials and styles extremely well, and this is echoed in the
museum's displays and layout.

On entering the museum the visitor
first sees a splendid Adams car made in
Bedford in 1907. The sales and enquiry desk is here, and a temporary
exhibition area where various exhibitions are shown throughout the year.
The museum has strong links with
local potters, who have not only exhi-

Farmland birds and mammals in the natural history gallery

Iron Age bucket handle from Felmersham

bited here but also sell items based on
the museum's collections at the sales
desk.

The Rural Life section takes the
visitor through the farming year of
preparing soil, planting, sowing and
reaping. These thematic displays are
complemented by room settings, which
add a social dimension to the agricultural tools and methods. A labour-

er's cottage with its all-purpose living
room, a dairy and a farmhouse kitchen
are sensitively re-created, with clear
explanatory boards and line drawings
supplementing the room settings
themselves. Just beyond this gallery is a
remarkable display on the Warden
Abbey medieval tile pavement. This is
made of 'picture tiles' that are like
giant jigsaw pieces and were excavated
from the floor of a Cistercian Abbey
near the village of Old Warden.

In the Geology and Archaeology
Gallery, on the first floor, the showcases are constructed of heavy, dark
wood echoing the exposed beams in
the ceiling above. Specimens are highlighted on glass shelves supported by
columns of white bricks. There is a
wealth of local material, and the geological displays are linked to the
archaeology of the region through the
Ice Age. The Roman bronze bowls
from Sandy are particularly eye-
catching, as is the Iron Age bronze
bucket handle (from Felmersham) decorated with two cow's heads, one of
which is licking its lips! Another fine
piece is the Old Warden Iron-Age
mirror. A Romanesque corbel head
from St Mary's Church in Bedford is

Dolls and large toys in the social history gallery

and Firefighting are illustrated with fine specimens and clear graphics. Intermittent views onto the central courtyard accentuate the displays. Lacemaking is picked up in a small cameo setting of equipment, which cleverly incorporates watercolour paintings that show how the various tools are used. An impressive display of lace bobbins is classified by the different types of decoration and of basic structure for which the East Midlands is famous. In contrast to these is the recently conserved Sharnbrook Village Fire Engine (ill. on cover), the largest and possibly the most colourful object on show. A display about the Bedfordshire Yeomanry is topped with a splendid black and white helmet plume.

The market town of Bedford, relying heavily on the river as its lifeline, changed with the coming of the old Midland Railway and the growth of industry. Straw-plait and agricultural machinery are amongst the exhibits in this section of the gallery. The Harpur Trust provided Bedford with comparatively cheap public schools, and this encouraged a particular type of resident to the town, as well as the trades to serve them. Bedford still retains an air of measured gentility that might more easily be associated with colonial Delhi than a light industrial town just off the M1. There is a section devoted to this aspect of the town as the displays move on to Family Life. A Victorian setting of musical instruments including a zither, cylinder musical box and an Edison phonograph is very atmospheric, as is the case of optical illusions. These examples of persistent vision, zoetropes and thaumatropes, were the forerunners of cinematography. An appealing display of dolls, toys and children's games for education and enjoyment end this family section, with ladies' accessories and gentlemen's smoking materials representing adult pleasures!

There is an enormous amount to see in this well-displayed and lively museum. It is informative and educational, and gives the visitor a sense of wonder in the objects that are shown. The building itself adds to the museum's fascination. (KH)

an example of the Anglo-Saxon style that lasted into the Norman period. The objects in the gallery and the way in which they are displayed cannot fail to catch the imagination. At one end of the room, in the mineral display, is a beautiful model of the Taj Mahal in soapstone, while one of the uses that gold has been put to is shown nearby in a full complement of porcelain teeth set in a gold plate.

The Natural History gallery is housed in the link block between the two wings of the original building.

Birds and mammals of the region are displayed in attractive habitat settings, which appeal very much to younger visitors. Particular habitats such as Chalk Downland – important for insect and plant life – are described on large colourful graphic panels.

In the Social History gallery on the first floor the emphasis is on the development of the local community as the town of Bedford expanded, particularly between 1870 and 1903. Community functions like Weights and Measures, Law and Order, Health Care

The Cecil Higgins Art Gallery and Museum

Castle Close, Bedford, Bedfordshire
MK40 3NY (0234) 211222
Closed mornings and all day
Monday. **F** **&W**
♿ preferably book in advance.
♿ book in advance: contact
Education Officer. ☺

The Cecil Higgins Art Gallery and
Museum combines a gallery of fine and
decorative art with a furnished Victorian
mansion, which was the Higgins family
home. The displays are based on the
collections made by Cecil Higgins, the
youngest son of a wealthy brewer, born
in Castle Close in 1856. When he died
in 1941 he bequeathed his collection to
Trustees, who still run the museum in
partnership with North Bedfordshire
Borough Council, who now own the
building. Cecil Higgins is described as
a tall, imposing man, autocratic, highly
competent, and a shrewd judge of both
men and works of art; above all, he
loved beautiful objects. The collection,
the house and the provisions made in
his will, ensuring the direction and
standards maintained in the gallery,
make this place very special. It is a
glorious array of beautiful objects,
some in traditional gallery settings,
others within rooms in the mansion.
There is an emphasis in the displays on
combining objects and pictures, making links between different periods,
materials or subjects. The richness of
the collections and the standards of
display are difficult to convey: allow a
whole day to enjoy the full impact,
especially given the setting in quiet
gardens. And there's the **Bedford
Museum** next door, which complements the gallery so well.

On entering the museum you will
find the sales point, where the full-
colour guide is well worth buying. The
entrance hall is in fact a link building
between the original brick-built brewery, which forms the left-hand wall,
and the brewer's mansion itself. The
hall is dominated by a giant Meissen
vase, designed by Gottfried Semper
around 1849, and a portrait by Glyn

Edvard Munch, Madonna – Eva Mudocci, *lithograph*

Philpot of Cecil Higgins, painted when
he was 79.

The watercolour gallery displays a
selection of about 100 drawings, watercolours and prints from the museum's
outstanding holdings. The collection of
British watercolours and drawings
ranges from 18th and 19th century
landscapes by artists such as Sandby,
Girtin and Turner to modern works by
Paul Nash, Henry Moore and Graham
Sutherland. Rossetti's Pre-Raphaelite

'Paolo and Francesca' (1862) and
Oscar Kokoschka's 'Lobster' (1946)
are just two examples that illustrate the
breadth and variety of this world-
famous collection. As a complement to
the British watercolours and drawings,
the print collection has works mainly
by foreign artists; there are examples
by Durer, Rembrandt and Goya, but
most of the prints date from Daumier,
Millet and the French Impressionists
onwards and include works by Degas,

Matisse, Picasso and Dali. Displays in the watercolour gallery are changed every six months or so, and the selection is based on a different theme each time – 'Faces and Fashion', 'Animals in Art' and 'Travel through Time' were three recent themes.

This gallery leads the visitor through into the Victorian mansion, which is a complete contrast to the ordered layout and low light levels of the watercolour gallery. The room settings are not reconstructions but have been arranged to give an impression of the home of a provincial, late-Victorian family like the Higgins family, who lived in the house from 1846 to 1910. Each room has an inventory of items on display, and the 'picture guides' that are also available give a sketch of each room with more detailed information on the main items of interest.

The rich panelling in the first area actually comes from the dining room of a Baring Brothers bank. Here it reflects the heavy atmosphere of the whole house and sets off beautifully a gilt-bronze clock of about 1770 designed by Paul Barbot. The clock is double-faced, and the jewels set on the central rosette revolve by clockwork. The Drawing Room embodies the domestic virtues so admired by the

Chelsea porcelain tureen of hen and her chicks, 1752–56

Dressing table by William Burges, c. 1867

Victorians; elaborate furnishings exude the prosperity and confidence of the Victorian gentry. Severe sofas are set beside the fireplace, and this area is well cluttered with porcelain, oil paintings and pole or fire screens. The long, gracious windows that look out into the gardens cast shadows across the Victorian toys scattered across the floor.

The creation of atmosphere is unmistakeable, especially in the hallway of the mansion. There are scarves and walking sticks on a bentwood stand, calling cards wait in a tray on the hall table, wooden bowls lie on the floor, as if brought in from a game, and the hall clock gently ticks away the minutes. Fresh flowers complete the sensitive recreation of respectability. If you have the good fortune to visit on a day when a school group is in the museum, you might even come across pupils wearing reproduction Victorian clothes.

The furniture and furnishings in the White Room convey elegance and quiet. As in all the rooms, the furniture here is quite beautiful. It would be impossible to list every eye-catching piece in the house, although in the Library the reading chair and the carved mahogany cabinet, which was designed by Alfred Waterhouse in

about 1872, are especially appealing. Most of the furniture in the Library was designed by architects. Before the Library, though, there is the Dining Room, with its rich red wallpapers, hangings and hunting pictures. The walnut dining chairs have original seat covers, one with the initials of the lady who embroidered it, 'EW', and the date '1722'.

The natural route at this point takes the visitor upstairs to large windows looking out onto the gardens, a break from the overwhelming interiors. A beautiful bronze by Henry Moore, 'Helmet Head', makes a stark contrast in its simplicity. The lace collections of the Cecil Higgins, which draw enthusiasts from far and wide, are located on the first floor. Thomas Lester and his sons revived the declining local industry during the 1850s, with a new type of lace that became known as Bedfordshire Maltese lace. It was easier and quicker to make, and incorporated exotic naturalistic designs. There is a racking system of examples for study, with the main displays in another room. Don't miss the dolls' house, which shows parts of a Victorian home that the Cecil Higgins Mansion doesn't include: the kitchen, scullery, servants' hall and a bathroom upstairs. The dolls' house is based on a local home, Oakley House.

The glass gallery is displayed chronologically but emphasises the techniques used in glass production. Colouring, gilding, enamelling, different types of engraving, or glass that imitates porcelain are shown by example. The collection's greatest rarities are two pieces of glass – a jug and a dish – made about 1676–77 by George Ravenscroft, the father of English glassmaking. Very few Ravenscroft pieces survive. These two are suffering from 'crisselling', a form of deterioration in which moisture rising to the surface of the glass gives a crazy-paving effect. This chemical reaction is stabilised by keeping the glass in a strictly controlled environment, hence the special case and measuring equipment. The glass collection has a particularly good selection of late 17th and early 18th century English glass. The later Jacobite and anti-Jacobite glass is also fascinating, while the Art Nouveau extends technical skills beyond belief.

Turning a corner from the glass there is a ceramic early-17th century watering-can, which brings the imagination down to earth! The ceramic collection, like the glass, is dealt with

Ravenscroft jug, c. 1676–77

chronologically but arranged in themes. There is even a life-size ceramic swan and ducks (manufactured at Chelsea, 1752–56), displayed over a fishpond. But nothing quite prepares you for the Burges Room, the finest collection of furniture and furnishings by the architect William Burges (1827–81) outside London. These items come from the Handley Read collection, a large part of which was purchased by the museum in the 1970s. Burges's Gothic-Revival pieces were mainly for his own use or part of grand interior-design commissions. Although most are simple in design, they are richly decorated with painted panels and other ornamentation. The Burges Room is dimly lit, and simply magic.

Arriving back in the original mansion, the Guest Bedroom uses the storyline of an unexpected guest arriving from London, and is arranged as if the maid has just begun to unpack – a splendid excuse to show clothes and accessories from the costume collection. The Nursery, too, is a delight and exudes an appropriate 'well-scrubbed' atmosphere, despite the clutter.

The Cecil Higgins Art Gallery and Museum is definitely not to be missed. Every part of the collection is a treasury of riches, and the standards and sensitivity of both the collections and displays are exceptional. (KH)

Lace cap by Thomas Lester, 1860–80

BIRCHINGTON

The Powell-Cotton Museum and Quex House

Quex Park, Birchington, Kent CT7 0BH   (0843) 42168
Open April 1st or Easter (whichever earlier) to end of September, Wednesday, Thursday and Sunday afternoons, plus Spring and Summer bank holidays, and Friday afternoons in August; Powell-Cotton Museum only open on Sunday afternoons in winter (Quex House closed during winter). ▣
▣ during summer season; ample space for picnicking. ▣
▣ but first floor of Quex House can only be reached by stairs; no **T**.
▥ & ▮ preferably book in advance: booking forms available from the Curator as well as information sheets for teachers; reduced admission for pre-booked parties; subject to availability of staff, the museum can be opened during mornings, evenings and weekends.

The Powell-Cotton Museum offers without doubt one of the most fascinating experiences for the museum visitor in Kent. Here are displayed the collections built up over many years by Major Percy Powell-Cotton (1866–1940), which provide a rare insight into the attitudes and interests of an Edwardian gentleman at the height of the British Empire. Powell-Cotton was in turn a soldier, big-game hunter, explorer, zoologist, ethnographer, and eventually pioneer conservationist. He organised and led numerous expeditions to Africa, including the Congo, Angola, Ethiopia and Tunisia, as well as travelling extensively in the Far East. Everywhere he went he found material for his collections of natural history, ethnography and decorative art.

While many similar collections have been sold or dispersed, Powell-Cotton had the foresight and concern for public access to turn his life's work into a museum, to ensure its long-term preservation. In 1894 he inherited Quex House and soon established a display pavilion in the garden. Over the years this has grown into an attractive range of eight galleries adjoining the main house. The result is a permanent memorial not only to Powell-Cotton's imagination but also to the constant care that is required to ensure the preservation of collections for the enjoyment of future generations.

A visit begins, appropriately, with a small display about the Major's expeditions. This includes the clothes he was wearing when mauled by a lion in Central Africa in 1906. One can only wish that this section will be expanded in future years to tell more about the Major's varied activities, latterly shared with his enterprising wife. In 1905 she travelled to Nairobi for their wedding and their honeymoon was spent on an expedition through Uganda and the Congo!

The first main galleries display the Major's animal collections, ranging

Part of the African plains diorama

Portrait of Major Powell-Cotton, 1908

from small monkeys to an African elephant over eleven feet high. The animals are grouped against painted backdrops (the largest seventy-five feet long) and for the first-time visitor, whether adult or child, these displays are undoubtedly the most impressive aspect of the museum. Powell-Cotton, although a hunter and superb marksman, was greatly concerned about the future of African and Asian wildlife and wanted to educate a largely ignorant Edwardian public. At a time before television and cheap illustrated books he pioneered the use of dioramas to display groups of animals in appropriate habitats. Although this approach has now spread to most natural history museums, his displays are still marked out by their quality and sheer scale. Different cases represent separate areas of Africa and India. They show a wide range of animals, whereas in the wild each type of animal would normally be found on its own, or perhaps with two or three other species. The group displays, however, allow a large number of animals to be included and provide the visitor with an instant safari. There are examples of giraffes, gorillas, rhinos, tigers and lions amongst numerous monkeys, antelope and other mammals. Even in an age of

high quality wildlife films these displays provide a fascinating opportunity to look at animals close to and compare different features and markings.

Attitudes to conservation have now changed radically: nobody would shoot such animals today as a means of studying them. But at the turn of the century this approach was considered perfectly acceptable in the absence of other methods of recording. Powell-Cotton felt that by preserving representative examples for study and exhibition he could raise public and scientific interest in species threatened with extinction. His life, moreover, spanned a period that saw wildlife in Africa change from an apparently inexhaustible resource to one threatened with almost complete destruction by population growth and industrialisation. The museum thus provides a fascinating starting point to consider changing ideas about conservation and the dismal future that faces many species.

Powell-Cotton also collected extensively amongst the various tribes that he met during his travels, and kept detailed written and photographic records. The objects reflect in microcosm the extraordinary clash of cultures brought about by the expansion of the British Empire in the 19th century. Perhaps most striking is the diversity of raw materials – wood, bone, shell, ivory, feathers, textiles, metals, pottery – used in an extraordinary range of ways to make anything from jewellery to musical instruments. One of the pleasures of the museum is its intimate scale, and you can compare products from the cultures of two continents within a few yards. There are objects reflecting every aspect of African life. Outstanding are five superb wooden fetish heads from Zaire, whose colouring is so fresh that they look as if they have just been painted (Powell-Cotton collected them in their original wrappings and this has ensured their pristine condition). Equally impressive is a reconstruction of a Fulani cavalryman: the horse is protected with a magnificent quilted cloth, which would do credit to a medieval knight, while the warrior's helmet is made from a recycled kerosine tin decorated with ostrich feathers. In contrast the adjoining case displays elaborate initiation costumes and masks from Angola, Zaire and Zimbabwe.

The African objects are complemented by a fine collection of material from the Far East, largely consisting of decorative art and weapons. Pride of place must go to the unique collection of nearly a hundred Imperial Chinese porcelain bowls and dishes, which originally came from the Summer Palace at Peking, looted in 1860 by a joint British and French expeditionary force. The pieces are remarkable for their simplicity of shape and design combined with a wonderful purity of colour (colour plate 9). Rank was denoted by different designs and there are particular bowls for the Emperor, Empress Dowager, and first, second, third and minor concubines. These superb dishes make an interesting contrast to the Chinese 'export' ceramics, designed for sale to western 'barbarians', that are also on show. Other material ranges from enchanting netsuke figures and scent bottles to Samurai armour. The museum also has an extensive collection of weapons, which ranges from swords and rifles to over sixty cannon (displayed in the surrounding garden and collected by John Powell Powell, builder of Quex House).

Quex House itself is a good example of a typical 19th century gentleman's residence. Largely Regency, it has an excellent collection of 18th century furniture and decorations, and is kept as it would have appeared at the turn of the last century. The oriental-style drawing room, built in 1883 and redecorated by Powell-Cotton in an eastern style, is a particularly interesting feature. There are plans to restore the extensive walled garden to its Edwardian appearance.

The museum and house offer an insight into a world and a way of life that have largely vanished. More importantly, Powell-Cotton's interests – conservation, the technological gap between the first and third worlds, the need for people to be better informed about other countries – are major concerns today and will ensure that his museum continues to entertain, interest and provoke people. Among comments in the visitors book are 'Mind blowing! must come again', 'My son and I are speechless and shall return': the Major would doubtless have been pleased. (GM)

CANTERBURY

Canterbury Heritage Time-Walk Museum

Poor Priests' Hospital, Stour Street, Canterbury, Kent (address for enquiries: *Royal Museum and Art Gallery, High Street, Canterbury Kent CT1 2JE (0227) 452747)* Open Mondays to Saturdays, and on Sunday afternoons June to October. ⬛
&: wheelchair access to ground floor only.
⬛ & ⬛ must book in advance; reduced admission for parties of 10 or more.

Every day, particularly in summer, visitors flock to Canterbury to visit the world-famous cathedral and wander through the narrow medieval streets. In the rush to get to the cathedral it is all too easy for visitors to miss the Roman mosaic, Norman castle, medieval walls, St Augustine's Abbey and other remains in this historic city. The Canterbury Heritage Time-Walk

Fetish head from Zaire

Interior view, Poor Priests' Hospital

Reconstruction view of Roman Canterbury, c. 300 AD

Museum, opened by The Queen in March 1987, aims to provide the general visitor, whether adult or child, with a rapid introduction to Canterbury's past, and to encourage exploration of the city with an understanding of the way in which it developed.

The Poor Priests' Hospital, where the Time-Walk is housed, was a medieval equivalent of an old people's home for the clergy. It was founded around 1200 and remained in use until 1575. The main element was a great hall with a superb 'crown post' roof; here the priests lived, ate and slept around a central open fire. Other rooms included a solar, where the master of the hospital lived, a private chapel dedicated to St Mary, and a service wing. After 1575 the building was used by a succession of different occupants, and a variety of new walls, floors and windows were added over the years. Trying to restore such a building to something like its original appearance whilst re-using it as a museum is difficult. A brave attempt has been made to preserve the feel of the medieval hospital without compromising its new function; display cases are deliberately restricted in number, with a muted design to avoid being too intrusive. A limited amount of restoration has been done to the building, with new timber additions coloured red so that they can be distinguished clearly. The building backs

Walter Tittle, Joseph Conrad, *1824*

onto an attractive branch of the River Stour, and provides a haven of tranquility from the nearby bustling High Street.

The Time-Walk story begins in the Roman period when Canterbury was established as *Durovernum Cantiacorum* – 'the marshy alder tree grove of the Cantii' (who appear to have had long-established trading links across the Channel, dating back to the Iron Age and beyond). Recent building development in Canterbury has facilitated a series of major archaeological excavations, which have revealed much about the Roman city, and have shown that the centre was only a stone's throw from this museum. Major buildings included the town hall, market place,

theatre, baths and temples. None of these can now be seen as they were subsequently demolished for their valuable building materials. However, large-scale reconstruction views convey a good impression of what it was like to live in this corner of the Roman Empire, and show the grandeur of many of the buildings. Finds on display include jewellery, a superb carpenter's set square, and a group of fine silver spoons, which were unearthed by chance in 1962 and bear Early Christian symbols, adding support to the existence of the remains of a Roman church somewhere under modern Canterbury.

With the collapse of Roman rule, Canterbury seems to have been largely abandoned but by about 650 AD there is plenty of evidence for Saxon settlers. Reconstruction pictures illustrate recent discoveries and show simple wooden houses scattered amongst the ruins of the Roman city. As the journey through time continues visitors increasingly meet the individuals who shaped the city's history. Of particular importance were the various early archbishops whose ambitious building projects resulted in the splendid cathedral and associated buildings, which spread over the entire northwest corner of Canterbury. A detailed model shows a cross-section of the 12th century cathedral choir under construction, and includes the various craftsmen whose combined skills created this enormous building.

On 29th December 1170, Archbishop Thomas Becket was murdered in his own cathedral at the hands of four knights; a hologram in the displays recreates the scene. The murder shocked the entire Christian world and transformed the site of his martyrdom into a major shrine. Pilgrims from all over Britain and Europe travelled to Canterbury and brought great wealth to the city. Large inns, such as the 'Cheker of the Hope' (mentioned in Chaucer's *Canterbury Tales*, and part of which still survives) were developed to house the travellers. Among items on the history of religion in the city are examples of the simple 'pilgrim badges' that were sold as souvenirs to visitors.

The Reformation and the destruction of the monasteries had a devastating impact on the economic life of Canterbury and as late as 1841 the city only had a population of 15,000. But among the residents were individuals who shaped British and, indeed, world history. Visitors to the Time-Walk encounter Christopher Marlowe (1564–93), the poet and playwright, who was the son of a local shoemaker and died at the tragically early age of 29. A local grocer, Robert Cushman, perhaps exerted greater long-term influence: Cushman was excommunicated for a time because of his strong puritan religious beliefs and fled to Holland; visitors will discover him sitting at his desk, writing a letter to hire the 'Mayflower', to allow the Pilgrim Fathers to emigrate to the New World. Displays from later centuries include memorabilia of the novelist Joseph Conrad, including the table at which he wrote *Lord Jim*, *Nostromo* and *Heart of Darkness*, and material relating to Mary Tourtel, the local girl who created Rupert Bear. Perhaps most surprising is 'Invicta', the world's first passenger steam engine, designed and built by Stephenson. In 1830, a 6½-mile railway line was opened linking Canterbury to Whitstable on the north Kent coast. It is extraordinary to learn that this apparently crudely-built 'boiler on wheels' could pull carriages, let alone be the ancestor of today's trains.

The time journey ends with a three-minute video on the Blitz of Canterbury in the Second World War. On 1st June 1942 a massive German air raid took place in retaliation for an RAF attack on Cologne; 6,000 incendiary and 100 high-explosive bombs were dropped, and their effect on the tightly-packed timber buildings was devastating. One quarter of the area inside the medieval city walls was destroyed, although miraculously the cathedral survived. Today, as Canterbury has to adjust to the new pressures of Britain's growing links with Europe, the Canterbury Heritage Museum provides residents and visitors with a reminder of the wealth that has resulted from the city's strategic location in the past. (GM)

CHALFONT ST GILES

Chiltern Open Air Museum

Newland Park, Gorelands Lane, Chalfont St Giles, Buckinghamshire HP8 4AD   (024 07) 71117
Open Easter to end of June and mid-September to end of October on Wednesday, Sunday and Bank Holiday afternoons; July to mid-September on Wednesday to Sunday afternoons inclusive. 🚻 ▣ 🅿

♿: wheelchair access possible to most buildings; gravel footpaths. 🏨 must book in advance. 🏨 must book in advance; museum open to pre-booked schools Monday to Friday throughout the year. ◎

A visit to this museum offers a combination of an easy country ramble and an opportunity to look closely at many historic buildings from the Chilterns gathered together on this 45-acre site. Visitors will usually be able to see buildings in the process of being re-erected, which is just as fascinating to see as the finished work. The museum has great plans for development, including a reconstructed Victorian village and an early industrial area, but the very high cost of reconstruction means that such major projects take a while to realise.

The museum was founded in 1976 by a small group of highly committed and enthusiastic individuals. It is frequently offered buildings, but its policy is not to move a building to the museum unless it is in imminent danger of demolition, since it is always better that a building should remain where it was built. Thorough surveys are carried out before the structure is carefully dismantled. Its numbered components are then re-erected, with replacement timbers used only where

Assembly of the Arborfield Barn's cruck frame

existing timbers are missing or beyond repair. New timbers and materials are not disguised.

One of the more recent additions is the Blythe Road Pavilion, which is now used as a visitor centre with displays about the museum, the buildings and the philosophy that guides the museum's work. Another recent addition is the Caversham toilets – this (useful!) little building is constructed of cast iron sections and stands close to the visitor centre.

There are a number of reconstructed buildings that are entirely 'new' and based on archaeological evidence. Such reconstructions are confined to one part of the site, and so far an Iron Age and Saxon house have been built. The Iron Age example is a round house with a steeply-pitched thatched roof, through which smoke escapes when a fire is lit inside. Some elements of the house's construction have to be based on educated guesswork, since the only archaeological evidence is a ring of post holes. The Saxon Bakehouse is also based on archaeological evidence, although its turf roof is again speculative.

Toll House and gates from High Wycombe

Volunteers re-erecting the Granary, 1980

A later form of construction was cruck framing, where the main structural timbers were long curving blades cut from a single oak tree. An example of this is the Arborfield barn (*c.* 1500), which was one of the first buildings erected at the museum.

In the middle of the site a 19th century farm area is being developed. The buildings here include a two-storey granary built in 1802 at Rossway Home Farm in Berkhamsted. The Granary stands on twelve mushroom-shaped stone supports (or staddles), which help to prevent rats and mice from getting at the stored grain and also help to keep the building and the grain dry. The large barn from Hill Farm in Chalfont St Peter was added to the farm complex in 1985. In fine weather the opened northern doors of this barn afford a splendid view of surrounding countryside. Near to these farm buildings is the Garston Forge, of about 1860, and the Gorhambury Cart shed. The cart shed was given to the museum by Lord Verulam and was re-erected by a team of three women volunteers during 1989.

One of the buildings most popular with visitors is the Toll House from High Wycombe, a four-roomed gothic-style cottage with the characteristic many-sided (in this case five) front facing the toll gate. This toll house was built in 1826, and the occupant was the collector of tolls on the London to Oxford road. Tolls were exacted on users of certain roads from the 18th century, and the toll fees went towards funding the cost of road repairs. Visitors can walk through the cottage, which is set out as it might have looked when in use in the mid-19th century.

An industrial area has been started near the museum's workshop and office centre. A furniture factory from Wycombe, which was originally used as an assembly shop for Windsor chairs, has been re-erected here and houses the museum's restaurant. In this area there is also a shop, and a granary from Haversham has been re-erected and adapted to house public lavatories.

Each season the museum runs special events, including conservation days, sheepdog trials and regular craft demonstrations. (NH)

CHATHAM

The Historic Dockyard, Chatham

Chatham, Kent ME4 4TE
(0634) 812551
Open Wednesdays to Sundays plus Bank Holidays in summer season, and on Wednesdays, Saturdays and Sundays in winter. 🚻 ▣ 🅿
♿ W: wheelchair access can be provided for most of the buildings open to visitors; close parking available.
🏚 preferably book in advance with Visitor Operations Manager; catering can be arranged.
†† book in advance: contact Education Officer, who will provide information for teachers. ☺

HMS 'Gannet' in dry dock for restoration

For over 400 years Chatham was one of Britain's key dockyards, building, repairing and servicing the warships of the Royal Navy. It therefore played a vital role in the maritime defence of the country and the expansion of the British Empire around the globe. Today, for the first time, visitors can penetrate inside the yard's high walls and discover the story of this remarkable place.

Over the centuries the dockyard was developed and adapted to meet the changing demands of new technology – iron, steam and steel. In 1860 a major extension was built to the north of the original site; the old part remained largely unaltered and visitors can now explore over eighty acres of the Georgian and Victorian dockyard, little changed since the days of sail. When Chatham was finally closed in 1984, a trust was established to preserve this unique concentration of historic buildings, which range from elegant officers' houses to a cavernous smithery. The work of the trust has only just begun and it will take a decade or more to restore the whole area. The aim is not just to conserve buildings but to breathe fresh life into them through working displays or re-use by appropriate modern industries. The site is therefore very much a 'living' experience. It will be fascinating to revisit the site at regular intervals to watch this process, and the huge amount already achieved augers well for the future. Although Chatham is only an hour from London, many people are still unaware of the range of features that can be seen.

A visit to Chatham will reveal as much about the people who worked in the yard as the ships that they built. It is often forgotten that before the industrial revolution the Royal dockyards were amongst the most technically advanced installations in the country, relying on a highly skilled workforce. The scale of operations required massive workshops, warehouses and stores, and first-time visitors are usually amazed by the size of the buildings. Shipbuilding was always extremely labour intensive; the simple tools on display are a constant reminder of the human skills needed to build a ship such as HMS 'Victory', launched at Chatham in 1759. It is often the personal items that bring the story to life as much as the buildings. One of the best features about the site is that you can always take a break to sit by the River Medway and watch the modern ships and yachts go past. It does not require much imagination to travel back 200 years and imagine the river full of wooden warships at anchor.

A tour starts at the visitor centre, which provides a short but comprehensive introduction to the whole site. You can then choose whether to roam at will or take a ninety-minute guided tour. The latter is excellent value and the friendly guides will not only entertain you but provide suggestions about how to spend the rest of the visit. The following selection of specific features gives a flavour of what is available.

Next to the Medway are five covered building slips (constructed 1838–55), which impress by their sheer size and the thought that over 400 ships were built here. These included fifty-seven submarines, the last HMCS 'Okanagan', launched in 1966. Today the slips house a variety of interesting displays, including a steam boiler repair shop. Regular 'Dockyard in Steam' days are held during the summer season, and a variety of traction engines are displayed as well as AJAX, one of the railway engines that worked in the dockyard.

Inside the Ropery, which has an overall length of 1,140 feet

ing displays. Without doubt the most spectacular is the ropery, where the whole production process can be seen. A typical sailing ship might have over thirty miles of rigging, and all the rope was made by hand until mechanisation was introduced in 1811. At Chatham the original equipment has been preserved in working condition, housed in a ropery nearly a quarter of a mile long that was built in the 1780s to make lengths of '120 fathom' rope. Close by is the sail and colour loft, which houses working demonstrations of the skills involved in sail and flag making.

Scattered across the rest of the dockyard are a number of 'mini-museums'. The Ordnance Gallery displays an impressive collection of cannon; the barrels of many ended their days as street bollards and the trust has rescued some for restoration as the dockyard has been redeveloped. In the Lead and Paint Mill is a collection gathered by the Chatham Dockyard Historical Society. Many of the members originally worked in the yard and act as volunteer staff; their recollections provide a vivid background to the displays, which concentrate on everyday life in more recent years.

In 1991 a major new exhibition, 'Wooden Walls', will open in the Mast House. This will recreate the story of the construction of a wooden warship, HMS 'Valiant' (built at Chatham in 1758–59), from laying out the ship's lines on the floor of the mould loft to the final launching. Also included will be many original items recovered from the wreck of HMS 'Invincible'.

The historic dockyard is a large site, so allow plenty of time to make the most of a visit. There are regular special events and weekends connected with the history of the site and the River Medway. And if after all the history you feel like getting out on the water, Chatham Dockyard is the home port of the 'Kingswear Castle', the last operational coal-fired paddle steamer in Britain. There are frequent trips along the Medway ('phone in advance to check availability), past sites as varied as Upnor Castle, 19th century forts and modern power stations. (GM)

There are also two historic ships, CMB103 – a 70-foot coastal motor boat, and the midget submarine XE8, built 1944–45. Next to the ships are the open drydocks, in one of which is HMS 'Gannet'. This sloop was built in 1878 and after a long and varied career has been brought to Chatham for complete restoration. The project will take several years, and a small exhibition describes the complex conservation work that will be needed to restore the battered ship to its original Victorian condition.

The trust are keen to explain the wide range of specialist skills that were needed in a dockyard, and several buildings have 'visitor friendly' work-

Royal Engineers Museum

Brompton Barracks, Chatham, Kent ME4 4UG   (0634) 844555 ext. 2312
Closed Saturdays and Mondays (except summer Bank Holiday Mondays). 🚲 🅿 ♿ W
♿ & ♿ preferably book in advance; reduced admission for groups over 10; Teacher's pack for sale; room available for school lunches and classwork.

Bedford Office Truck and Folding Boat Equipment in the museum's Second World War gallery

The Royal Engineers' motto, *Ubique* (everywhere) would be an appropriate title for the museum, since it draws together material illustrating the work of the 'sappers' all around the world. First-time visitors may find it surprising to see Chinese silks and Ashanti gold weights alongside more conventional military material. The Royal Engineers have travelled the world, constructing anything from roads and railways to palaces, in addition to direct military operations. Over the years they have been responsible for buildings as diverse as Wormwood Scrubs prison and the Bombay Silver Mint. The museum, therefore, not only tells the story of the Royal Engineers but reflects the broad sweep of Britain's military, political and imperial history over the last three centuries.

The museum was moved to its present location in 1986 and now occupies the ground floor of the old electrical school next to the modern military base. The building was constructed in 1904 in an Anglo-Indian style, which is very suitable for its new function. The domes on the roof originally housed powerful searchlights for training and to help guard Chatham dockyard. On arrival the scale of military engineering operations is immediately brought home by a massive Centurion Bridge Layer and an A.V.R.E. tank flanking the entrance gates. Inside, the modern-style galleries tell the story of Britain's soldier engineers from the Norman conquest to V.J. day in 1945. The museum is currently being ex-panded to show the recent history of the Royal Engineers, including their emergency relief work, as in the aftermath of the Mexico earthquake.

The first galleries show how military engineering skills developed out of castle building and became increasingly sophisticated to counter ever more powerful artillery. The Royal Engineers were founded in 1716, and with their function of 'helping the army live, move and fight' became increasingly important as military operations grew in complexity. One display is devoted to the defence of Gibraltar in the 1770s and shows the vital role of the 'sappers' in turning this tiny site into one of the cornerstones of British maritime power.

The galleries include reconstructions, models, maps, prints and many other items. There are also uniforms, the earliest original one dating to around 1820. One prize exhibit is the 'Waterloo Map', an original plan of the battlefield made from individual field surveys stuck together. It was recovered from a corpse after the battle. The map is a graphic reminder of the difficulties faced by commanders in controlling their units when they only had limited knowledge of the geographical terrain. An example of the range of engineer activities, even in the 19th century, is shown by a display on early diving. This includes a wonderful print of divers in extremely crude outfits working in 1840 on the wreck of the 'Royal George', which sank at Spithead in 1782.

Four galleries trace the Royal Engineers' extensive role in the development of the British Empire. They contain material as diverse as items looted from the Summer Palace in Peking in 1860 and mementoes from the Battle of Rorke's Drift during the Zulu war. Pride of place, perhaps, goes to the items relating to Major General Charles Gordon, which include exquisite sets of Court dress presented to him in 1864 by the Chinese emperor. Gordon was not renowned for his modesty and there are examples of the photographs he circulated to his friends showing him wearing these clothes. There are also items connected with Gordon's tragic death at Khartoum in January 1885, which shocked the entire country. The picture of him facing his assailants on the steps of his house was to become one of the icons of British imperialism.

The ever-increasing pace of military technology in the late 19th century is shown by a massive Brennan torpedo. Developed in the 1870s, it was in effect Britain's first guided missile. Torpedoes, launched and controlled from riverside facilities, were extensively deployed. An original launching site still survives on private land about seven

Recruitment poster, c. 1907

miles from Chatham at Cliffe, where it was constructed to defend the Thames.

The last section of the museum describes the two World Wars. During the First World War the Royal Engineers were involved in everything from observation balloons to tunnelling and mining. Visitors can walk along the duckboards of an accurately reconstructed trench on the Western Front. Most horrific is the display about gas warfare. Gas (chlorine) was first used by the British at the Battle of Loos in September 1915. The gas masks and cylinders perhaps symbolise better than anything how the red-coated soldiers of distant imperial campaigns were transformed into the technological warriors of the 20th century.

The display on the Second World War begins on the Home Front with a reconstruction of a typical Medway house, its front living room complete with a Home Guardsman toiling over his paperwork. At the start of the war the Government were expecting a massive German aerial attack, and a searchlight battery is a reminder of the Engineers' role in protecting Britain at this critical time. This is followed by large exhibits, vehicles and engineering equipment set in realistic landscape displays. One can discover the role of the 'sappers' in bomb disposal, build-

ing roads and laying out airfields. Their position at the fighting edge, facilitating an advancing army's progress across difficult terrain, is illustrated by a section of the war-winning Bailey Bridge. Perhaps most dramatic of all was the huge floating Mulberry harbour built to supply the D-Day invasion of Normandy in 1944. Its construction and use is explained by detailed models and photographs. The engineers were also involved in many commando raids and there are small displays on attacks, such as the 1942 Bruneval raid on a German radar installation.

There is a separate gallery devoted to an extensive collection of British campaign medals and gallantry awards, including twenty Victoria Crosses. The non-specialist would probably wish for more background information in this section: how does one become a Grand Officer of the White Elephant, Siam, and what was the 1894 Hong Kong Plague Medal awarded for? Generally, however, the museum achieves an excellent balance, compressing a vast and varied story into the available space while using individual personalities or events to highlight key developments. For anybody who is wary of visiting military museums, this is a good place to start: with the variety of material on display there is something to interest almost anybody.

The museum is situated next to the 'Chatham Lines', a massive defence built in the 18th century to protect Chatham dockyard from landward attack. The Royal Engineers played a major role in its design and construction. Although most of the fortifications are inaccessible, Fort Amherst is currently being restored. This fourteen-acre site, a few hundred yards from the museum, preserves one of the finest examples of a Georgian fort in the country. Occupation of the site did not finally cease until the end of the last war. Tours are given of the massive ditches, bastions and tunnels, and the site provides a fascinating complement to visiting the Royal Engineers Museum. Visitors should 'phone in advance (0634 847747) to check opening times. (GM)

CHELMSFORD

Chelmsford and Essex Museum and *Essex Regiment Museum*

Oaklands Park, Moulsham Street, Chelmsford, Essex CM2 9AQ

Chelmsford & Essex Museum
(0245) 353066
Essex Regiment Museum
(0245) 260614
Open daily. **F**
& S: wheelchair access to ground floor only.
& book in advance.

Oaklands Park in Chelmsford offers two museums in one building, Oaklands House – the Essex Regiment Museum and the Chelmsford and Essex Museum.

French eagle captured at Salamanca, 1812

Palmer Challenge Cup, 1894–95

The Essex Regiment Museum is a purpose-built extension to the main house and was opened in 1973. It houses a splendid array of costumes, medals, colours and mementoes that trace the history of the Essex Regiment. The 44th (East Essex) and 56th (West Essex) regiments were formed in 1741 and 1755 respectively. The two came together in 1881 to form one Essex Regiment, which itself was amalgamated into the 3rd East Anglian Regiment in 1958. In 1964 the Regiment became the 3rd Battalion Royal Anglian Regiment.

The gallery has been designed to protect the costume on display from the fading and deterioration that are caused by too much exposure to light: it is windowless, with dark walls and ceiling. But the darkness also serves to highlight most effectively the colour and the embroidery of uniforms, sashes and banners, and the polish of weapons and metal objects.

At the far end of the gallery is the Salamanca Eagle, captured from the 62nd French Infantry Regiment on 22nd July 1812 during the Peninsular War. The gilded eagle, which would have sat at the top of the colour staff, is a central feature of the displays and rotates gently under strong lights that emphasise both shape and colour. The museum has recently acquired the Military General Service Medal presented to the officer who captured this

highly-prized trophy. Further trophies include the ceremonial sword of Field Marshall Von Runstedt, captured by Chelmsford's own 5th Territorial Battalion on crossing the River Elbe in 1945. Among other exhibits are the solid silver drums presented to the County of Essex in memory of soldiers killed in the Boer and Great Wars.

There are also less obviously 'military' objects on display, for example one of the boxes of chocolate sent by Queen Victoria in 1900 to the soldiers fighting the Boer War – still unopened. Among various cups is the Palmer Inter-Company Challenge Cup, highly decorated and one of the many items that will appeal to those interested in the decorative arts.

The Chelmsford and Essex Museum is in Oaklands House itself. Built in 1865–68 by Alderman Frederick Wells, a local brewer, the house is Italianate in style and stands in a park setting just off the old A12. The displays in the museum show only a fraction of the vast collections that the museum holds. These range from natural history and archaeology to social history, costume, ceramics and glassware, and British model soldiers.

Glasses from the Tunstill Collection

Given the layout of the house, which has had little structural alteration, the visitor faces a series of rooms that are easy to manage individually, if a bit confusing when viewed 'en masse'. It is a real pot-pourri of a museum, with a little of something for everyone.

On the ground floor, one room is displayed as a Victorian sitting room. In another, the archaeology room, there is a small collection of local finds including 4th century jet, excavated in 1972. The pre-history room has a small selection of elephant fossils, flints and material from the Bronze and Stone Ages. Next door, the geology room has shells, fossils and some eye-catching rocks and minerals.

There is a temporary exhibition gallery on the ground floor, with regularly changing exhibitions on different aspects of the museum's collections. Passing some of the museum's portrait collection on the stairs, you arrive on the first floor where there are three natural history galleries, a temporary exhibition room, a costume gallery, a social history gallery, a collection of ceramics and coins, and a lovely collection of 18th-century English drinking glasses.

The natural history galleries concentrate on birds and mammals, but don't miss the bees: there is a working beehive, which lets you look at a section of honeycomb with the bees at work. The local history room has topographical pictures, photographs and postcards of Chelmsford. There are some gracious watercolours, a distinguished picture of 'Shire Hall' (1794) by P. Renigate, reminding one that Chelmsford is the county town, and a huge Chapman and André map of the county, surveyed in 1777.

Displays in the costume gallery are changed every year, so that fragile clothes are not exposed for too long. More durable is the kitchen from the turn of the century in the social history room. Finally there are the ceramics – a mixed display, with some interesting Hedingham ware – and the glass. The Tunstill Collection of 18th century drinking glasses is very special, pretty and informative; if I only had time to visit one room, this would be it. (KH)

COLCHESTER

Colchester Castle Museum

*Castle Park, Colchester, Essex
CO1 1TJ   (0206) 712931/2*
(address for correspondence &
enquiries: *Colchester and Essex
Museum Service, Museum Resource
Centre, 14 Ryegate Road, Colchester,
Essex CO1 1YG)*
Closed Sunday mornings, and all
day Sundays October to March. ⬛
Hourly guided tours at weekends
April to September & daily in July
& August.
&: wheelchair access to ground
floor only.
⬛ Book in advance, reduced
admission for pre-booked groups
of 20 or more.
⬛ book in advance with Schools
Officer; talks & other resources
available.

Exterior view of Colchester Castle

It would be difficult to visit the historic
town of Colchester without noticing
one of the five museums run by the
Colchester and Essex Museum Service, which all stand within the town
centre. The rich and varied collections
of the museum service are housed in
buildings that are in themselves an
attraction and have their own story to
tell; the most spectacular of these is
Colchester Castle.

Colchester Castle Museum is located inside the remains of the largest
Norman keep in Europe, begun by
William the Conqueror around 1076
and built over the platform of the
Temple of Claudius, Britain's first and
largest Roman temple. Part of the
archaeological collections of Colchester and Essex Museum are displayed
here on the ground and first floors.
They boast 'one of the best groups of
Roman remains north of the Alps':
Colchester was the capital of Roman
Britain during the reign of Claudius
and remained an important city
throughout the Roman occupation.

A museum was opened to the public
in the Castle crypt in 1860, when the
records of the Essex Archaeological
Society also came here. The Vint collection of local and foreign Classical
antiquities, which can be seen on the
ground floor, relates to the foundation
of the museum: it was bequeathed in
1852 by Alderman Henry Vint, 'on
condition a fireproof museum building
be found'. Charles Grey Round made
the Castle available to house a museum
in 1855, and the building was finally
presented to the Borough in 1920 by
Viscount Cowdray. The Castle's chequered history is well documented in
the 'History, Description and Guide',
which is on sale in the museum shop.
The growth and various uses of the
Castle can best be absorbed by going
on one of the guided tours (see above).
The tour route takes the visitor down
into the Roman vaults and up onto the
roof, and makes it easier to understand
the construction and layout of the
building. There is great excitement in
seeing the Roman temple foundations,
the re-use of Roman building materials, the great stairway with contem-

Replica of a bronze head of Claudius

porary engravings on its walls, the early
fireplaces, or in standing where prison-
ers were held in most periods of unrest
in English history. It is difficult to
escape the sense of history and won-

Bronze statuette of Mercury, 3rd century AD

Medieval, Tudor and later material, but it is the local Roman finds that really stand out. Among those that particularly catch the imagination are the 1st century Rossette brooches that have given their name to the Brooch Grave excavations, and the Red Hills finds, including pedestals and fire bars used in the production of sea salt. The Colchester Mercury is a bronze figure with fine delicate lines. Found by a local ploughman in 1946, the figure reflects the more aesthetic side of Roman life in the town. Amongst larger items the Sheepen cauldron is bold and immensely practical, while the highly decorated Colchester Vase, though still practical, is also decorative, showing scenes of gladiatorial combat and hunting.

Many of the treasures on display have been retrieved during the archaeological work in and around the town itself. A colourful publication by the Colchester Archaeological Trust superimposes the Roman streets and walls onto a modern aerial photograph. This is a manageable area to walk around, with plenty of sites and buildings still visible. The museum's Tombstone of Facilis, a centurion of the 20th Legion, originally stood near the modern Lexden Road. It is a sombre reminder of the thousands of men who lived and died in Britain during the Roman occupation. Another memorable item on display that relates to life in Roman Colchester is the mosaic pavement found on North Hill in 1925. It is one of many examples that have been found in the town and recalls some of the richness and textures within Roman buildings that are hard to imagine from today's fragmentary remains.

One section of the ground floor is devoted to Colchester's role in the Civil War, when occupying Royalists were besieged by Parliamentarian forces. Through objects, graphics and models a true-life drama is unfolded. The exhibition is housed in the room from which two of the Royalist commanders were finally led out to be shot in the Castle bailey, having held the town for twelve weeks against the Parliamentarians.

Gold coin struck at Colchester c. 10–40 AD

It is difficult to absorb the magnificent collections and the building itself on one visit. There is so much to catch the imagination that it is well worth allowing yourself plenty of time to wander around the Castle and its treasures. Then there are the other museums close by to visit: **Hollytrees Museum**, next to the Castle, and the *Natural History Museum* opposite, housed in the former All Saints church, with permanent displays concentrating on the effect of man on the environment and including dioramas of local places painted by a Colchester artist. This is a town steeped in history. Its museums, sites and monuments are real treasures that excite and inform. (KH)

Colchester Vase, c. 175 AD

der, and unless you come in winter you should try to make the tour an essential part of your visit.

The displays in the main part of the building are traditional and reveal only the tip of the huge archaeological collections cared for by the Museum Service. (There are exciting plans to develop the displays over the next few years.) Exhibits range through Roman,

Hollytrees Museum

High Street, Colchester, Essex
CO1 1VG   (0206) 712931/2
(address for enquiries: see
Colchester Castle)
Closed Sundays. ◪
& **S**: five steps to entrance;
displays on three floors.
◫ preferably book in advance.
◫ book in advance: contact
Education Officer.

Hollytrees mansion is 'the best 18th
century house in town' and stands
adjacent to **Colchester Castle**. A
gorgeous, elegant building, Hollytrees
contains 18th and 19th century material from Colchester and Essex
Museum Service's collection, and
houses the library of the Essex Society
for Archaeology and History.

The building is early Georgian, dating from about 1718. The main part of
the house was built by Elizabeth Cor-
nelisen, who left it to her niece Sara,

19th century Meerschaum clay and amber cigar holder

Candle sconce designed by Mackmurdo, 1884

then married to Ralph Creffield.
Widowed in 1723, Sara was remarried
to Charles Gray, 'a man of learning –
much interested in antiquities'. Sara's
mother bought Colchester Castle for
her new son-in-law as a wedding present, and in doing so linked Hollytrees
to the Norman Keep. This link was
finally cemented in 1920 when Hollytrees was acquired by the Borough.
The atmosphere of the museum is
dictated by the living spaces within the
house, and by its architectural features.

The ornate ceiling in the 'Garden
Room' was actually removed from a
house in the High Street and re-
erected in Hollytrees by the Friends of
the Museum. The ornate shuttered
window in the 'Music Room', however,
is contemporary with the house. Both
rooms have views out over the castle
park, and it is easy to imagine the
house as a gracious yet friendly home.

The front gallery on the ground
floor has on show part of the Mackmurdo Collection, given to the
museum in 1932. Mackmurdo was co-
founder, with Selwyn Image, of the
Century Guild and the collection contains furniture, ceramics, designs and
paintings by makers from the late 19th
century Arts and Crafts movement.
There are pieces by Mackmurdo and
Image, along with others by William de
Morgan and the Martin brothers (ill.
on cover).

The large room facing the main
entrance of the house is called the
Garden Room, but is full of toys. Here,
as in other rooms, there are occasional

clocks and paintings that refer to other
parts of the museum's collections. In
this setting they are easily overlooked
as part of the 'furniture', yet they are
often important in their own right. A
painting by Lucien Pissarro hangs
amidst the prams and hobby horses.
The Victorian dolls' house is fascinating, furnished in fine detail inside and
out. The boat-shaped double pram on
display was made by a local boatbuilder
for his twin offspring, who no doubt
wore sailor suits. There are soldiers
and sailor dolls in one case, with model
boats alongside. Other cases include
dolls, games and early mechanical toys.

On the half-landing, the Music
Room does have some musical instruments, many of which have survived
from local Church bands. Part of a very
special collection of caddy spoons, the
Lewer Collection, is displayed in this
room; it is surprising to find such a
variety of design and ornamentation on
such a simple object. This is also true
of the selection of pipes and cigarette
holders – some of the ornamentation
completely swamps the object itself!
Colchester-made guns, kitchen tools,
clay pipes and scientific equipment all
vie for attention. On the stairs and
landing the walls are bedecked with
portraits and local topographical paintings. One particularly charming portrait is of a Colchester Blue Coat
schoolgirl holding a piece of red knit-
ting.

In the Costume Gallery on the first
floor, evening wear from 1805–1940 is
shown on carefully grouped manne-

Victorian boat-shaped double pram

quins. At the back of this display is part of a large screen, embroidered by 100 ladies in Essex, and presented to Sir Henry Smyth, the local MP, on 28th January 1843. It is signed 'a token of friendship from a Century of Ladies'. The Costume Gallery is full of sumptuous needlework, particularly the wedding and christening cases. The wedding case has a poignant unfinished wedding dress from 1905; the white net dress, sewn with sequins, is draped alongside a veil and bridal accessories, with no clue as to why it was never completed. There is an important collection of military uniforms and accessories dating back to the late 18th century, during the Napoleonic wars. Those of the local volunteer regiments are very special, particularly as they are complete: volunteers apparently tended to re-use their uniforms for home-based activities after their military service was over, and very few complete sets survive.

In addition to the museum displays, Hollytrees provides an important research facility in the library of the Essex Society for Archaeology and History. The Society is part-owner of the collections, and the library may be used by prior appointment.

Hollytrees has an air of faded elegance. Its dimmed lighting and domestic layout give an impression of exploring a private collection in a private house, and it is full of atmosphere and unexpected treasures. (KH)

Tymperleys Clock Museum

Trinity Street, Colchester, Essex CO1 1JN (0206) 712943 (address for enquiries: see **Colchester Castle**) Closed November to March, and otherwise closed Mondays. ▣ A: access by three steps; displays on one floor. ▦ preferably book in advance. ♛ book in advance: contact Education Officer.

'Tymperleys' is just lovely. Built in the 16th century, the house was adapted to the Georgian style in the 18th. 'Old Tymperleys' had been the home of William Gilberd (1544–1603), the distinguished Elizabethan scientist, who was Elizabeth I's physician and the first man to use the word electricity. The name Tymperleys, however, came from Bernard Mason, who bought the property in 1956. Bernard Mason's interest in clocks began in 1927, when he bought a lantern clock from a local clockmaker. He went on to build up the splendid Mason collection of time-pieces made by Colchester craftsmen, which he bequeathed to the town along with the house. Part of the collection is now displayed in Tymperleys Clock Museum.

Colchester's clock-making industry can be traced back to the rise in popularity of the pendulum clock, which came to London in 1658. The pendulum movement was more accurate and cheaper than others. It is thought that basic clock parts were made in London and Birmingham, while dial-engraving, cog-cutting, case making and assembly were handled by local craftsmen.

The displays are confined to the ground floor, and as you enter the building the stained boarded floor and the chorus of ticking clocks create a hushed, almost religious atmosphere. The museum was opened in 1987 and the displays, though modern, use the building well. Simple text explains how the various movements work, in a way that can be understood even by the layman. There are panels that set the

Exterior view of Tymperleys Clock Museum, built c. 1500

Deatbeat clock by Joseph Barrister

collection and the house within the context of the town, and space is also devoted to information on Bernard Mason himself. This includes his establishment as an Honarary Freeman of the Borough of Colchester, the company of E. N. Mason & Son, and Mr Mason's 'Band of Hope' card and his school records, adding a very human touch to the inanimate objects on display.

This is perhaps unfair to the 'grandfather' clocks, and certainly many of the clocks at Tymperleys have very definite characters. The Joseph Barrister Deadbeat Escapement, for example, patented in 1836, stands aloof and distinguished, while a Woodcock longcase clock has a delightful balloon motif celebrating the increasingly fashionable balloon ascents in the 18th century. The museum sells a small publication that gives the personal de-

tails of each clockmaker: Joseph Barrister, for instance, was a borough councillor in Colchester; another clockmaker rescued a man from drowning; yet another contracted a secret marriage. These touches of the social history that surrounded the clock trade and its place in the town's history give the collection a breadth of interest that will appeal to any visitor.

The displays include a charming cameo of a customer's house, set around 1810, and a workshop from the same period. These settings harmonise with the atmosphere created by the house itself, which is set in an enclosed garden. Across the drive the former stable building houses the Turret Clocks. Again, photographs are used to help place the mechanical objects in their social setting. The whole experience of a visit to Tymperleys left me reflecting on the nature of time, and I was reminded of the lines by Sir Thomas Browne (1605–1682), 'Time, which antiquates antiquities, and hath an art to make dust of all things hath yet spared us these minor monuments'. Above all, I was left with the sounds of the place.

The museum is off Trinity Street, a quiet corner lost in time amidst the bustle of Colchester's two new shopping precincts. Midway between the two stands the 11th century Saxon tower of Holy Trinity Church, where William Wilbye, the Elizabethan composer, was buried in 1638. Converted in 1873, the church now houses the *Social History Museum*, with its displays of Essex country life and crafts. (KH)

A customer's drawing room, c. 1810

COMPTON

The Watts Gallery

Compton, Nr Guildford, Surrey
GU3 1DQ   (0483) 810235
Open afternoons on Mondays, Tuesdays, Fridays and Sundays, mornings on Wednesdays and Saturdays. ⓕ Can be opened at other times by arrangement and ⓢ. ⓟ
&: most of Gallery accessible by wheelchair; sculpture gallery and drawings by arrangement.
⚇ & ⚇ should book in advance; information sheet available.

Despite the widespread revival of interest in many Victorian painters, the work of George Frederic Watts (1817–1904) remains stubbornly out of favour. Yet in his lifetime he was one of the pillars of the Victorian art world, immensely popular with the public, and his picture 'Hope' was one of the best known in the world. Watts was elected a Royal Academician in 1867

Watts, Clytie, c. 1868

and received the Order of Merit on its creation in 1902. His one-man exhibition in 1884–85 at the Metropolitan Museum, New York, was seen by over half-a-million visitors. Indeed, the Tate Gallery had an entire room devoted to his work until 1939.

Today the Watts Gallery at Compton continues to attract devotees of Watts, but is largely unknown to the general public. It offers visitors the opportunity to examine a wide selection of Watts' paintings, and to come to their own conclusions about his importance. Even if the interests and concerns of Watts fail to strike a chord, a visit to the gallery provides a fascinating insight into the Victorian art world and the way in which popular taste changes. As a review displayed in the gallery puts it, the paintings 'may move you and fill you with a sense of awe, or maybe leave you with the feeling that your view of the artist as a recluse living in an ivory tower and dedicated to the propagation of heavyweight Victorian virtue and ideals have finally been confirmed'.

Despite the expansion of Guildford and the heavy traffic on the A3, the village of Compton and the woodland setting of the gallery still retain much of the charm that attracted Watts to the area in his old age. For forty years he had lived and worked in Kensington, but from 1886, following his second marriage to Mary Fraser-Tytler (his first marriage, to the 16-year-old Ellen Terry in 1864, had been disastrous), he spent increasing amounts of time at Compton. In 1891 he had a house, Limnerslease (not open to the public) built there as a winter residence. It was his second wife who was largely responsible for the creation of the gallery. In 1896 Watts presented collections of his work to the National Portrait Gallery and to the recently-established, as yet unopened Tate Gallery. Watts conceived the idea, probably prompted by Mrs Watts (who regarded her husband as the greatest painter in the world), that it would be of great benefit to the public if his studio collection was preserved – that year the studio collection of Lord Leighton, President of the Royal

Watts, The Denunciation of Cain, *1872*

Academy, had been sold and dispersed following Leighton's death. A gallery was built at Compton in the grounds of the Watts' house, and was opened on Good Friday 1904, a few weeks before the death of Watts at the age of 87. Although the gallery was never the artist's studio, it is one of only a handful of galleries in the country devoted to the work of a single artist. Mrs Watts continued to live at Compton until her death in 1938, aged 90. Over the years she extended and improved the gallery, and established a charitable trust to maintain it for the public. She also established an 'art' pottery nearby, which finally closed in the 1950s.

Today the range of one-storey galleries is surrounded by an attractive garden. The works displayed range in date from 1834 to 1904 and thus span the entire Victorian era. The earliest works include a self-portrait painted when the artist was 17, and Watts' first exhibited painting, 'The Wounded Heron', shown at the Royal Academy in 1837. There is a wide variety of works on display, including some sculpture. A few contemporary paintings by other artists include the delightful 'Jasmine' by Albert Moore and 'Washing Day' by Edward Stott. Watts' pictures fall into three main groups – allegorical paintings, portraits and social commentary. The latter group, hung in the main gallery, are perhaps the most readily accessible. They include 'The Song of the Shirt' – an exhausted seamstress with her head in her hands; 'Under a Dry Arch' – an old woman in a bonnet shivering in the cold; 'Irish Famine' and 'Found Drowned (all 1848–50). The pathetic figures not only evoke immediate sympathy but reflect the darker side of Victorian life.

Much more difficult to categorise are Watts' huge allegorical paintings such as 'Progress' (1903), 'Love and Death' (1887), 'The Good Samaritan' (1849–1904) and 'Destiny' (1904). With their dramatic use of paint, many have an almost futuristic quality. These large compositions, often with elaborate symbolism, are difficult to appreciate today. Some appear over-sentimental, although Watts was convinced of the seriousness of his work and wrote of his earlier donation: 'All my paintings in the Tate Gallery are symbolical and for all time ... Their symbolism is, however, more suggestive than worked out in any detail. I want to make people think. My idea is really the Book of Ecclesiastes with a higher impulse.'

Whatever their effect, the galleries certainly have a unique atmosphere. This is particularly true of the main gallery, which has the proportions of a village hall combined with extraordinary pictures and a colour scheme of green, silver and gold – a recent re-creation of the original. Here the fascinating 'The Sower of the Systems' is hung, painted by Watts in 1902, near the end of his life. The swirling mass of

Watts, Under a Dry Arch, *1850 (one of a group 'painted in sympathy with human misery')*

blue paint speaks of a different age, and as one reviewer has remarked 'is one of the pictures that kicked Victorian painting into the 20th century'.

One gallery is devoted to Watts' portraits and includes many famous Victorians. Among them are individuals as diverse as John Burns MP and Socialist reformer John Stuart Mill, Thomas Hughes, author of *Tom Brown's Schooldays,* and the Hungarian violinist, Dr Joachim. Perhaps most appealing today is the charming portrait of the actress Lillie Langtry; the strange design of her bonnet is the result of Watts removing all its feathers. Scattered around the gallery are many fascinating objects and mementoes connected with Watts. These include his palette, awards and decorations. There is a fine bronze of Watts by Henry Poole, showing his proud but rather sad face, and close by a death cast of his hands, the wrinkled skin seeming to mock their former skill. There is also a complete list of all Watts' output, with details of exhibitions. A small display of photographs, selected from an extensive archive, shows scenes from the Watts' domestic life, meeting with friends and relaxing.

The final gallery contains a dramatic surprise – two of the artist's massive plaster models. One is a huge figure of Lord Tennyson, worked on from 1898 to 1903, the bronze cast of which is outside Lincoln Cathedral. The second is Watts' huge equestrian piece, 'Physical Energy', now in Kensington Gardens (worked on from 1870 to 1904). The scale of these works is an education in the sheer physical effort involved in creating major pieces of sculture.

Love it or hate it, few visitors will leave the Watts Gallery without a strong reaction. Even those who do not find Watts generally to their taste will probably have one or two favourites. And if nothing appeals, the Gallery at least provides a rare opportunity to study an artist's changing technique over seventy years.

Visitors should not miss the remarkable Watts mortuary chapel a few hundred yards away. This must rank as one of the strangest buildings in England; the interior was designed and decorated by Mary Watts with the assistance of local villagers. She described the design as 'Some fragments of the story, of the spiritual life, on the wing of which, in the passage between the mystic of death, material life is lifted to the glorious consciousness of its affinity with the infinite' – a reminder that if it is difficult for museums to give accurate ideas about the development of technology in history, it is far harder to convey past beliefs and aspirations. (GM)

1   Egyptian antiquities from the Myers Museum Collection, including a funerary female portrait head, a seal, a pectoral ornament, various vessels, and amuletic figures. Pre-Dynastic to Roman period, c.3500 BC–2nd century AD. Eton College Collections, Eton.

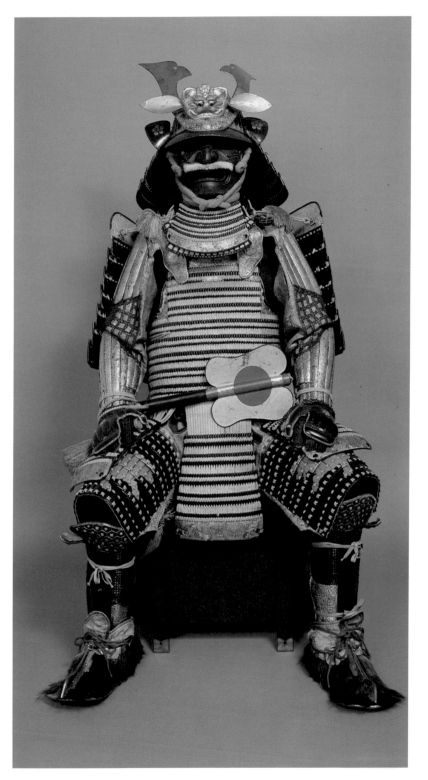

2 Above   Roman enamelled manicure brooch. Letchworth Museum and Art Gallery, Letchworth.

3   Japanese Samurai warrior's suit of armour, c.1750. Pitt Rivers Museum, Oxford.

4   The Deposition of Christ *by The Master of Delft. Dutch school, early 16th century. Christ Church Picture Gallery, Oxford.*

5　A Vase of Flowers with two Carnations *by Abraham Mignon (1640–79). Ashmolean Museum, Oxford.*

6 *Below*　A Hunt in a Forest *by Paolo Uccello (1396/7–1475). Ashmolean Museum, Oxford.*

7   The Alfred Jewel, believed to have belonged to King Alfred the Great (871–899 AD). Ashmolean Museum, Oxford.

8   *Display of dairy equipment. Institute of Agricultural History and Museum of English Rural Life, Reading.*

9   *Imperial Chinese porcelain bowls from the Summer Palace at Peking. The Powell-Cotton Museum and Quex House, Birchington.*

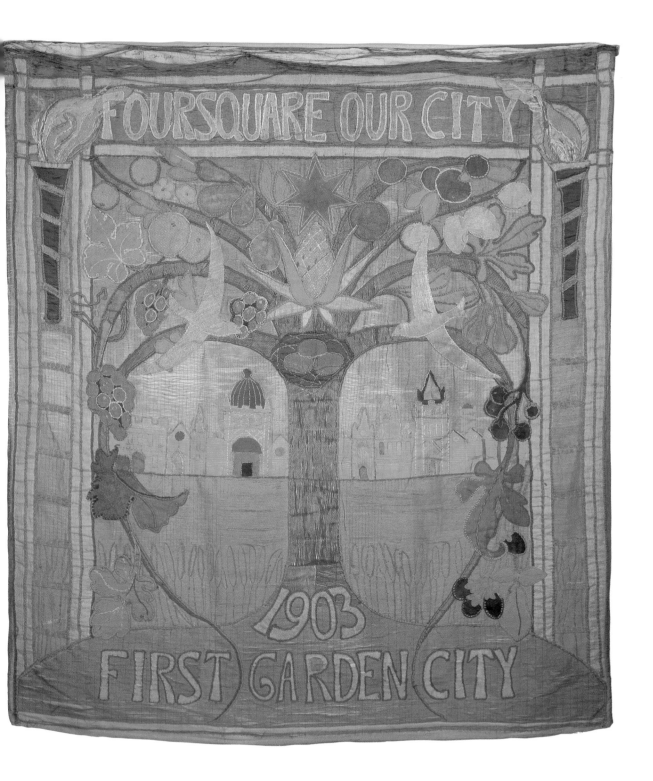

10 *Letchworth First Garden City banner. First Garden City Heritage Museum, Letchworth.*

11   No. 5900, 'Hinderton Hall'. Didcot
Railway Centre, Didcot.

12   Keen Ordinary, 1871. Mark Hall
Cycle Museum and Gardens, Harlow.

COOKHAM-ON-THAMES

Stanley Spencer Gallery

King's Hall, High Street, Cookham-on-Thames, Berkshire SL6 9SJ
(062 85) 20890/20043
Open daily Easter to October, and at weekends and public holidays November to Easter (or by appointment). 🅿️ ♿
♨️ & 🍴 book in advance with Manager.

This little gallery is a gem! It is also unique, being the only gallery in Britain devoted entirely to this artist, and is in the village where he was born and spent most of his working life. The Gallery has a permanent collection of Spencer's work, together with letters, documents and memorabilia. Summer and winter exhibitions are mounted; winter ones are drawn mainly from the permanent collection, while in the summer additional important works are borrowed from other collections around the country. This means that although the gallery is small, it is well worth visiting again and again.

Stanley Spencer was born in Cookham in 1891 and as a child spent many hours in the King's Hall (now housing the Gallery) when it was still a Wesleyan Methodist Chapel. Religion, music and literature were key interests for the young Spencer, particularly since his education was somewhat rudimentary. He and several contemporaries were taught by his sisters, the garden shed doubling as a schoolroom. The Spencer family lived then at 'Fernlea', just a little way along the High Street from the gallery.

Spencer went to the Slade School of Art, London, in 1908, commuting daily from home in Cookham. Though he was at first a reserved and quiet student, he went on to win a scholarship in 1910 and two prizes in 1912.

During the First World War

Stanley Spencer, The Last Supper, *1920*

Spencer served in the army and his experiences were reflected in the murals that he painted in the Sandham Memorial Chapel at Burghclere, near Newbury (for which there are preparatory studies in the collection). The chapel is a memorial to Henry Willoughby Sandham, who died in 1919 from an illness that he developed during the War. The mural on the east wall shows soldiers rising from their graves at the Resurrection; those on the north and south walls depict the daily tasks of a medical orderly, including polishing taps and cleaning floors (Spencer was an orderly from 1914–16). Students at the Royal College of Art presented Spencer with his own key to Burghclere Chapel (now displayed in the gallery together with other memorabilia).

In 1925 Stanley Spencer married Hilda Carline, also a Slade-trained artist, who, according to Spencer, was an extraordinary person; their relationship was apt to be a stormy one. In 1932 they came to live in Cookham. Increasing difficulties between them resulted from Spencer's developing relationship with Patricia Preece, another

Stanley Spencer, Marjorie Metz, *1958*

Slade-trained artist who lived in Cookham. This finally led to divorce in 1937, followed within a week by Spencer's marriage to Patricia. Spencer's ideal would have been to share his life with both women; in fact, he lived mainly on his own in Cookham, Patricia living with a friend. He was always devoted to Hilda and nurtured the hope that they might remarry one day. Hilda died in 1950, nine years before Spencer himself died of cancer.

The Gallery has an important collection of Spencer's work, both paintings and drawings, some owned by the gallery and others on loan; a number of these are permanently on display. It has a number of examples of Spencer's early works, which are particularly important as relatively few have survived. The largest and most intriguing painting is 'Christ Preaching at Cookham Regatta' (ill. on cover). This huge painting is unfinished, so one can study the pencil outlines of figures that were never completed. The poem by Alfred Boxer describes the scene:

'They stand, they sit, they stare and
    yawn and pray
A motley gathering on a summers day
He talks with thrusting zest and fearful
    eye
The river runs, the boatman passes by.
Two thousand years of gospel his
    refrain
Their bland indifference crucifies
    again.'

There are also early sketches and studies for this painting, and you can see how images were developed and altered. 'The Last Supper', painted in 1920, is another important early work that, like 'Christ Preaching at Cookham Regatta', has an associated poem by Boxer. A series of studies for 'The Last Supper' are displayed alongside the painting. Continuing the biblical theme, Spencer's Bible is on display, inscribed: 'From E. Moss to Spencer/14th March 1906/Thou therefore endure/hardness as a good/soldier of Jesus Christ/2 Timothy 2 v 3'.

The late Marjorie Metz was a personal friend of Spencer's, who became

Spencer going painting in Cookham

Chairman of the Friends of the Gallery after Spencer's death. In 1958 Spencer painted her portrait. It is a striking and fine picture, and is on permanent display in the gallery. Spencer is well known for the rather stylised figures in his later paintings, but the picture of Mrs Metz and some of the drawings here show what a fine portraitist Spencer was. His series of five paintings of Englefield House reveal another aspect of his work and skill; 'Wisteria at Englefield' is one of the series usually on display.

Spencer's skill and importance were recognised by the award of a CBE in 1950. He also received an Honorary Doctorate of Letters from Southampton University, which is on display along with the CBE. He is remembered by many local people, and was often seen painting in the area. He transported easel and equipment in a pram that now stands in the gallery, together with his large black umbrella and handwritten sign: 'As he is anxious to complete his painting of the Churchyard Mr Stanley Spencer would be grateful if visitors would avoid distracting his attention from the work.' (NH)

DIDCOT

Didcot Railway Centre

Didcot Parkway Station, Didcot, Oxfordshire OX11 7NJ
(0235) 817200
Open Tuesdays to Sundays plus Bank Holidays April to end of September; weekends only remainder of year. 🚆 🖼 🅿
NB Children under 12 must be accompanied by an adult.
♿: wheelchair access not generally possible, but special days held with transport laid on – 'phone for details.
🍴 & 🚻 book in advance; Education service. ◉

Isambard Kingdom Brunel designed the Great Western Railway (also known as GWR and 'God's Wonderful Railway') from 1833 and construction began in 1835. The GWR line ran from London to Bristol, and it was the Bristol merchants who promoted it as they were keen to have access to the London markets. The GWR remained an independent company until the nationalisation of the railways on 31 December 1947.

Brunel was an entrepreneurial genius who was determined that his railway would be the finest in the country and would carry the fastest trains. He employed a 'broad gauge' of seven feet between the rails, and viaducts and bridges were designed on a suitably grand scale. The broad gauge was in fact abandoned by GWR in 1892 and standard gauge (of 4ft 8½ inches) was adopted; this marked a turning point in the fortunes of GWR, with a new phase of expansion and building taking place in the 1890s.

The GWR line ran through Didcot, with the first Didcot station being constructed in 1844. The Railway Centre is accessible via Didcot Parkway BR station, and the sight and sound of today's 125 trains make an excellent contrast to the Railway Centre's collections. The Centre collects GWR-related equipment and associated ob-

Locomotives 'ready for action' on a steam day at Didcot

jects, and the distinctive, well-organised collections make any visit particularly memorable. Among the main features of the Centre is a visitor complex comprising a shop, refreshment room and small relics museum. There is also a section of broad gauge line, a signal box from Radstock, and a main line that allows a round trip of one mile.

The story of the origin of the Railway Centre is an appealing 'Boy's Own Adventures' sort of tale. After nationalisation the new British Railways decided that a limited number of old GWR locomotives would be preserved for posterity. In 1961 four train-spotting schoolboys noticed an old GWR 'push and pull' or autotrain in sidings in Southall; it seemed to be forgotten but the boys felt it should be preserved and that if no-one else wanted to do it, they would. They raised money towards the project, and eventually the Great Western Society was formed. In 1964 the Society bought its first locomotive, and was offered the use of an old engine shed at

Didcot to store it. In the twenty-five years since then the Railway Centre has developed and thrived. Many volunteers are involved in keeping the Centre and the trains running, and it is beginning to build up a small team of paid staff.

The museum has a fascinating range of GWR equipment and ephemera. The GWR company needed a veritable army of staff to keep the railway running smoothly, and some of their uniforms and equipment are displayed in the museum. It seems that the logo 'GWR' was stamped, printed or embossed on almost everything the staff used, ranging from leather over-boots for use when working with gunpowder vans (GWR was stamped on the sole) to pen-nibs in the station-master's office.

A railwayman's work could be hazardous, especially in the shunting yards and engine sheds, so GWR established a comprehensive first-aid network. During the First World War trains were specially adapted as ambulance trains to transport wounded sol-

diers home from the front; the museum has photographs and objects relating to these.

A railway journey often involved a night or two away from home, so the GWR owned a number of hotels around the country. The best known of these was the Great Western Royal Hotel at Paddington, where 'the bedrooms are decorated and furnished in the latest modern designs and the beds equipped with Vi Spring mattresses to ensure comfort. Generous provision is made in the matter of bathroom accommodation.' It really does seem to have been a more elegant age for travellers in the early decades of this century. All the plates were china and the glasses *were* glass, not plastic. The passenger could even order light lunch boxes or tea baskets – a pot of tea, bread and butter, a cake or bun and some fruit, all for the princely sum of 1s 3d (or about 6–7p).

In the 1930s the GWR was not slow in publicising its services. Among the publicity material were posters extolling the virtues of trips by rail to Porthcawl or Plymouth. Another poster in the museum's collection recommends a visit to 'Bertram Mills' Circus and Menagerie, with Koringa, the only female fakir in the world'. Less direct forms of publicity were also used. There were GWR jigsaw puzzles of all sorts, playing cards, models of locomotives, and even full model railway sets. GWR had a tremendous impact on children's toys of the 1920s and '30s. Another publicity vehicle was books – on winter resorts served by GWR, and on camping and rambling holidays that were possible using the GWR line to get away from it all.

Some of the GWR tickets displayed around the museum are reminders of stations that have long since disappeared, such as Hampstead Norreys. The railway did have a considerable impact on the local community, as evidenced by the 'Market Didcot' watch. When the GWR line reached Didcot four local farmers paid for a local Corn Exchange to be built so that farmers no longer had to travel to London for such business. The project was so successful that the profits of the

Display of GWR hotel equipment and ephemera in the small relics museum, Didcot

DORCHESTER-ON-THAMES

Dorchester Abbey Museum

The Monastery Guest House, Dorchester-on-Thames, Oxfordshire (0865) 340056
Open May to end of September Tuesdays to Saturdays, Bank Holiday Mondays and Sunday afternoons; also weekends from Easter to May and first two weekends in October. ▣ ▣
&: 2 steps at entrance, then all on one level.
▟ & ▟ welcome; if a guide is required contact the Rector, 10 Manor Farm Road, Dorchester-on-Thames, Oxfordshire OX9 8HZ   (0865) 340007.

first year of operation were used to make special commemorative watches for the four farmers.

The museum has a fine range of locomotive models, including the 'King Richard I', a fine GWR King class locomotive in the form of a 5-inch gauge steam model. One case of smaller models sits on a table that could easily be overlooked: this is one of the only surviving tables from a GWR ladies' waiting room.

The small relics museum, opened by John Craven in 1982, is an excellent complement to the collection of locomotives. The Centre has over twenty GWR locomotives including the 'Drysllwyn Castle', which worked between South Wales and London. The engine was purchased from a scrapyard in Barry, South Wales, and was restored between 1977 and 1980. The GWR pioneered the use of diesel

GWR posters

railcars and the Centre has No.22, which saw service in the Worcester area. The Centre also has a wide variety of GWR coaches. The oldest dates to 1887 and was designed for broad gauge use. Some early-20th century coaches (such as No. 1941) were designed with 'clerestory' roofs, which gave additional head space. No. 1941 originally had oil lamps, which were replaced by gas, and the elaborate gas light fittings are still to be seen.

The Centre often has a number of trains on loan from other railway centres. These visiting locomotives provide new and changing interest for the visitor. There are regular steam-days, evening and early morning photographers' sessions, and many other events throughout the season. (NH)

Dorchester Museum is tiny, but can be the basis of a whole day out because of all the things that there are to see and enjoy in and around Dorchester. The village and its surroundings are picturesque and steeped in the history that 6,000 years of continuous human occupation have generated. The museum provides a brief overview of this history, and the volunteers who run the museum and gift shop will happily provide the visitor with tips on local sites that should not be missed, plus leaflets to guide your explorations.

The museum's founder was Edith Stedman. She was not, as you might suppose, a born and bred local but was the Director of Radcliffe College Appointments Board – in America. Miss Stedman had friends who moved to Dorchester and she soon fell in love with the place herself. For seventeen years she spent six months in Dorchester and six in America. One of her first enterprises was to raise money for the creation and maintenance of the abbey cloister garden. Then she helped raise money for the restoration of the Abbey's East Window (contributions came, among others, from General

GWR model railway items

Front of the museum, incorporating the remains of the Abbey Guest House

and arctic fox. Even in prehistoric times this area was an important one. Evidence of early man's activities comes from the Neolithic/Bronze Age henge and cursus complex, including the Big Rings henge monument. This site was discovered from the air and excavated before destruction by gravel workings. The Bronze Age (so called because of the widespread use of bronze for tools, weapons and ornaments) has also left its mark in the form of field systems, round barrows and ring ditches. A map and aerial photographs displayed in the museum show that Dorchester is surrounded by cropmarks of many periods. Finds from the late Bronze Age include two fine shields found in the River Thames (now in the **Ashmolean** and British Museums). The dominating feature of the early Iron Age was the hillfort on the 'Wittenham Clumps', across the Thames to the south of Dorchester. The southern 'clump' provides a magnificent view over the Thames Valley, including the site of a large British settlement (*c.* 50 BC–50 AD).

Roman Dorchester was an important regional centre. Initially there was a fort here, but the military phase ended by about AD 78 and a small civilian settlement, with streets laid out on a grid pattern, developed. A modified Roman way of life continued in Dorchester after the end of Roman Britain in AD 410; it was one of the few towns where this was so. An interesting coin in the museum's collec-

Eisenhower). The next project was the Monastery Guest House, built in 1400. With help from the **Ashmolean Museum** and the Bodleian Library, Dorchester Abbey Museum was founded there in 1959 and, in Miss Stedman's words, 'was a howling success!' (Edith Stedman received an OBE for her services to the community; she died in 1978.)

The Monastery Guest House was originally linked to the Abbey tower by an archway, and although traces remain the arch itself has long since gone. After the Dissolution in 1536 most of the monastic buildings disappeared. The Abbey Church itself survived, thanks to Richard Beauforest, who bought the chancel in 1536 and gave it to the parish. The remains of the Guest House were incorporated into a new grammar school, which operated there from 1652 until the mid-18th century. Later it was used as a boys national school. The museum has a photocopy of the origin-

al school register of 1653–1714, now in the Bodleian for safe keeping. Another reminder of the school is a set of small wooden drawers used by the pupils, which can still be seen in the central pillar of the original schoolroom. Most of what remains of the Guest House now forms the front wall of the museum. There is a deep window with a small window seat and it was from here that the 'Abbey Dole' – bread and beer for the pilgrims – was handed out.

The museum describes the development of the village and its surroundings. Many of the exceptional archaeological finds from the area are now in the British Museum or **Ashmolean**, but Dorchester retains some items of particular interest. There is a small but fine collection of Acheulian hand-axes, made of flint and dating from the Paleolithic or 'Old Stone Age'. Local gravel deposits have yielded remains that indicate contemporary animal life included mammoth, woolly rhinoceros, cave bear, cave lion

Roman coin of Magnentius (350–353 AD)

tion is that of Magnentius, a usurper in Gaul around 350 AD. The coin has the Chi-ro monogram on the reverse – one of the early symbols of Christianity, which can still be seen in churches today. The town was garrisoned by Germanic mercenary troops in the early 5th century; their burials have been found at Dyke Hills and to the north of the town. It is uncertain how long this phase lasted, but the sunken huts found within the town walls show that new Saxon settlers had arrived by the mid-6th century.

In the 7th century Dorchester was part of the Kingdom of Wessex, and became an early centre of Christianity in AD 635, when Cynegils, king of the West Saxons, was baptised here by St Birinus, a missionary bishop sent by Pope Honorius I to convert the English. Dorchester was first the cathedral-church of the West Saxons and later of a great Mercian diocese. The bishop's seat was moved to Lincoln in the 1070s, and the church was refounded as an Abbey of Augustinian canons around 1140. The Abbey Church is rich in medieval glass and sculpture, and has some interesting and unusual features, including a lead font depicting eleven apostles (only about thirty lead fonts of the period still exist in England and this is one of the finest), and the splendid effigy of an unknown knight (*c.* 1280), a 'lively' cross-legged figure in chain mail, with his hand about to draw his sword.

By the 9th century Dorchester's importance had declined, and Oxford and Wallingford came to the fore. More recently, farming was the dominant way of life. The village also had two water-mills working into the 19th century. One unusual feature (which visitors can make use of!) is the survival of many long-established inns; by the 18th century there were ten in this small village. Among those surviving today are the George Hotel (*c.* 1500), the White Hart (1691) and the Fleur-de-Lys (run by one family from 1850 to 1900). So by the time you leave, you can feel well fed and spiritually refreshed, having learned a good deal about Dorchester's history into the bargain! (NH)

ELSTOW

Elstow Moot Hall

Elstow Green, Elstow, Bedford, Bedfordshire   (0234) 66889 (address for enquiries: *Bedfordshire Leisure Services, County Hall, Bedford MK42 9AP   (0234) 228330*)
Open April to October, afternoons on Tuesdays to Sundays and Bank Holidays. 🄵 🄿
♿ S: limited access for wheelchairs to ground floor and none to first floor.
♿ & ♿ must book in advance (0234) 228330; reduced admission rates; every effort made to accommodate visits out of normal opening hours.

Elstow Moot Hall is one of four historic sites in the care of Bedfordshire County Council. The 15th or early 16th century building stands in the middle of Elstow Green, and contains furniture and furnishings from the 17th century, and documents and books that refer to the life of Elstow's most famous resident, John Bunyan. The Moot Hall, or Green House as it was formerly known, was used as a market house at the centre of life in Elstow. The ground floor was originally divided into 'bays' or 'shops' which served as storage space for the stalls and equipment used at fairs held on the green; a single room above was used for hearing disputes, testing measures and checking merchants' credentials. Similar buildings, with a long open chamber above and shops below, are rare.

Bunyan was born near Elstow in 1628 and returned to a house on the edge of the village after his marriage. He rang bells in the abbey, and played games on the green until his spiritual development and preaching, and arrest on 12th November 1660. Released in 1671 under Charles II's Declaration of Indulgence, a warrant was issued for his arrest in 1675 and again in 1676. Two friends stood surety for his re-

Exterior view of Elstow Moot Hall

Interior view of the upper floor, showing the medieval roof

the edge of the room and portraits hang on the walls. The effect conjures up the heaviness of 17th century interiors while maintaining a sense of space. The furniture is mostly dark oak, carved and turned in varying degress of richness. The lovely barley-twist chairs contrast with the straighter gun-barrel turnings of the occasional joint stool. The portraits include one of Sir Samuel Luke, MP for Bedford in 1640, painted by Gerrard Soest, and a rather jolly head and shoulders of 'Bunyan in Prison' by Andrew Geddes (1789–1844).

Elstow Moot Hall is a good starting point to explore Bunyan's Bedfordshire. There is another museum devoted to his life in the *Bunyan Meeting Rooms* in Mill Street, Bedford, and other 'Bunyan' sites in the town are detailed in publications on sale at Elstow. This is a somewhat underestimated part of the world, often visited only on the way to somewhere else, but Elstow Moot Hall and the other historic sites throughout the county make Bedfordshire well worth visiting in its own right. (KH)

lease after he had spent six months in prison, during which time it is thought that he wrote *Pilgrim's Progress*.

The Moot Hall contains many papers relating to these turbulent times in Bunyan's life. They are displayed in well-lit cases, with models or period artefacts to give them context. The warrant for his arrest, signed by eleven magistrates, is particularly striking with its eleven red seals. John Bunyan is described in it as 'Tynker' of Bedford. Also on display are editions of *Pilgrim's Progress*, Bunyan's most popular though not only book. There are copies in Punjabi, Sotho and Swedish, perhaps the result of English missionaries' zeal. Various artists' impressions of the Pilgrims' route are striking, as is the plate from an edition illustrated by William Blake. It is strange to see the variety of ways in which one set of words can be presented. In the same room is a door from the county gaol in Bedford. Behind this, or one similar, the character of Christian and his progress to the

Celestial City were born. On the wall there is a helpful list of notable people from Bunyan's lifetime, including Sir Christopher Wren, Isaac Newton and Oliver Cromwell.

The rest of the building concentrates on giving the visitor a feeling of Bunyan's contemporary world. One room on the ground floor is furnished with table and benches, a child's cot, lacemaker's stool, and various chairs, chests and implements, to give the effect and atmosphere of a 17th century room. The upper storey of the building is a large open chamber, which in its time has been used for the manor court hearings, as a place of worship, and as a National and a Night School. The gorgeous medieval roof is largely intact, with exposed 'trusses', 'collars' and 'purlins'. It gives a rare opportunity to examine the construction techniques of medieval carpenters. The chamber is left open, with a long refectory table in the centre of the cambered polished floorboards. Items of 17th century furniture are placed at

Christian and Hopeful escape from Doubting Castle

Illustration by Blake to Pilgrims Progress

ETON

Eton College Collections

*Eton College, Windsor,
Berkshire SL4 6DB
Office of Keeper of the College
Collections (0753) 869991 ext. 117
Tourist Manager (0753) 863593*

Brewhouse Gallery (including *Myers Museum*): in Brewhouse Yard; open Saturday & Sunday afternoons during term, & at other times by arrangement. **F**
&: wheelchair access to ground floor only.
Museum of Eton Life: in Brewhouse Yard; open every afternoon from 1 April to first Sunday in October (out of School term also open mornings). as part of general admission fee.
Natural History Museum: adjacent to the Lower Chapel in South Meadow Lane; open on School half-holidays during term. **F** &

& book in advance: contact Tourist Manager.

Eton College has four main collections accessible to the public (although it is wise to check the opening hours in advance). There is the **Brewhouse Gallery**, where part of the College's extensive and fine collection of watercolours and prints is exhibited, as well as the **Myers Museum** collection of Egyptian antiquities. There is also the **Natural History Museum**, where in baronial splendour a fine collection of zoological and geological specimens is displayed, and finally the **Museum of Eton Life**, which is a museum of social history.

The **Museum of Eton Life** was opened in 1985 and tells the story of the College, from its foundation in 1440 by the nineteen-year-old Henry VI, up to the present time. This is done by means of a wide variety of documents, books, objects, models, pictures, photographs and video presentation. It is housed in what was the old

beer cellar under the College Hall, and is a well designed, attractive introduction to the college and school.

Henry VI founded both Eton College, which he intended to be one of the finest religious centres in England, and King's College in Cambridge. He made provision in the original statutes, which date from 1443, for the free education and support of seventy boys, chosen when between the ages of eight and twelve, called the King's Scholars. These still exist and today are selected for their high academic promise and performance. Henry also allowed that others who wished their sons to be educated at Eton could send them to board in the town: hence the word *Oppidans*, derived from the Latin word *Oppidum*, meaning town. Today there are about 1200 of these, who pay fees (although in some cases these too are subvented by the College). The documents that relate the early history of the College are preserved in the College Archives, and some are shown in the Museum.

From the foundation right up to the 1840s the King's Scholars lived in one long room, the notorious Long Chamber. By the 18th century there were established in the vicinity of the College boarding houses run by women 'dames', and eventually in the 19th century by masters. This was done on a basis of private enterprise, and it is only this century that the College has taken control of all boarding houses, where every boy has his own room. The museum has a reconstruction of a boy's room of 1900: a bare minimum of furniture was provided – a fold-up bed, a flap table, a hard chair, each boy having to provide his own bureau, curtains and other furniture.

For centuries the scholar's life was rigorous – early rising, poor food and severe discipline. From the 15th to the 19th century the birch was used to punish miscreants: for example, boys were beaten for drinking or going out of bounds. Interestingly enough, smoking was not punishable in the 1660s but was indeed compulsory for boys as a protection against the bubonic plague.

Until the 19th century the boys

learned only Latin and Greek. It was certainly possible from the 17th century to learn some modern languages and some arithmetic, as well as fencing and other gentlemanly pursuits, but special arrangements, and extra payments, had to be made. This situation was finally changed in the 1860s, and today the curriculum is very wide.

Fayyum mummy portrait, 2nd century AD

The **Brewhouse Gallery**, which is immediately adjacent to the Museum of Eton Life, was once the College's brewhouse where beer (the staple drink for all until well into the 19th century) was brewed. It lies next to the medieval kitchen, which is still in use. From about 1870 until the 1960s the brewhouse was used to house the Choir School maintained by the College, but in 1969 it was turned into a picture gallery.

The ground floor of the building is devoted to changing exhibitions that draw on the College's artistic treasures, while on the top floor one room contains an exhibition of late 18th cen-

Paul Sandby, Eton College from Crown Point, *after 1768*

tury watercolours and prints of Windsor and Eton, and another a changing exhibition of photographs and other materials. Of the two rooms on the first floor, one, which has recently been renovated, contains a selection of the extensive collection of English watercolours given to Eton by Alan Pilkington. This collection includes many fine and important pictures, by artists such as Girtin, Cotman, de Wint, Callow, Gainsborough and Prout, as well as the work of many other artists. As a rule about forty of these are displayed in exhibitions organised around a particular theme.

In the adjacent room on the first floor is displayed the bulk of the collection of Egyptian antiquities that form the **Myers Museum**. William Joseph Myers was at Eton from 1871 until 1875. He became an army officer, and in the 1880s was on the staff of the General commanding in Cairo. It was there that his passion for collecting, which embraced many different fields, was centred upon Egyptian artefacts. His particular interest lay in faience ceramic ware, with its brilliant blue glaze. In 1899 he was killed in the Boer

War, but he had bequeathed his collection to Eton, to be an inspiration to future generations. And inspiration it certainly is. The Myers Museum is one of the finest and largest private collections of Egyptian art in Britain, and numbers some 1500 objects ranging in date from the Stone Age to the Coptic period. Its use as a unique teaching aid is actively encouraged.

The items on display reflect many aspects of Egyptian daily life and religion (colour plate 1). There are small models, for example, of a granary and a basket weaver's workshop, both dating from 1987 to 1640 BC. Another wooden model of the same date is of a funerary barge, a reflection of the religious ceremonies of the Middle Kingdom. Religion permeated all aspects of Egyptian life: there were official state cults (such as Amon Ra) centred on the temples, but these were remote from ordinary people, and for them there were cults with smaller shrines and lesser gods. Many objects could almost be modern – the wooden wig support, the trinket boxes, or the dice (from the Roman period). Another especially attractive item is a small painted

wooden statue, dating from between 2705 and 1987 BC, of a serving girl with a basket on her head, with a duck in her hands, and a goat walking in front. One of the most famous objects is the Fayyum portrait of a young bearded man. This is painted on wood, and was placed over the head of a mummy and held in place by bandages. It dates from the early Christian era (before *c.* 395 AD).

The **Natural History Museum** is the oldest of the museums at Eton. There are stuffed birds here, as well as birds' eggs, butterflies and moths, and skeletons of large mammals, together with sizeable collections of rocks, minerals, and fossils. Part of the museum has been adapted for teaching biology, but the rest remains a marvellous specimen of a now more or less vanished approach to the natural world.

The museums of Eton College, combined with the splendid buildings of the College itself – the famous chapel dominating everything, make for a full and varied visit. It is a short walk from Eton to **Windsor**, where there is also much to see. (NH)

FARNHAM

Farnham Museum

*38 West Street, Farnham, Surrey
GU9 7DX (0252) 715094*
Closed Sundays and Mondays. ☐
&: wheelchair access to ground
floor only, including garden; **T**;
access to first floor only by original
staircase.
⊞ & ⱦ preferably book in
advance.

Farnham is a very attractive market
town on the Surrey/Hampshire border
that still retains a great deal of its
original character. Despite the considerable expansion of the town, the
High Street remains the natural focus
and has not yet been neutered by
building society offices and fast-food
outlets. The small museum provides a
useful introduction to exploring the
town and the surrounding area.

Visitors to Farnham are immediately
attracted by the large number of fine
Georgian brick buildings, many constructed with profits from local hop
growing. Closer examination, however,
will reveal that a number are re-
frontings of much older buildings,
often dating back to medieval times. It
is fascinating to walk along the High
Street and then to look at the rear of
the same buildings from backyards or
lanes; many owners in the past simply
added an up-to-date front but did not
waste money on the parts that most
people would not see. As well as the
wealth of domestic architecture, the
medieval castle (begun in 1138) and
Waverley Abbey (the first Cistercian
abbey in England) should not be missed.

Farnham Museum occupies Willmer House, a Grade I listed building
and one of the finest houses in the
town. It was built in 1718 by a local
merchant, who made and subsequently
lost his money in the fickle hop trade.
The front, built of 'Kentish Rubbers',
is one of the best cut-brick façades in
the area. Willmer House, with its
equally impressive neighbour, domin-

Exterior view of Farnham Museum

ates the west end of the High Street
today in much the same way as it must
have done when originally constructed.
Once inside, you get a good sense of
the living space available in a house of
this type in the 18th century and realise
that outside appearances can be decep-
tive, for there are only a small number
of rooms. With an imposing staircase
taking up one corner of the house, each
of the two main floors has only three
rooms. The top floor (not open to the
public) would originally have been
used by the servants.

The building houses a small collection of material largely connected with
the history of Farnham. A painting of
the town from the south by an unknown artist, dated 1773, shows a
typical 18th century market town
dominated by the church and ruined
castle, which are surrounded by a mass
of houses and inns. The observant will
notice Willmer House, with its long
garden running down to the river,
standing out amongst the cottages.
Farnham then was a compact unit with
a population numbered in hundreds
and fields running up to meet the
gardens. It was at this period that the
town produced its most famous son,
William Cobbett (1762–1835), the

Farnham Pottery pig

essayist, politician and agriculturalist.
Cobbett was born at the Jolly Farmer
Inn (which still survives, renamed 'The
William Cobbett') in Bridge Square,
and is buried in the churchyard. He
spent his life fighting against the economic changes that were reshaping
England, and particularly the countryside. Many will be familiar with Cobbett's descriptions of his travels across
England, published as *Rural Rides*,
which are full of acerbic comments on
the changing pattern of rural life. The
fine panelled dining room here contains a small collection of mementoes
relating to his life, including carica-

Detail from one of James Gillray's caricatures of scenes from William Cobbett's life

GOUDHURST

Finchcocks Living Museum of Music

Goudhurst, Kent TN17 1HH
(0580) 211702
Open afternoons only on Sundays from Easter to end of September, Bank Holiday Mondays, and Wednesdays to Sundays during August. (Private visits can be arranged from April to October on most days, though preferably not on Mondays or Tuesdays.) ▣ ▣ and special catering can be arranged. Picknicking in grounds, or cellar during bad weather. ℗ ♿: wheelchair access to ground floor only (access to first floor by original stairs only).
♙ & ♙ are strongly advised to book as Finchcocks is very popular with groups; ♙ reduced admission. ◎

tures, his portrait and various publications. The William Cobbett Society is based at the museum, and one can only hope that the displays about this fascinating character will be extended in the future. A copy of his American publication, *The Porcupine's Gazette*, gives a clue to his character. Although Cobbett was not elected to Parliament until 1832, he was always in the thick of political debate and founded *Hansard*. Objects include a silver inkstand presented to him in 1819 by the 'Female Reformers of Manchester', a group described by a contemporary opponent as 'petticoat reformers ... degraded females guilty of the worst prostitution of their sex'.

A century later another Farnham resident, George Sturt (pen-name 'George Bourne'), a local wheelwright, recorded the passing of a later golden age. Sturt (1863–1927) had his first book, *A Year's Exile*, published in 1898, followed by another ten that describe the rapid development and change in the Farnham area as waves of middle class residents, seeking an escape from the spawling suburbs of London, moved into the locality. Books like *Change in the Village* and *A Small Boy in the Sixties*, which have recently been republished, paint a remarkable picture of this area. Today it is difficult to believe how an area so close to London could have been so isolated only 100 years ago. The museum has a small display of related material, including a

photograph of Sturt's remarkable gardener, Frederick Glover, who was the source of much of the dialect stories and observations contained in the trilogy of Bettesworth books.

This unspoilt corner of Surrey attracted many members of the Arts and Crafts Movement in the late 19th century and the town still has an important art college. The museum has a small collection of Farnham pottery. Although local production dates back to the Roman period, pottery manufacture was re-established by Absalom Harris in 1873, and Farnham was soon supplying art wares to progressive London stores such as Libertys and Heals. Unlike most similar ventures, the pottery still survives, run by the fifth generation of Harris potters.

The scale of the museum building does not allow for large exhibitions on any one subject, but there are small displays on local geology, archaeology and history, including local hop growing, which only died out finally in recent years. Many children and adults will be charmed by a superb dolls' house, built about 1788 and based on Sandford House, next door to the museum. Although the original contents have disappeared and been replaced by more recent furnishings, it is an excellent early example and even features a pull-out garden. Special exhibitions are regularly held in a separate gallery in the attractive walled garden behind the museum. (GM)

The moment you see the grand brick façade of Finchcocks from the approach drive you expect something special – and this museum does not disappoint. Finchcocks is unique, and combines aspects of visiting a country house, a museum and a concert to make a hugely enjoyable experience. The museum is the creation of the pianist, Richard Burnett, and his wife Katrina, who aim to provide anybody, from the general visitor to the specialist musical student, with an entertaining and informative introduction to the keyboard instruments of the 17th to 19th centuries.

The story of the collection begins in the 1960s when Richard Burnett started to acquire early keyboard instruments. There was a growing interest in performing early music on original instruments and he began to restore many of his acquisitions to playing condition. The collection soon expanded to considerable size, and now includes virginals, spinets, harp-

Grand piano by Clementi, 1822

The collection stops around 1850 with the introduction of the first metal-framed pianos, the immediate antecedent of the modern concert piano. To some extent the collection is complemented by the late Frank Holland's Musical Museum at Brentford, Middlesex, which concentrates on the late 19th to early 20th centuries, with particular emphasis given to mechanical instruments.

During a normal afternoon at Finchcocks one may hear anything from six to ten instruments being used to illustrate how keyboard playing developed. Special performances can be arranged for individual groups, concentrating on particular instruments, periods or composers. Additional impromptu performances also take place as Finchcocks is now a musical centre of international repute and musicians are often at the house for teaching or recording purposes. In between performances, one has the opportunity to examine the collection in detail and talk with the pianist. It should be stressed that during normal opening the afternoon is aimed at the ordinary visitor without any specialist knowledge. Families with children are actively encouraged and the sequence of three performances separated by breaks allows information to be digested easily. Parents of babies and very young children should bear in mind the enjoyment of others, but there is plenty of space in the grounds to run off excess energy. The house is located in one of the most beautiful areas of Kent and there are extensive views across the park to the farmland of the Weald.

For most people a visit will be a revelation about the style and sound of keyboard music in the past. It is fascinating to see the types of instruments that Haydn and Mozart would have played on. The pianos include a grand made in 1826 in Vienna by Conrad Graf, which is virtually identical to the instruments on which Beethoven, Schubert, Schumann and Chopin composed and performed. All the instruments have wooden frames and the quality of their sound shows the enormous care with which they have been restored and maintained. The collec-

sichords, clavichords, chamber organs and a wide variety of pianos. Today there are nearly seventy historic instruments, together with a few modern copies, and over thirty are kept in playing condition. In 1970 Richard Burnett bought Finchcocks to house his expanding collection, which was soon recognised as one of the most important in the country. The house is a fine example of a Georgian country seat and dates to 1725. It is a Grade 1 listed building and is particularly noted for its fine quality brickwork. Finchcocks was opened to the public in 1977 and the collection, activities and facilities have been gradually developed as resources permit.

The essential part of a visit is not just to look at the collection but to hear original music played on appropriate contemporary instruments. All the instruments date from before the appearance of large public concert halls and were designed to be played to small audiences. They are therefore much quieter than modern concert pianos and are inappropriate for most modern concert venues. However, the large rooms at Finchcocks are typical of the original settings for which these instruments were designed and the fine acoustics allow visitors to hear performances as they would have sounded 200 years ago. On a typical afternoon when the house is open there are 1½–2 hours of playing, broken into three sections. The performance takes a broadly chronological journey, starting with virginals and early harpsichords, and finishing with pianos from the early to mid-19th century.

tion provides not only a comprehensive range of types but has examples from most of the main manufacturing centres, including many from Vienna. Each instrument is a superb piece of craftsmanship and reflects general developments in design and technology. Among particularly attractive items is a 1668 virginal from Naples with a superbly decorated case, including a range of classical buildings painted on the underside of the lid. In sharp contrast is a piano made by William Southwell in Dublin around 1800. Although it is of inferior quality as an instrument, it is a fine example of the cabinetmaker's craft, decorated in marquetry with a design of musical instruments. It is interesting to see how the use of iron inside the piano steadily increased during the 19th century and eventually led to the introduction of the complete iron frame. This allowed a much louder tone and consigned earlier keyboard instruments to rapid oblivion. Craftsmen such as Graf would not use iron in their pianos and eventually went out of business. However, most makers were happy to incorporate the latest technology made possible by the Industrial Revolution. Looking at pianos by Clementi or Broadwood it is extraordinary to realise that they were built in London workshops in the heart of Soho and the City.

When the Burnetts moved their collection to Finchcocks there was no original furniture as the house had previously been used as a ballet school. They are slowly decorating the interior with paintings and displays relating to the collection, although most of the rooms are filled with the instruments. In one of the first floor rooms there is an amusing collection of satirical prints featuring early pianos.

One of the particular pleasures of a visit to Finchcocks is that many of the instruments have been used for period recordings which are for sale in the shop. There are few museums in Britain where you can take home such an accurate sound of the past. Most visitors probably leave the house not only having learnt a great deal but also with the desire to learn more about this fascinating subject. (GM)

GUILDFORD

Guildford Museum

*Castle Arch, Guildford, Surrey
GU1 3SX   (0483) 444750*
Closed Sundays. ▣
♿: wheelchair access to ground floor and part of upper floors.
▥ & ♥ preferably book in advance; information sheets available and classroom for ♥.

The sea of new executive housing estates encircling Guildford is an eloquent testimony to the enduring attractions of this medieval town. Guildford maintains a distinctive character despite extensive redevelopment in the town centre, and the cobbled High Street, with its famous clock, is still lined by many historic buildings.

Set in a prominent gap in the North Downs, Guildford was laid out as a planned town in the medieval period. A

good idea of the original street pattern can be gained by climbing the imposing castle mound. The huge stone keep here, dating to the 12th century, is roofless, but there are hopes to restore it one day to its original appearance. The castle was a favourite royal residence, and both King John and Henry III stayed there. Nestling close to the castle, and indeed partially built onto the castle gate, is Guildford Museum.

Despite the importance of Guildford, which is the county town of Surrey, the museum is very small and the displays therefore cannot do justice to all its collections. It was founded in 1898 by the Surrey Archaeological Society and provides a home for finds from all over the county. The galleries occupy a rambling set of rooms within a 17th century house and an extension added in 1911. There is a fine fireplace in the parlour, dating from around 1630, carved from clunch – a hard type of chalk. There have been various schemes to rebuild the museum but despite the evident wealth of the mod-

Working model of a roundabout made by Mr Finzer in 1915

Local horse-drawn fire engine, 1863

ern town nothing has happened. Current plans focus on redesigning the existing space. At the time of writing the archaeology gallery is being redisplayed; check which areas of the museum are open before you visit.

The existing displays include an eight-minute audio-visual presentation, which provides a rapid guide to the history of the town. Guildford was important enough to have a mint in Saxon times and was the main population centre in medieval Surrey, albeit with only 1,000 or so inhabitants. Since it was halfway between London and the royal dockyards at Portsmouth, Guildford became an important staging post, and by the 18th century had half a dozen coaching inns. Only the Angel survives today; the rest were put out of business by the railways. Material on show in the museum highlights most of these major developments. Medieval sites in Guildford and Surrey have produced a wide range of finds, including superb pottery from local kilns. During the late 15th and 16th centuries the area had a flourishing glass industry and was also one of the centres of the iron industry that stretched

Cover of Wonderland postage-stamp case

across Surrey into Sussex and Kent. Looking at the modern town and the countryside it is strange to think of this area as a forerunner of the Industrial Revolution.

The museum is particularly fortunate in having been given the important collection of local rural-life material collected by Gertrude Jekyll (1843–1932). Although she is best remembered for her innovative garden designs, she was also an acute observer of social life. Living and working around

Godalming she realised how traditional life was being eroded by the continuous stream of affluent immigrants moving into the area to enjoy the rural beauty of the Weald. Her book, *Old West Surrey*, published in 1904, is still well worth reading. Items such as rush-lights, collected from farms and villages, reflect the ending of centuries-old rural self-sufficiency as mass-produced goods swept local products of wood, bone, iron and horn into oblivion. This collection is complemented by a small display about Surrey folklore and traditions (subjects on which the present Curator is an expert).

The late 19th century also saw the arrival of one of Guildford's most famous inhabitants, the Revd Charles Lutwidge Dodgson, otherwise known as Lewis Carroll. In 1868, shortly after *Alice in Wonderland* was published, Dodgson leased The Chestnuts, a house that still stands a short distance from the museum. He died there on 14th January 1898 and was buried in the town's cemetary. A variety of personal items are on display, including a sketchbook and the family's zoetrope.

The museum also has a specialised needlework collection, which aims to preserve a representative selection of British and foreign manufacture. Most examples date from the last 300 years, although there are fragments of embroidery from ancient Egyptian tombs. There is a particularly good collection of countrymen's smocks, and the displays also include samplers, patchwork, whitework and a variety of coloured embroidery.

Guildford Museum provides an absorbing introduction to the town, but lack of space and a temporary exhibition area limits the museum's full potential being achieved at present. Next door is the Guildford Muniment Room (part of the County Record Office), which contains a fine collection of local records and maps available by appointment only, while a few streets away is *Guildford House Gallery*. Located in an historic townhouse, this has a small permanent collection matched by an impressive temporary exhibition programme. (GM)

Women's Royal Army Corps Museum

Queen Elizabeth Park, Guildford, Surrey GU2 6QH (0252) 24431 ext. Guildford 8565

Closed Saturdays and Sundays. F P ♿

& must book in advance.

The WRAC Museum depicts the role played by women as part of the army. It is the only museum in the area covered by this guide that is devoted entirely to an aspect of women's history. The army's ambivalent attitude to women serving has resulted in the corps having a disjointed history, relatively little early material surviving. The museum therefore has to rely on photographs and two-dimensional displays for a large section of its story. It has recently been redisplayed in an attractive modern style.

The museum is small and housed in a single gallery, but the importance of its story is out of all proportion to its size. The opening up of the army to females was a major step in the general development of opportunities for women in the 20th century. Despite Florence Nightingale's pioneering work in the hospitals of the Crimea, British society was slow to recognise equal rights for women, or women's worth as a valuable skilled workforce. The period prior to 1914 saw intense political lobbying by the suffragettes but the outbreak of war turned the government's attention elsewhere.

However, the increasing losses on the Western Front resulted in pressures on manpower, and a growing number of people saw that women could be used to release non-combattant men for front-line duties. Concern started, perhaps predictably, in the kitchen, when the Quartermaster General, Sir John Cowans, became alarmed at the appalling standard of army cooking and the subsequent waste. In consultation with the Marchioness of Londonderry, plans were drawn up for the Women's Legion. This was to be a voluntary organisation to provide 'a capable and efficient body of women to take the place of men' by providing canteen and ambulance staff. By August 1915 the first twenty cooks were at work under the control of Miss Lilian Barker, Commandant of the Military Cookery Section. Photographs indicate that the new organisation took its work very seriously, and one hopes that culinary standards rapidly improved.

Members of QMAAC tending war graves in France, c. 1919

Due to the massive losses of men during the Battle of the Somme in 1916, the Women's Army Auxiliary Corps was established in January 1917 to supply cooks, clerks, accountants, typists and waitresses. Recruits were rapidly trained and the first draft left for France by March of that year. By the end of the war over 7,500 WAACs were serving overseas. However, if they married a soldier they could not serve in France and were sent back to England. Although the press seemed mostly interested in the moral standards of the women, the Corps performed a valuable role and began to shift the attitude of the army high command towards the idea of female soldiers. Life in France, even far behind the front line, was not comfortable or even safe. Photographs show the WAAC camp at Abbeville after bombing by German aircraft in 1918, which killed several people.

Unfortunately, few objects have survived from those early days and the displays have to rely largely on official photographs. There is, however, a small section of personalia including diaries, certificates, Christmas cards, and a Royal Doulton 'A WAAC's match tray' depicting a woman and her beau. There are also examples of the first WAAC uniforms and insignia. The Corps was given Royal patronage and renamed Queen Mary's Army Auxiliary Corps in 1918. One of the last functions of the camp at St Pol was as the temporary home of four unidentified bodies from different sectors of the Western Front. One of these was finally selected to be the 'Unknown Soldier' buried in Westminster Abbey in November 1920. The QMAAC was finally disbanded in September 1921, and one wonders whether any more records of these pioneers of opportunities for women survive in attics and cellars. It is a sad irony that the records of service by women in the First World War were destroyed by enemy bombing in the Second World War.

In the 1930s, as the threat of war began to grow, the army's attention began to turn again to the role of women in wartime, particularly as it was clear that this time civilians would be under direct threat. The Auxiliary

Territorial Service (ATS) was initially established in 1938 to release Territorial Army soldiers for active duties by providing clerks, cooks, drivers and orderlies. By the end of the Second World War over a quarter of a million members were being trained in over a hundred skills throughout the army. A series of displays concentrate on the main areas of service where the ATS worked in conjuction with male units. These included the Royal Artillery, Royal Corps of Signals and Royal Army Service Corps. In March 1945 the then Princess Elizabeth was commissioned as a 2nd Subaltern in the ATS; the museum displays the motor chassis on which she trained at Camberley and some of her uniforms, together with those of Princess Mary, Princess Royal. Winston Churchill's daughter served in an Ack Ack battery, and there is a detailed model of an anti-aircraft gun sight of about 1942.

Other displays of photographs, post-ers, documents and further items illustrate the work of the ATS around the world during the war. In 1949, in recognition that women were to be considered as a permanent part of the army, the Women's Royal Army Corps was established with its motto *Sauviter in Modo, Fortiter in Re* – 'Gentle in Manner, Resolute in Deed' – the official view of women's involvement in the army over the previous forty years.

The final section of the museum illustrates the post-war and contemporary role of the WRAC and includes a selection of proposals for and completed uniforms. The originals were designed in 1949 by Norman Hartnell and there are a number of his elegant outline sketches. Perhaps most impressive is the WRAC officer's mess dress designed by Owen Hyde Clark of the House of Worth.

The scale of the museum does not make it worth a long specific journey for the average visitor. However, for anybody in the vicinity of Guildford it shows a fascinating chapter in the story of the changing role of women in 20th-century Britain. Some skill is needed to find the museum, and the best advice is to follow the A322 north out of Guildford towards Bagshot or the A320 towards Woking and ask for directions after a mile or so. Visitors will appreciate the need for security checks since the museum is within an operational army base.

The WRAC Museum is only one of a number of military museums spawned by the concentration of army facilities around Aldershot. Some are highly specialised but many offer exhibits or locations of great interest. The *Museum of the Royal Army Chaplain's Department* is housed in Bagshot Park. This sombre house was built for Queen Victoria's son, the Duke of Connaught, and includes a superb Indian-style billiard room designed by Kipling's father and carved by Indian craftsmen. In contrast the Museum of the Royal Army Dental Corps at Aldershot (included in *Exploring Museums: Southern England*) contains an extraordinary set of drawings (*c.* 1917/18) by Henry Tonks of the first attempts at plastic surgery. (GM)

Uniform of Chief Controller, WAAC, c. 1917

HARLOW

Mark Hall Cycle Museum and Gardens

Muskham Road, Harlow, Essex
CM20 2LF   (0279) 39680
Open daily. 🅵 🅿 ♿W
♿ & ♿ book in advance.

Mark Hall Cycle Museum is one of two museums run by Harlow District Council. Opened in 1982, the museum's unique collection illustrates the development of the bicycle from its beginnings in the early 19th century to the present day. The collection was purchased by the Council in 1978 from a local bicycle business, Collins of Harlow – a family that had set up as wheelwrights in Market Street, Harlow, in 1816. Five generations later one of the same family, John Collins, still cares for the collection as Curator at Mark Hall. Although a specialist collection, the museum has wider appeal than one might at first imagine, with bicycles of all shapes and sizes, an extensive collection of accessories, and a lovely building with three walled gardens to wander in.

Sundial by Nathan David in the garden

View down Gallery 5, with multi-seaters and racers

Mark Hall itself was a medieval manor, but all that remains today are the 19th century stable block and coachmen's houses; the manor house itself was demolished in 1960. The conversion and history of the site are well documented through photographs and text in the reception area. The shop is here, too, with a selection of souvenirs and publications that relate to the subject of the museum or to the town of Harlow.

The collection is displayed in five galleries, which are best followed in sequence. The first room concentrates on the early history and development of the bicycle, with the Denis Johnson 'Hobby Horse' of 1818 as the earliest example. This is not really a bicycle: it was propelled by the rider pushing his feet on the ground. The next example, the Hedges' Velocipede or 'Boneshaker' (1865), has developed pedals, the change reminiscent of natural selection in the development of huge metal insects! The wooden Penny Farthing in the gallery is a rare example of 1869, but Penny Farthings really take over in

the next gallery, where there are twelve examples of the type of machine that reached its peak of popularity in the 1880s. With no gears, the front wheel was enlarged to give greater speed, but a limitation to size was of course the rider's length of leg. In later models the front wheel was geared and therefore became smaller.

The museum's earliest bicycle, the Denis Johnson 'Hobby Horse' of 1818

Gallery 2 also contains a 'Dunlop Corner', which displays material donated to the museum by John Boyd Dunlop's daughter. Dunlop began his career as a qualified veterinary surgeon at the age of 18, but is remembered here as the inventor of the pneumatic tyre in 1888. The company that carried his name through to the 20th century had planned to set up its own museum, and commissioned ceramic models from Charles Forster to illustrate different aspects of the history of the bicycle. Some forty of these ceramic models were made before Dunlop was taken over and the plans forgotten. The models were given to Mark Hall in 1984 and are displayed throughout the galleries; they give a charming light touch to the subject.

At the end of this gallery there is a lovely view down Gallery 5, a modern plate glass extension to the original building, which provides an attractive display space that shows the machines in an 'outdoor' setting. It is better, though, to follow the sequence of galleries and bicycles into Gallery 3. Here, the tricycle and safety bike have brought the rider closer to the ground – although 'safety' also refers to rear-wheel drive. The Rover Safety of 1885 was the first rear-driven safety bycycle that went into mass production, and shows that the basic design of bikes has remained the same for a century.

The National Royal Tricycle (1884), manufactured by the Starley brothers of Coventry, is an early example of an ejector seat on a bicycle. When the brakes are applied hard, the seat tips forward, throwing the rider over the handlebars! It was the Starley brothers who invented the differential, enabling the wheels that are being driven to corner efficiently. There is a display case showing various types of differential. Other, less technical displays of accessories include an array of bicycle bells in Gallery 4. This gallery has bicycles that fold, bicycles made of plastic, 'recumbent' bicycles designed to reduce wind resistance, and bicycles designed to look like mopeds. The Scoo-Ped of 1958 was a small wheeled machine that carried a fibreglass body to protect the rider from weather.

Gallery 5 concentrates on multiseaters and racers. The 'Rudge Tandem' of 1905 can be steered from the back or front seat, demanding a sense of harmony from the riders. The Pashley Unicycle of 1985 contrasts well with the Ariel Quintuplet of 1898. This was used by the Dunlop Racing Team during the 1890s and is nicely complemented by a Dunlop ceramic model portraying both men and machines (ill. on cover).

Returning into the main building, the visitor is invited to walk through the three walled gardens, which were developed during the late 18th and 19th centuries as part of the estate. The largest walled garden (approximately one acre) has been stocked to demonstrate various gardening styles and techniques. It includes a model allotment, rose garden, herbaceous borders and a cottage garden. The 17th century garden has been laid out with authentic plants researched from existing 16th and 17th century gardens. It uses a low box hedge as edging, with rosemary and lavendar infilling the beds. The pattern of the layout is best seen from a specially constructed viewing platform on the east-facing wall of the Cycle Museum. A bronze sculptured sundial created by Nathan David stands in the centre of this atmospheric little garden. The third walled area is the unusual Fruit Garden, an idea born from the ancient fig stools found growing in the garden and thought to be the same as those listed in 1822 and 1823.

Both the museum and gardens have a great charm, not usually associated with the modern environment of Harlow New Town. They encourage visitors to pick up a Heritage Trail from the museum shop and follow the cycle tracks or paths that explore the town. The main museum in Harlow, *Passmores Museum*, is on one of the main trails and well worth visiting. In a lovely parkland site, occupied since Domesday, it houses displays on local history and archaeology. The prehistoric and Roman material is of much more than 'local' interest: it comes from the Harlow Temple site and includes a lifesized limestone head of the Goddess Minerva. (KH)

HASLEMERE

Haslemere Educational Museum

78 High Street, Haslemere, Surrey GU27 2LA   (0428) 2112
Closed Mondays and Sundays (except Sunday afternoons April to October). 🗓
Grounds open for picnics.
♿ **A**: ramps for smaller flights of stairs; assistance can be given with flight of 8/9 steps by prior arrangement; access best from rear by prior arrangement.
♟ & ♟ preferably book in advance; quiz sheets available. ☺

This museum, situated in a pleasant small town on the Surrey/Sussex/Hampshire border, provides an individual introduction to natural and human history. It was founded in 1888 by a local resident, Sir Jonathan Hutchinson, an eminent medical doctor who had advanced ideas on the role of museums in education. At the time, Haslemere was still a rural backwater but was becoming an important centre of the Arts and Crafts revival. Hutchinson wanted to provide the town with a comprehensive introduction to the story of the Earth. He supplemented the museum displays with extensive programmes of free talks and demonstrations for the local inhabitants. The museum is still independently managed, and although it moved to a new site in 1926, it still retains the atmosphere of its founder's original ideas.

The museum makes no concessions to modern fashion in terms of design, and still concentrates on the principle of learning through the careful examination and comparison of objects. This traditional approach may not find favour with every visitor, but generations of children have used the museum to learn the value of careful observation with their own eyes. Hutchinson built his museum for the benefit of the local area and it continues to function as a social centre for the district, with an extensive series of special events, and many societies using its facilities.

The bulk of the collections are connected with natural history: Haslemere is surrounded by some of the finest countryside close to London. The museum thus provides a useful starting point for exploring some of the thousands of acres of public open

Unknown artist, Chichester mail coach at Haslemere, *c. 1700*

Schoolchildren at the teaching pond

space in the area. It has ten acres of its own attractive grounds, which connect directly with extensive National Trust property. Visitors can therefore explore a range of habitats including lawn, meadow, woodland and pond. Groups can use a laboratory to examine specimens.

The museum is located in an attractive 18th-century house in the High Street, with additions at the back to accommodate the extensive collections. There can be few museums of this size where you can explore the mouth of a shark, the neck bones of a giraffe (only seven but very large), amulets carved from giant clams, goliath beetles, a Japanese giant crab and an Egyptian mummy, all within a few yards. The museum is well organised, with each subject – zoology, geology, botany – separated into individual sections. Hutchinson set himself the task of covering the whole world and the diversity of material reflects his ambitions. Under some showcases are drawers that contain study collections ranging from butterflies to prehistoric stone tools.

The first of the main galleries contains the geology exhibition, which provides a guide to the entire history of the earth's crust. A 'Space for Time' chart along one wall is drawn to a scale of one foot to a million years. The one inch devoted to the presence of humans is a striking reminder of the immense length of geological ages. Much of the Haslemere area was shaped during the Cretaceous period (140–65 million years ago), and there are specific displays on the shaping of the local landscape and more generally the Weald. In the middle of the gallery are showcases looking at particular themes, such as the development of fossils and rock-building minerals. Relief models, maps, photographs and specimens show the relationships between scenery, vegetation, agriculture, local industry and architecture. This gallery also contains a small display of botanical specimens from the Haslemere area.

The zoology gallery includes sections on fish, amphibians, reptiles, birds and mammals, as well as insects, molluscs and very simple animals. The wide variety of specimens shown within a relatively small space emphasises, particularly for children, the extraordinary diversity of organisms on the earth. The museum is fortunate in having an extremely fine collection of mounted British birds. Although some people always find taxidermy rather artificial, it does allow close examination, which is rarely possible in the wild. To gain most from such a collection one must be prepared to invest some time and concentration. A good way to start is by picking on one particular aspect, such as beaks, feet or plumage, and comparing the range of types that are present even within apparently similar specimens. Once children start to realise the reasons behind the variations in different species they soon appreciate the importance of habitats in determining what birds they are likely to see in the wild. There are also two dioramas, of Frensham Great Pond and Chichester Harbour, depicting typical habitat groups at these favourite bird-watching locations. Even experienced ornithologists will probably be able to learn more about the fine detail of different species, which will help them in observing living birds. Next to the bird gallery is a small annexe, with a beehive that has glass sides so that bees can be seen.

The history gallery is set out on a 'space-for-time' basis, as in the geology gallery. It covers world history up to the Hiroshima atomic bomb. Although many ideas have changed since the gallery was designed, it is still interesting to see, and the Egyptian mummy complete with exposed toes proves of enduring fascination to children. There are also examples of items made by local industries, especially glass, and a Victorian kitchen.

The museum has one specialist collection comprising examples of 'peasant art'. In the 1880s and 1890s Haslemere was a centre of the 'Arts and Crafts' revival. Many potters and weavers had local workshops. The Peasant Art Society was founded to try and preserve peasant craft production at a time when mass-produced objects were reaching every corner of Europe. Its members assembled an extensive collection of domestic objects, textiles and woodwork from all over Europe, particularly Scandinavia. It is remarkable how recently such traditions survived in many countries, and Haslemere's display is a rare opportunity to see this sort of material in Britain. The collection also illustrates an interesting example of late Victorian middle class artistic concern. While one may smile today at their enthusiasm, the Society did ensure the survival of a fascinating group of objects.

Haslemere Museum has a distinctive character that is well worth sampling. The surrounding area forms part of the Surrey Hills Area of Outstanding Natural Beauty and varies from heathland to the Wealden pattern of farmland with hedgerows and coppiced woodland. Within a few miles are Hindhead Common, with marked nature trails, Witley Common with its National Trust information centre, and Winkworth Arboretum, a 'living' tree museum. Whichever you visit, a trip to Haslemere Museum will help you see and discover a great deal more about the local environment. (GM)

HATFIELD

Mill Green Museum and Mill

*Mill Green, Hatfield, Hertfordshire
AL9 5PD   (07072) 71362*
Closed Mondays. ⬛
♿: wheelchair access to all parts of
museum and ground floor of Mill.
👤 & 👥 welcome; guided tours by
prior appointment. ◎

Mill Green Museum has a working
water mill with museum displays on the
ground floor of the adjoining mill
house. The displays consist of two local
history galleries, which cover life and
work in the area from prehistoric times
through to the present day. A third
room is used as a temporary exhibition
gallery, with a regularly changing programme of events.

The size, position and atmosphere
of this museum make it particularly
endearing. The building is tucked into
the middle of Mill Green hamlet, one
mile from Hatfield railway station and
just off the A414, about one mile east
of the A1 M. The domestic size of the
building gives a friendly approach; the
front door on the left leads to the sales
point and galleries, to the right the
workings of the mill itself.

There has probably been a mill on
this site since Domesday, but this particular building is thought to have been
altered to its present shape in 1762.
Further work was done in 1824, but
with the decline in water- and wind-
powered milling, the mill fell into dis-
repair until it was rescued by the Hatfield Rural District Council. Restoration was begun in 1976, when the
Hatfield & District Archaeological
Society took over the lease. After extensive work on the building, machinery and water supplies, Mill Green
began producing its own flour again.
Milling generally takes place on Tuesdays and Wednesdays (10.30am–
12.30pm and 1.30–3.30pm) and again
on Sundays (2–5pm). It is always exciting to see mill machinery turning, with

Exterior view of Mill Green Museum and Mill

all the accompanying clanks and
groans: this mill, with it subtle lighting,
is no exception.

The local history galleries complement the mill and the mill house. They
are truly 'local' history displays, closely
related to life in the area from earliest
times, and feature local businesses and
industries – blacksmiths, wheelwrights
and saddlers – and the railway. Many
of the items on display have a very
personal quality: whether school certificates, underwear, wartime memorabilia, craft tools, or an Iron Age jar,
they all have close connections with
people who have lived and worked in
this area. One case, including a shaving
stand, china washing-jug-and-bowl
set, razors, shaving mug and a long
nightdress, gives a lovely atmosphere
of the well-scrubbed bedtime that one
associates with young children. The
nightdress in fact belonged to an elder-
ly lady who suffered from arthritis and
was glad of the warm woollen cloth.
Throughout the museum, the visitor
can easily identify with the themes and
objects, and gain a real sense of life as
it was lived in different historical
periods.

Part of the local history display

Interior view of the mill

The museum organises special craft displays and demonstrations throughout the summer, and has special quizzes and worksheets, which encourage the visitor to look more closely at specific objects. There is a well-stocked sales point with a good selection of relevant publications and postcards.

If you are visiting Mill Green with your own transport, it is worth travelling a few miles north to Welwyn Roman Baths – an archaeological site preserved beneath the A1 M in a specially-constructed steel vault. Here are the remains of a suite of baths that were originally part of a Roman villa, and date from the 3rd century AD. They clearly show the layout of hot, warm and cold rooms, hot and cold baths, furnace room and hypocaust underfloor heating system. As at Mill Green (likewise run by Welwyn Hatfield Museum Service), this site shows a very personal part of life in the area. There are graphic panels to explain how this particular Roman dwelling fitted into the surroundings, and displays of Roman material excavated from this and other sites in the district. (Open afternoons Tues-Sun & Bank Hols.) (KH)

HENLEY-ON-THAMES

Fawley Court Historic House and Museum

Fawley Court, Henley-on-Thames, Oxfordshire RG9 3AE
(0491) 574917
Open March to end of September, Wednesday, Thursday and Sunday afternoons. 🅟 ▣ 🅿
& ST: wheelchair access to ground floor only.
🛈 & 🚻 book in advance.

This is an extraordinary place, well worth going out of your way to visit. The house and main park were bought in 1953 by the congregation of Marian Fathers, a Roman Catholic order of Polish origin, as a school for Polish boys. Gradually the Marian Fathers bought more of the estate and began the painstaking task of restoration. The school itself (the divine Mercy College) closed in 1986 and the Marian Fathers now run religious retreats here.

The museum is one of the handful in this country that tell the story of another nation. The collections are wide-ranging and immensely impressive; they include manuscripts, medals, books, and arms and armour.

Fawley Court stands on a site that has been occupied for over 1,000 years. After the Norman Conquest in 1079 the Manor of Fawley was given to Sir William de Sackville. The Sackvilles built a fortified manor house; all that remains of it is the undercroft or cellars. Some of the museum displays occupy these rooms, with their fine stone arches and central pillars. The Sackville family retained Fawley for some 400 years, but in 1616 it was acquired by Sir James Whitelock, whose son, Sir Bulstrode, eventually inherited it. Sir Bulstrode was a supporter of Parliament, so during the Civil War Fawley was caught in the crossfire between Prince Rupert and his Royalist troops, and the Round-

heads. Fawley Court was severely damaged as a result.

Sir Bulstrode's support for Cromwell stood him in good stead as he became Ambassador to Sweden, but on the restoration of the monarchy Charles II imposed heavy fines on him. Bulstrode's son was forced to sell Fawley Court to Col William Freeman, who invited his great friend, Sir Christopher Wren, to design a new house. The Wren-designed house was completed in 1684 and by 1690 also boasted a magnificent ceiling by Grinling Gibbons in the drawing room. The ceiling is decorated with large panels of intricately carved wood, painted white to resemble high-relief plasterwork. It is exceptionally fine and is one of only three such ceilings in the country. Don't let the splendid view across the ornamental waterway draw your attention away from the ceiling – it is certainly worth spending time gazing heavenwards in this room.

Another famous architect to enrich Fawley Court was James Wyatt. He designed some of the most distinctive interiors, including the painted ceiling in what is now the library/museum room. Over the years some new wings were added, the Capability Brown landscape was enriched, and the building was re-faced in a rather vivid red brick. Appropriately enough, the museum's present curator is himself a retired architect, who relishes both the building in which he spends so much of his time and the collections on which he lavishes so much care and attention.

In the early years of the school, Polish families (many now living in this country) began to give their private collections to the Marian Fathers. The museum holdings steadily grew and were cared for by volunteers; today, it represents a unique exhibition of the achievements of a great European civilisation. Do arrive in time to join one of the regular 3pm tours – it is well worth it – though of course you can browse on your own.

The first museum room houses a fine collection of books, manuscripts and medals, and also has some poignant reminders of the many Polish

The Drawing Room at Fawley Court, with ceiling by Grinling Gibbons

HERTFORD

Hertford Museum

*18 Bull Plain, Hertford, Hertfordshire
SG14 1DT   (0992) 582686*
Closed Sundays and Mondays. ▣
& S: wheelchair access to ground
floor only; T scheduled for 1990.
▥ & ▥ book in advance: contact
Administrative Officer.

The building on Bull Plain in Hertford
was converted into a museum in 1913
by two brothers, Robert and William
Andrews. Their collection, begun in
1888, formed the basis of Hertford
Museum, which opened in 1914. It still
provides the core for the interpretation
of Hertford's past and gives a fascinating insight into both the past and the
past's collectors.

The shop-like frontage of the
museum gives a sense of 'looking in' on
history, just as the displays allow the
visitor to 'look in' on the museum's
rich and varied collection. The
museum's reserve collections are available for study by appointment and are
stored in another building in the town,
the Seed Warehouse, where the large

citizens who died in the concentration
camps of the Second World War.
Among the manuscripts are documents
bearing the seals and signatures of
Polish kings from the 15th century
onwards. These documents were saved
from destruction during the Second
World War: many others were destroyed, so this collection represents a
unique record outside Poland. There
is a numismatic collection, and a particularly fine collection of medals, many
of which cannot be seen even in
museums in Poland. Among the books
are some of the earliest printed in
Polish, dating from the 15th century.
One of the most important books is the
original Laski's Code of Laws of 1506.

The first floor display room, new in
1989, houses a magnificent collection
of arms and armour. The collection
was given to the museum recently and
consists of over 400 items, including
swords and daggers from Persia, Turkey, the Middle East and Indonesia,
many of them richly decorated. There
is also a collection of weapons and
helmets dating from the 16th to the
18th centuries.

Downstairs in the 12th century
undercroft is a fine collection of Polish
weapons, saddlery and other militaria,
including a splendid collection of Polish sabres from the 16th to 18th centuries, which were presented to the
Marian Fathers by the late Col W.A.D.
Buchowski, VM, KW, to whom the

room is dedicated. Among the objects
here is an example of the Polish Military Cross, *Virtuti Militari*, the equivalent of the Victoria Cross, awarded
only for valour. Another is a Patek
Philip watch inscribed with the Polish
national anthem (the equivalent of the
Marseillaise) which is still in working
order, despite its 140 years.

In the militaria room there is a collection of objects relating to General
Haller, including his Grand Cross of
the White Eagle, which was one of
Poland's highest orders. General Haller was a hero general of the First
World War. In the Second World War
he was a member of the Sikorski
government-in-exile in London and
his London desk is among the collections. Objects relating to the Second
World War include a chaplain's field
altar cross made of spent bullet cases
and candle sticks of spent shells. The
Polish Army, Navy and Air Force
served with the Allied forces between
1939 and 1945, and there are uniforms, photographs and other objects
recording some of their activities.

The museum and house are relatively little known, but really are worth
seeking out. The Curator finds that
visitors are always very surprised and
glad to find such rich collections, and a
house with such interesting and rare
features. Do make the discovery for
yourself – it is a treat! (NH)

*Sedan chair made for Henry de Gray,
a local landowner who died in 1741*

object store is open to the public on a regular basis during summer months. The reserve collections reflect the interests and occupations of some members of the Andrews family. Robert Andrews formed a fine collection of 17th-century trade tokens and brought together a large number of architects' drawings, plans and documents relating to buildings in and around Hertford. William concentrated on maps, prints and drawings, forming a valuable body of research material and objects for display. The museum holds a vast collection of local photographic material and some 4,500 postcards relating to Hertfordshire; these are available for research or as reprints.

Urban and rural craft tools, 17th century printed Bibles, geology, archaeology and ethnography were all aspects of the Andrews' acquisitive instincts. The ethnographic items are particularly fine, some of them having come to the collection through the several members of the family who were active missionaries in the Far East. Other items were given to the museum by local residents, like the plaited ivory prayer mat, the gift of an MP who had been presented with it by the King of Siam. Another special area of the Andrews' interests was the Hertfordshire Regiment; the museum cares for the regimental loan collection, rich in medals, uniforms and photographs.

Hertford Museum is on two floors with a sheltered garden area at the rear. The ground floor includes a space for regularly changing temporary exhibitions and a well-stocked sales desk. 17th century oak pilasters from a coffee house in Hertford are used as a striking feature in the displays and to inform about the popularity of coffee-drinking in the late 17th century. The town sported three such houses; the pilasters came from a building in Honey Lane, as does the beer engine, now sadly disconnected. Hertford has a strong tradition of brewing, complemented by the malting in neighbouring Ware. An early 18th century Sedan chair is parked in this section of the museum, the property of one Henry de Gray, a local landowner. Costumes and textiles on display are

Chinese export porcelain of c. 1745, decorated with the arms of Sir William Baker

changed regularly, and included a charming set of 1911 trousseau garments when I was there.

On the other side of the ground floor galleries there is a magnificent orrery, a clockwork model of 'The Planetary System and Celestial Globe', designed by Jeremiah Cleeve of Welwyn around 1800. The piece rather immodestly includes Jeremiah's portrait within the inlaid wooden mount. Nearby, fragments of an alabaster calvary dating from the 14th century are laid in a flat cabinet. They were rescued from Layston Church and still have their coloured paint in places. The ecclesiastical tone continues in a display on Hertford Priory, which includes a number of 14th century floor tiles. The adjacent wall cases divide pottery into 'before' and 'after' 1767, when the Lea Navigation was constructed. Before this date most pottery was made within twenty miles of the town, whereas after 1767 examples from much further afield travelled into the area by canal, along with fuel, building materials and other goods.

Non-conformity has shaped the history of the Borough since the 17th century, particularly that of the Quakers and Independents (or congrega-

tionalists). The Brown Coat School of Industry for Girls was founded in 1793, and is prettily illustrated by a dressed doll. Another famous academic institution, Christ's Hospital, Hertford, was founded here in 1553 by Edward VI. The boys' Preparatory School taught from 1682 to 1902 and Christ's Hospital girls' school from 1697 to 1985, when it moved to Horsham. School cap, buttons, monitor badges and commemorative mugs are used to illustrate the lives of pupils and staff. The East India Company founded a college at Haileybury, close to Hertford, in 1806; this became a public school in 1862. Many of the company's directors and chairmen held lands in and around the town and one director, Sir William Baker, had some lovely Chinese porcelain specially made in 1745; several pieces on display bear his crest.

A human skull stares gloomily from a case concentrating on Saxon Hertford, which includes two Saxon brooches, a Viking sword found in the river Lea near Hertford, and a splendid array of Saxon silver pennies – examples from the Hertford Mint, in production until the reign of William II. More of the town's past is retold by

Orrery by Jeremiah Cleeve of Welwyn, c. 1800

maps, prints and drawings. Views of Hertford Castle, built just after the Norman Conquest for William the Conqueror, show change, decay and re-building, while Thomas Rowlandson's 18th century depictions of the Bell Inn and the Market are real treasures. The Health and Welfare of Hertford is covered in various documents and photographs relating to the notable town doctors, including a photograph of the very large isolation hospital.

Upstairs the displays put Hertford in its regional context as County Town. This gallery and part of the ground floor are to be refurbished and redisplayed during the next year or so, integrating displays on the archaeology, geology, natural and social history of Hertford and the rest of the county in a 'Hertfordshire Gallery'. In addition, detailed plans have been drawn up for restructuring the museum garden area to provide essential facilities and access to the main feature – a Jacobean knot garden. The garden will be designed and planted to be consistent with a date of around 1610, to match the earliest part of the museum building. (KH)

HIGH WYCOMBE

Wycombe Local History and Chair Museum

Castle Hill House, Priory Avenue, High Wycombe, Buckinghamshire HP11 2DX   (0494) 23879
Closed Sundays and Bank Holidays. 🅵 🅿
&: wheelchair access to ground floor only.
🚻 & 🚻 must book in advance.

Chair making has been an important Chiltern craft since before 1700. Daniel Defoe (author of *Gulliver's Travels*) noted in 1725 that there was 'a vast quantity of Beechwood which grows in the woods of Buckinghamshire more plentifully than in any other part of England' providing raw material for the chair industry. During the 18th century chair parts were made in High Wycombe but were sent to London to be made up. At the end of the 18th century a far-sighted local farmer decided to make premises available in Wycombe so that the whole process of chair making could be completed locally.

Children's chairs

Bodgers encampment at Speen, c. 1905

From 1800 to 1860 the number of factories grew from one to 150, and by 1870 the Wycombe factories were producing 4,700 chairs a day. Large orders were taken, such as 8,000 chairs for Crystal Palace, and special commissions such as designing and making presentation chairs for the wedding of Edward, Prince of Wales (later Edward VII). An extraordinary sight greeted royalty when they visited the town, as a huge arch of chairs would be built in the High Street between the Guildhall and the houses opposite. (The Guildhall, by the way, has an exhibition on local history open to the public from May to October, which is also worth a visit.)

It is quite reasonable to ask 'why *Windsor* chairs in High Wycombe?'; unfortunately there is no certain solution to this conundrum. One theory is that when they were assembled in London the chair parts travelled from High Wycombe along the Windsor Road (the same principle applying to 'Bath' buns). The museum shows the special history of these chairs – who made them and who used them. There were three main craftsmen involved in making a chair. The first was the 'bodger', who usually worked out in the beech woods cutting and preparing the timber. He made the chair legs and other

KNEBWORTH

Knebworth House

Knebworth, Hertfordshire SG3 6PN
(0438) 812661
Open daily during Easter period,
then only open weekends and Bank
Holidays until end of May, after
which open Tuesdays to Sundays
until beginning of September;
open weekends only during
September. Closed October to
Easter. 🔊 P
& S: wheelchair access to ground
floor only.
🛏 & 🍴 book in advance. ☺

Ceremonial chair arch erected in the High Street to welcome Edward, Prince of Wales, 1880

turned parts – the sticks at the back
and the stretchers that connected the
chair legs. The origin of the term
'bodger' is not clear, although the term
'badger' was still in use to describe a
travelling pedlar in the 1930s. The
verb 'to bodge' refers to a job that is
not properly finished – and indeed
chair bodgers completed only part of
the chair-making process. The next
craftsman involved was the benchman,
who roughly prepared the chair seat
and back. Finally the framer assembled
and finished the chairs.

Many styles of chair were produced
locally, not just the Windsor, including
cane or rush-seated chairs, and chairs
in the style of Chippendale and Sher-
aton. The museum has a varied collection of 19th century chairs, including
Hutchinsons Champion chair, which
won its accolade at the Great Exhibiton
of 1851.

There were also many variations on
the theme of Windsor chairs. In the
19th century several new styles were
introduced within the range. The
museum has a comprehensive collection of these different styles, including
the low-back Windsor and the stick-
back Windsor. The low-back was
especially popular in America, while

the type known as the smoker's bow
was the traditional chair of the office,
reading room or club about 150 years
ago. The stick-backs were usually
heavier-looking, and were frequently
used in club rooms or as a strong
armchair for the home. The Wycombe
chair factories produced many chairs
for the War Office; some of these
chairs had only one arm, for the use of
officers in uniform complete with
swords.

The chair industry offers a window
on the social history of the town, for
most people – two-thirds of the residents in one particular street, for example – worked in the furniture industry. The museum also highlights other
local crafts, such as straw plaiting and
lacemaking, and has a collection of
treen (domestic wooden items). In
addition there are period room settings.

One of the objects that is not easy to
miss is the Wycombe Lion. The red
lion was carved locally in about 1800
and stood above the entrance to the
Red Lion Hotel. 150 years later it was
beginning to show its age, so a new lion
was carved by Frank Hudson and the
original now stands imposingly in the
museum. (NH)

Knebworth is a place of fantasies. The
building and its collections tug at the
imagination: it is a place to weave
dreams. From the massive 17th century English oak screen in the Great
Hall, to tiny painted miniatures, Knebworth is full of contrasts and colour. It
sits amidst glorious parkland and has
that peculiar atmosphere created by
the continuing history of a 'family seat'.

Knebworth has been the home of
the Lytton family since 1490 when a
Sir Robert Lytton bought the Estate.
He transformed the medieval fortress,
which had been surveyed by the Nor-
mans in 1085, into a Tudor Mansion.
Sir Robert was a counsellor to Henry
VII and Keeper of the Great War-
drobe. He built a four-sided house
with a central courtyard, which stood
for over 300 years. It was Mrs Elizabeth Bulwer Warburton Lytton who
demolished three of the wings, retain-
ing the great hall and encasing the
remaining section in cement. This gave
an impression of a stone-built house in
'Gothick' style. Her son, the famous
novelist and eccentric Bulwer Lytton,
inherited the house in 1843 and set
about realising the romantic idyll that is
Knebworth. Turrets, heraldic beasts,
domes and gargoyles crave attention on
the exterior cladding that hides the red
Tudor brickwork. Inside, furniture and
fittings range from the 17th century
oak screen and panelling of the Great
Hall, to the elaborate high Victorian

Heraldic beasts on the roof

decoration of the State Drawing Room and the elegant quiet of Mrs Bulwer Lytton's Empire-style bedroom. The mixture is quite extraordinary, and part of the building's great charm. It is difficult not to imagine the ghosts of ages past, whether visitors in political discussion in Bulwer Lytton's study, or children playing with the nursery toys on display in the Hampden Room.

The Great Hall is for me the most stunning room of all, in its proportions and dignity rather than its furnishings. The vast table, the family portraits and barley-twist chairs remind the visitor that this is a room *used* by people; the house may be of stately proportions but it's still a home. There is a painting by Winston Churchill of the Great Hall, hanging on the far wall. Churchill was a friend of the second Earl's wife, and visited Knebworth during the 1930s. The White Drawing Room leads off this room and was the dining parlour of the original house. Here Hepplewhite and Italian furniture are presided over by a fine portrait of Ruth, Lady Lytton (*c.* 1635), painted by Sir Peter Lely. This room was transformed by the architect Edwin Lutyens at the beginning of the 20th century. Son-in-law of the 1st Earl, Lutyens' influence can be

seen in various parts of the house and Knebworth village.

From the lightness of the Drawing Room, with its views out over the open parkland, the Library is wonderfully overpowering. The walls are lined with books, and furniture and furnishings are heavy and lush; only the old Library steps give a clue to its previous decoration. There is a sketch by G. F. Watts over the fireplace for a portrait of Robert, first Earl of Lytton and Viceroy of India from 1876–80, a wistful impression heightened by the unfinished nature of a sketch. Son of Bulwer Lytton, Robert was a poet who wrote under the name of Owen Meridith. Bulwer Lytton himself wrote over seventy volumes of plays, essays, poems and novels; editions of each are housed in this room. An ornate Dutch musical clock (*c.* 1775) lurks in a dark corner of the room, and it is easy to overlook the case of miniatures, among them a gorgeous jewelled crucifix that belonged to Mary Queen of Scots. Do look below eye level as you go round: the twisted, carved and decorated feet of furniture are quite amazing.

In the hallway and stairwell armour and portraits do their best to intimidate the passer-by: a painting of the second Earl in Garter robes is particularly imposing. At the top of the stairs there are two contrasting rooms: the State Drawing Room, spacious with large windows, and Bulwer Lytton's study, a small, somewhat overpowering room. The portrait of Bulwer Lytton by Maclise on the landing is one of the artist's best-known portraits. It shows the Earl as a young man, standing hand on hip with a thoughtful but direct gaze. In the study there is a very different image of the writer: E. M. Ward's painting shows a much older man sitting in this room, with the panelling, table covering and chairs as they remain today. Bulwer Lytton holds a long cherry-wood pipe, which is displayed in a cabinet alongside the crystal ball he would gaze into for hours. Reproductions of letters from his great friend, Dickens, are kept here, with manuscripts of many of Lytton's novels. Bulwer Lytton is fascinating in his own right: romantic novelist, poet, essayist,

politician and mystic, he was a Tory MP for Hertfordshire at the time of the Corn Laws and the Crimean War. His life is outlined in a publication on sale at Knebworth and reads rather like one of his own novels.

The State Drawing Room is 'one of the finest surviving examples of Victorian interior decoration, and a perfect embodiment' of the 'revival of interest in High gothic'. The rich red chairs, highly decorated ceiling, stained glass and heavy paintings make this room quite spectacular. Everything is worth time and attention, not least the painting by Maclise of Edward IV visiting Caxton's printing press (1850). This is one of the great English history paintings and fits the room perfectly. Maclise wrote that every 'personage' was derived from Bulwer Lytton's book, *The Last of the Barons.*

The gallery that looks down into the Great Hall is hung with portraits of the various 'Ms Lyttons' and is a good area to pause and take breath, before tackling the bedrooms. En route to the bedroom area there is a small display on the Lytton family's influence on early ski-ing. Before the First World War, skating was the main winter sport; the Lyttons' expertise and enthusiasm helped popularise ski-ing as an enjoyable if expensive alternative.

Here the house takes on a more private air. The Falkland Bedroom, named after the Viscountess Falkland, is hung with 18th century hand-painted Chinese wallpaper. This is supposedly the room where Dickens slept and was inspired enough by the room's Chinese pagoda cabinet to mention it in *David Copperfield* as a residence for Dora's dog. The china and glass collection here includes a Meissen lapdog (*c.* 1850), traditionally made for Catherine, Empress of Russia. The Child's Bedroom or Hampden Room (in reference to Sir William Lytton's association with the Parliamentarian cause in 1624) is now dressed as a nursery. Amongst the toys, christening robes and dolls' houses, there is a tiny Napoleonic uniform worn by Antony, son of the second Earl, when he was six. Recent renovation has revealed part of the original

The State Drawing Room, 'one of the finest surviving examples of Victorian interior decoration'

LETCHWORTH

First Garden City Heritage Museum

*296 Norton Way South, Letchworth
Garden City, Hertfordshire
SG6 1SU   (0462) 683149*
Open daily. 🇫 ♿
🍴 & 🚻 book in advance.

Letchworth's First Garden City Heritage Museum nestles in one of the tree-lined avenues that radiate from the town's centre. It is housed in the drawing offices built by the architect Barry Parker (1867–1947) who, in partnership with Sir Raymond Unwin (1863–1940), made real the Garden City dream conceived by Ebenezer Howard (1850–1928).

The Garden City principles of domestic and public planning, of straight main roads and curving minor ones, of pedestrian paths and carefully

'Winter' from the 'Four Seasons' window

black and white wall decoration of around 1550.

Mrs Bulwer Lytton's bedroom was furnished for her during her thirty-year stay here at Knebworth as a widow. Many of the objects were collected by her, and two paintings of her favourite Italian pug dog were painted by her. The last bedroom is the Queen Elizabeth Room, also full of atmosphere. Elizabeth I may have visited Knebworth, although there are no clear records. Portraits of Sir Philip Sydney and Edward VI hang on the dark panelling, and the great carved bed has ornate heavy hangings. A painting with particular charm is 'The Nun, the Monk and the Baby', a piece of anti-Catholic propaganda from the time of Queen Elizabeth.

The Knebworth experience doesn't end in the house itself. There is the Indian Exhibition, which, with its silver throne, gifts and photos, refers in particular to the career of Robert, first Earl and Viceroy of India. The estate also contains a narrow gauge railway, an adventure playground, and an historic church, as well as the herb and formal gardens of the house. (KH)

Barry Parker's private office, designed by him in 1907; furniture includes his desk and chair

designed as drawing offices for the Parker and Unwin partnership. It was extended in 1936 to provide residential accommodation, but Barry Parker's private office in the original building is still furnished and decorated as it was when first used. Much of the furniture was designed by Barry Parker, and his watercolour paintings hang on the walls. The 'Four Seasons' stained glass window is not contemporary with the building, as it was installed by Barry Parker in the early 1920s. Manufactured by Heasman of Harpenden in 1914, it is the only one of its type still complete. Also on display are Ebenezer Howard's desk and his own invention, a shorthand typewriter.

The museum confines its collecting to the development of the Garden City and only has a small collection of artefacts. Photographs and documents supplement the displays on the general life of the town, home of Spirella Corsets and Dent's, the publishers. There is an interesting selection of banners (colour plate 10) and mementoes of special events, such as May Day, Civic Week, or the opening of Letchworth's famous pub without beer, The Skittles Inn, in 1907 (Letchworth was for many years a temperance stronghold). Great emphasis is placed by the museum on the importance of architecture and housing, and researchers, students and interested visitors can examine by arrangement countless photographs, plans and drawings that are part of the museum's archives.

The museum also runs a programme of changing exhibitions exploring aspects of the Garden City theme.

You need not have a prior knowledge of the Garden City movement to enjoy this museum. The garden and the house, along with its displays, exude a particular atmosphere and enable the visitor to absorb something of the enthusiasm and commitment that went into creating Letchworth. Maybe it isn't quite the Utopian city that Ebenezer Howard wrote about in 1898, but the museum gives a valuable insight into Letchworth Garden City and town planning in general. (KH)

preserved or planted trees, controlled all development, both of layout and architecture. In Garden Cities, it was believed, the inhabitants would have the 'health of the country and the comforts of the town'. Letchworth covered some 3,818 acres when work began in 1904 on the first modern 'planned' town – the birthplace of the profession of town planning. Letchworth Garden City Corporation was set up by an Act of Parliament in 1962 to replace the original First Garden City Ltd. Any surplus made by commercial management is ploughed back into the amenities provided for the community. One such amenity is the museum, which opened in 1977.

The museum building itself is a fine example of Arts and Crafts architecture, and has great atmosphere and charm. The original building was

Howard's shorthand typewriter (patented 1923)

Letchworth Museum and Art Gallery

*Broadway, Letchworth, Hertfordshire
SG6 3PF   (0462) 685647*
Closed Sundays and Bank
Holidays. ⬛
&: wheelchair access to ground
floor only.
⚹ & ⚹ preferably book in
advance.

Letchworth Museum has two great strengths: natural history and archaeology. The museum is the centre for the North Hertfordshire Museum Service, and many of the displays refer to the open landscape, villages and towns that make the northern part of the county so distinctive. The material in the exhibition galleries gives the visitor a chance to understand the history of the surrounding area, both in terms of its natural landscape and habitat, and man's history within it.

The museum building itself was purpose-built from 1914–20. Begun by the local Natural History and Antiquarian Society, the museum's emphasis still lies in this area. Unlike most museums, the entrance plunges the visitor straight into a gallery – a bright new natural history gallery, which begins its story some 135 million years ago. Through the geology of prehistory, through hedges and verges, farmland and woodland, the gallery explains aspects of the natural history of North Hertfordshire in a lively and clear manner, right up to present day issues of conservation. There are examples of species and habitats under threat of extinction, as well as those that have already been lost, and a 'Find Out More' section for anyone with a deeper interest. One exhibit peculiar to Letchworth is the Black Squirrel, only found in this area. The colour variation is apparently caused by melanism, which is clearly explained on graphic panels. There is even a pub in Letchworth named after this local eccentricity.

Other galleries are on the first floor, reached via the stairs, as is the sales point, which has an ample selection of

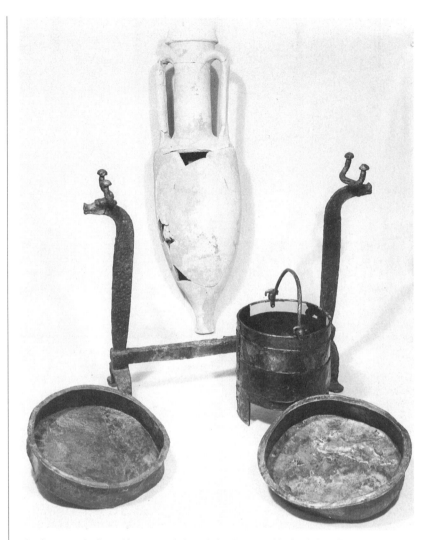

Amphora, iron firedog and bronze vessels from the late Iron Age 'Chieftain's Burial', Baldock

publications, postcards and souvenirs. The Art Gallery at the top of the stairs has changing exhibitions that draw on the museum's reserve collections of art and archaeological material, or show the work of local and regional artists.

The History of Man in North Hertfordshire is the all-embracing title of the next area. Beginning around 200,000 years BC, the archaeological displays take you through to 1900. At this point the history of Letchworth is taken up by the other museum in the town, the **First Garden City Heritage Museum**. There is a series of diagrammatic panels explaining what archaeology is, how sites are found and excavated, and what happens to the finds and information after the excavation has finished. Finds from local Iron Age sites are accompanied by information and aeriel photographs, while pottery-making and other techniques are explained with the help of matchstick-men graphics. There is a general feeling of being helped to

Spencer Gore, Letchworth – The Road, *1912*

understand, not always apparent in archaeology galleries. One of the results of the Iron Age pottery-making is an elegant cordonned pedestal urn from the 1st century BC. It was used for burying a cremation, and stands amidst the subtle colours of other pottery examples from the same period.

Letchworth's prize in terms of archaeological sites and finds is the 'Chieftain's Burial'. This site was uncovered in 1968, and the material found reveals valuable evidence about Iron Age society. Many of the items buried with the Chieftain were to provide him with food and drink in the afterlife, including storage containers for food and wine, and cooking utensils. Two of the containers have recently been conserved – huge, flat circular dishes, fit for a banquet. Chainmail was a rare find at this site, and is thought to have been a prized possession.

Some of the Iron Age sites in the area continued to be used as Roman civilisation took hold, and they have yielded a wealth of material that gives us an insight into Roman life in North Hertfordshire. Full explanations of the Roman 'villa' are presented as a context to the more delicate personal items on display, such as small bone gaming counters, a bronze mirror, and bracelets from a child's grave. The remains of a Roman theatrical mask certainly capture the imagination. Only a few such examples have been found, and those elsewhere in Europe. This mask came from Baldock, which was not a large enough town to have a

theatre: did it belong perhaps to strolling players, or to a 'resting' Roman actor? The site of Roman Baldock was discovered in 1925 by the then Curator of the Museum, W. Percival Westell, and research continues into the site and finds.

Opposite a collection of Roman coins from the whole Empire is a cabinet of English coinage, ranging from Edward IV silver groats to our 20th century threepenny pieces and 20p coins. A very lovely display of Roman jewellery includes an enamelled manicure brooch (colour plate 2), a small reminder of the colour that was used by Roman craftsmen and has perished on other found items. A Romano-British skeleton from the 4th century AD, found in Clothall Common, punctuates the Roman displays. The Anglo-Saxon and Medieval-period displays have more fine examples of craftsmanship. A pilgrims badge formed like a feather and a 15th-century copper alloy sword scabbard-end from Ashwell are particularly lovely. Amidst the more modern post-Medieval archaeology, an 18th century iron finger ring bears a face with an expression of wide-eyed astonishment – appropriate to the end of a museum visit! Clay pipes abound at this end of the displays with an interesting number of variations in shape, all relating to different dates of manufacture.

The 'Collectors Corner' is a friendly touch in this final gallery. It provides a space for local collectors and enthusiasts to display their treasures. Another link with the community is created in the Craftsman of the Month exhibition space at the top of the stairs.

Letchworth is a traditional but immensely friendly museum. Bright colours and occasional chairs provide the visitor with a sense of welcome that is often difficult to create in museums. The archaeological and natural history collections are of high quality; the huge cauldrons and chieftain's dishes, the tiny finger rings and flint arrowheads all help to send visitors out into the surrounding countryside with a much clearer understanding of the area's history and man's life within it. (KH)

LUTON

Stockwood Craft Museum and Gardens

Stockwood Park, Farley Hill, Luton, Bedfordshire LU1 4BH
(0582) 38714
Open Easter to October, Wednesdays to Sundays and Bank Holidays. 🄵 ▣ (weekends only) 🅟 ♿W
♿ & ♿ book in advance: contact Luton Museum Service, Wardown House (0582) 36941. ◉

Stockwood Craft Museum is housed in a former stable block in Stockwood Park. The stables were part of Stockwood House, which was built in 1740 and until it was demolished in 1964 was one of the remaining four Luton 'mansions', along with Luton Hoo, Wardown House (now *Luton Museum*) and Whitehill House. Photographs and text help the visitor to interpret the rebuilding of Stockwood's stable block and there is an excellent scale model of the original building on display. It is good to see some of the architectural features from the mansion re-used in the new museum building, which will eventually include a reconstructed 17th century timber-framed merchant's house rescued from Luton's town centre (to be re-erected in 1990/91).

Displays at Stockwood concentrate Bedfordshire's crafts, many of which developed to supplement the basic income of farm labourers. The crafts include lacemaking, rush weaving and the plaited straw that was the basis of the Luton Hat Industry. One of the nicest aspects of this museum is the links that are made between the crafts and the people of Luton. There are references to the people and firms that used the items in the displays, and to the man who collected the majority of them. Thomas Bagshaw came from a family that owned an engineering company in Dunstable; over a period of some thirty years he assembled a fine collection of rural trade items. He be-

View of the gardens at Stockwood

Part of the Timber Trades display

Bedfordshire Hedger display

came honorary curator of Luton Museum in 1935, and his collection now forms the basis of the Stockwood Museum displays.

The main exhibition area is in the courtyard of the original stable block. The covered open areas house larger items associated with brickmaking and water supply, while inside the buildings various galleries interpret rural life and rural crafts. The Rural Life Gallery links crafts and activities with the different seasons of the year – hunting and trapping, draining, sowing and harvesting. The 'Bedfordshire Hedger' section has a personal tale behind it. The working clothes and tools all belonged to Mr Harry Cheshire, a local hedger. Thomas Bagshaw met him one day and bought everything he was wearing and using; Harry Cheshire was given a fresh kit, and the originals preserved as

part of the museum's collection. The Rural Crafts section concentrates on crafts such as thatching, plaiting and saddlery, which use the raw materials available in Bedfordshire. The mainly traditional displays are enlivened at weekends by visiting craft workers.

Before the 19th century, Luton was a milling and brewing town, and one display uses equipment from J. Horton and Co., Corn and Seed Merchants of Luton. Another direct link between the collection and the people who lived and worked around Luton is made in the Blacksmith's Forge – a reconstruction

of Toddington Forge in Bedfordshire. The forge is occasionally in operation, and on the day I visited was being put to good use repairing the park gates that had been struck by a corporation skip!

There are many interesting items on display that are not necessarily part of a setting. Among them is the dress coach built for the 7th Earl Cowper of Silsoe in Bedfordshire, and an itinerant knife-grinder's bicycle, which was taken by train to London and ridden back to Luton via large houses and country estates. A Burton-type gypsy living caravan has been lovingly refurbished and it is worth climbing the steps to see the interior. The Timber Trades are dealt with in open displays of working areas complete with tools, lathes and benches. A former garage inspection pit makes a credible saw pit in one display area, and video film is used to supplement the static display to give the visitor finer detail on wheelwrighting.

If all this 'museum type' activity proves too much, there is a glorious escape route via a series of period garden settings. They include a 17th century knot garden and a Victorian cottage garden, all surrounded by the original mansion's kitchen garden walls. Beyond the walls is the less formal approach of the 18th century garden, where recent sculpture by Ian Hamilton Finlay melds into the surroundings. And don't leave Stockwood without visiting the Craft Courtyard, where a number of workshops are leased to present-day craft workers – a direct link between the past and the present.

Stockwood Museum is the latest development of the Luton Museum Service, which has its main collections at Wardown House. These cover the traditional museum subject areas of natural history, archaeology, social history and decorative art, and there is also the Bedfordshire and Hertfordshire Regimental Collection. There are many fine items, particularly the collection of lace, and there is also a large library and archive and the County Herbarium, which can be used by prior appointment. (KH)

MAIDSTONE

Maidstone Museum and Art Gallery

*St Faith's Street, Maidstone, Kent
ME14 1LH   (0622) 54497*
Closed Sunday mornings. **F**
&: wheelchair access to ground floor only; close parking by arrangement.
ᛞ preferably book in advance.
ᛞᛞ book in advance: contact Education Officer to book facilities and obtain information. ◉

16th century Great Hall, with the pair of Panini paintings of Roman ruins

Maidstone has been extremely fortunate in having a succession of wealthy local residents, whose generous donations over the last 130 years have created the finest general museum in Kent. Indeed, it is one of the best in the Home Counties, and visitors can enjoy a wide selection of displays of high quality. The Kent Archaeological Society is based at the museum, and it provides a good starting point for anybody wishing to explore the human or natural history of the county.

The museum was severely damaged by fire in 1977 and parts of the building are still being redisplayed. The important archaeology, ethnography and Japanese collections remain largely in store. Visitors should check if they wish to see specific items; the staff are extremely friendly and helpful, and welcome enquiries. Specific visits can be arranged to see the parts of the collections that are not on public display.

Maidstone Museum is housed in Chillington Manor, a rambling range of buildings, the oldest part of which dates back to Tudor times. Indeed, the building is an interesting exhibit in its own right, and the Great Hall has been kept free of cases to show it off to best advantage. A small collection of appropriate oak furniture and paintings complements the wooden floor and panelling, and conveys a good sense of the bareness of such a room in the 16th

century. A free leaflet is available describing the building and its development over the centuries.

The galleries are divided along traditional subject lines into art, social history, natural history and archaeology. It would be invidious to compare them, and every visitor will have a different order of preference. The fine picture gallery is, however, a good place to start. The museum was given over 200 paintings in 1897 by George Bentlif and has received several other important donations. Maidstone has the tenth largest collection of foreign paintings outside London, and the small gallery has recently been redecorated to provide a luxurious setting for a selection of works. The finest are perhaps an 18th century pair by Giovanni Paolo Panini, depicting fanciful arrangements of ancient ruins in Rome, bathed in golden sunlight. They were originally brought back as souvenirs from Italy by a wealthy Kentish gentleman. The gallery makes a rare attempt to introduce its pictures to a general visitor, and the range and quality of exhibits makes it an excellent

place to introduce children or school groups to classical painting. A large proportion of the pictures are by relatively unknown artists, and many people would find them less intimidating to discuss and criticise than the accepted 'masters' in the national collections. There are a variety of Italian and Dutch paintings, the latter including a very attractive 17th century picture of 'A Musical Party', and a work of particular local interest, 'The Dutch in the Medway', showing the attack by Admiral de Ruyter on the British fleet at Chatham in 1667.

The museum also has a temporary exhibition gallery, where a regular programme of modern art displays is shown, and a small area is devoted to 18th and 19th century sculpture. The latter includes the remarkable figure of Lady Godiva by John Thomas. In addition there is a gallery devoted to the work of George Baxter (1804–67), a printer who pioneered the manufacture of high quality coloured reproductions. Prior to his work, prints had to be laboriously hand-painted by teams of women and children. Baxter developed a block-printing system using oil-based paints. He was obsessed by quality, a concern that eventually led him into bankruptcy. Starting with book illustrations, Baxter expanded over the years into a wide range of prints appealing to Victorian taste, including 'religion, royalty, romance and rural scenery'. The Mote House in Maidstone was for many years the home of the 1st Viscount Bearsted, the co-founder of Shell. His wife was an avid collector of Baxter's work, and in 1919 she presented a large group of books and prints to the museum. A selection dating from 1830–59 is now on display and provides a fascinating insight into mid-Victorian middle-brow taste. The illustrations of the 1851 Great Exhibition are particularly interesting.

The art galleries are complemented by a ceramics gallery, which displays the largest range of ceramics on show in Kent. Although the layout is somewhat stiff, it does provide a comprehensive introduction to the subject and allows the interested visitor to grasp easily the chief trends and developments. The main display shows examples from about 1650 to the present day. There is also a range of Chinese ceramics, which offer a striking contrast to the crude Kentish earthenwares made in local kilns.

A complete contrast is provided by the two natural history galleries. One is devoted to a general introduction to the whole county, covering geology, plants and animals, and includes fragments of fossil mammoths recovered from North Kent gravel pits. The displays are the most comprehensive in the county, and include a plant table and a range of live specimens, such as snakes, eels and fish, which are very popular. The second gallery contains a massive collection of mounted birds, largely from one collection given by Guy Mannering. It includes every common bird likely to be seen in Kent, and many rarities. It is sad to see the number of species, such as the Peregrine and Montagu's Harrier, that were still breeding in Kent when Mannering was collecting fifty years ago but now only nest in more remote areas.

The local history displays are crammed into a small space that could not do justice to half of the subjects covered. There are currently plans to redisplay this material and to provide the town with an exhibition worthy of its past. The best section is that on paper manufacture, which remained an important industry until recently. The local firm founded by Albert Reed in the late 19th century grew to become the massive company, Reed International. The most attractive objects are without doubt the pattern books from a Kentish silk and calico printers. Dating

1960s costumes

from the 1840s, the small samples of cloth show a range of intricate and beautiful designs. These lead one naturally into the costume gallery, which houses the collection of Lady Brabourne, murdered with Lord Mountbatten in 1979. The displays concentrate on the 20th century and provide a brief synopsis of fashion, decade by decade, up to the 1970s. Many visitors particularly enjoy the more recent styles, which are all too often absent from costume exhibitions.

Elsewhere in the museum are small displays on the history of photography, arms and armour, archaeology, and much more. The museum also contains one gallery devoted to the Queen's Own Royal West Kent Regimental Museum. Although the displays of uniforms, medals, swords and ephemera are traditional, they seem to be very popular with the public. The prime object is a superb Indian field gun, the 'Sutlej Gun', captured during the Sikh War of 1845–46.

Maidstone is a fine example of a county museum, and offers a full range of temporary exhibitions, special events and an enquiry service. There is much else of interest to see in and around Maidstone, including the **Rural Life** and **Carriage Museums**: enough to provide a full day's outing. (GM)

Baxter colour print of the Great Exhibition, 1851

Tyrwhitt-Drake Museum of Carriages

Archbishops's Stables, Mill Street, Maidstone, Kent ME15 6YE
(0622) 54497
Closed lunchtimes and Sunday mornings; closed all day Sunday October to March. 🔒
&: wheelchair access to ground floor only.
🏛 preferably book in advance.
👥 book in advance: contact Education Officer.

Yellow landau by McNaughton and Co., Worcester, c. 1885

If you have ever wanted a closer look at the elegant carriages that clatter across the television screen in historical dramas, this museum provides the opportunity. It has one of the best collections of domestic carriages in the country and includes a particularly wide range of types. Even if after a visit you are still not quite sure of the differences between a landau, gig, barouche, brougham, hansom cab or phaeton, you will have gained a vivid insight into the methods of travel for the rich before the advent of the railway and the internal combustion engine. In addition, the museum shows the wide variety of craftsmen – coach-builder, wheelwright, carver, gilder, saddler, harness maker and many others – whose skills were combined to create these expensive items.

The collection was formed by the remarkable Sir Garrard Tyrwhitt-Drake (1881–1946), sometime mayor of Maidstone. In the 1940s he realised that as a result of the development of the car and the sale of country houses, 'thousands of fine examples of the coach-builders' craft have been broken up since the end of the First World War, and I am satisfied that within a very few years the only examples in existence will be those in museums'. He rapidly gathered a fine collection of carriages, many from Kent, and the museum was opened to the public in 1946. Although Sir Garrard could not have foreseen the recent revival of interest in carriage driving and the resulting demand for vehicles, his concern and enthusiasm saved many items from destruction.

The museum is currently housed in a fine 15th-century stable block, part of the complex of medieval buildings surrounding the Archbishop of Canterbury's manor house in the centre of Maidstone. Unfortunately, the site is divided by a busy inner ring road, which provides a continuous reminder of the contemporary descendants of the coach-builders' craft. Although the stables and carriages have horses in common, the present exhibition space is far from ideal and the displays have mostly remained unchanged since the original opening. It seems strange that when so many towns are desperate to develop visitor attractions, Maidstone keeps this remarkable collection in such cramped conditions. This should not, however, deter visitors, since the carriages largely speak for themselves and convey an immediate sense of quality and grandeur.

There are over thirty carriages on display, with the larger examples on the ground floor. Particularly fine exhibits include a semi-state landau of about 1865, built by Holmes of Derby and London, and formerly owned by His Royal Highness the Duke of Con-naught, and a dress landau built around 1870 in London and used by Queen Victoria. One is impressed not only by the coach-builders' skill but also by the combined effect of paint, brass, leather and the superb decorative 'hammer' cloths. The Marquis of Lansdowne's dress chariot (*c.* 1850) is equipped with footmen in full Lansdowne livery. Originally, they would have carried staves to ward off any undesirables that might have impeded the Marquis's journey.

Other notable exhibits include a coach built for Napoleon's son, Count Walewski, who was French ambassador in London in the mid-19th century. There is also a fine example of a late 19th-century hansom cab, the London taxi of the turn of the century. With its characteristic pair of huge wheels, the hansom was drawn by one horse and could carry two passengers, with the driver perched high up at the back behind the carriage. Hansom cabs were also built for private use, and this particular example was owned by Sir Henry Stanley, the African explorer. Looking at the carriages at rest it is easy to forget the skills needed to drive them and to control one to four horses and up to a ton of wood in crowded city streets or poorly surfaced rural roads.

Although the bulk of the collection is Victorian, there are a few earlier examples, mostly on loan from the Victoria and Albert Museum. These include a highly ornate Italian gig of about 1675, which is one of the earliest carriages in existence. Comparison with later carriages shows the gradual improvement in comfort and safety achieved over successive decades. Even so, most carriage trips must have been uncomfortable, noisy and tiring, especially in bad weather. The unsophisticated braking devices are also a reminder of the importance of a skilled coachman.

An interesting feature of all the carriages is that they are displayed in their 'used' condition without any modern restoration. The low level of wear and tear shows how carefully carriages were looked after, and maintenance must have been as big a financial worry as running a modern car. One carriage, a late 18th century travelling chariot of George III, shows a dramatic change in fortune. At present it is completely covered in dark paint, perhaps for a funeral, but one can just detect the original elaborate gilding and coloured decoration underneath.

The first floor displays a mixture of smaller carriages, including six loaned by Her Majesty the Queen. Amongst these are two 'garden chairs', which would have been pulled by a donkey and were originally used by Queen Victoria, as well as a Japanese rickshaw given to Queen Alexandra when Princess of Wales, in 1875. There are also sledges, sedan chairs, and a small group of commercial vehicles ranging from a local butcher's cart to a bier for the final journey.

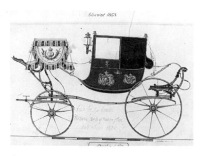

Carriage design by Barker & Co., c. 1820

Detail of museum exterior

Apart from the coaches there are a large number of objects connected with carriage construction or use, including tools, harness, whips, horns, coachmen's uniforms and decorations. There are also a small number of paintings and coaching ephemera. Particularly attractive are the finely-drawn carriage designs by London builders, such as Barkers. In an age when each carriage was custom-built, these drawings formed pattern books of previous designs from which prospective purchasers could select or adapt. It will come as a surprise to many that the centre of London carriage production was located around Long Acre in Covent Garden.

Tyrwhitt-Drake acted just in time and it would be difficult, if not impossible, to assemble such a collection today, only forty years later. One can only wish that the present generation will redisplay the museum to reveal more about the carriages and their owners, builders and drivers. It would be fascinating to see a carriage partially stripped down to reveal the basic underlying framework. Even then, however, one suspects that most visitors will still leave wishing to climb inside one of the exhibits and head for a long straight road. (GM)

NEWBURY

Newbury District Museum

*The Wharf, Newbury, Berkshire
RG14 5AS   (0635) 30511*
Closed Wednesdays; closed Sunday and Bank Holiday mornings (and all day Sundays and Bank Holidays October to March). ▣
& S: wheelchair access to ground floor only.
▥ & ♥ book in advance: contact Museum Secretary.
Tourist Information Centre on ground floor.

Newbury District Museum is housed in a delightful old building. At the time of writing, the Granary is like an oasis among the car parks and busy roads; this may change as there are hopes to develop this area into an attractive cultural centre for the town, and there are also plans to bypass the A34, which should reduce congestion into Newbury considerably. The Granary has an overhanging gallery, which gave access to store rooms on the first floor. Here were stored goods to be transported up and down the Kennet Navigation (completed in 1723) and the Kennet and Avon Canal (completed in 1810). The Wharf used to be exactly that, and in the 18th century would have been a hive of activity with boats being loaded and unloaded just in front of what is now the museum.

The ground floor galleries are to be redisplayed in 1990–91. At present they are not especially inviting, which is a pity as some visitors are no doubt deterred from venturing upstairs where the more attractive new displays are to be found. Nevertheless, there is some interesting and important material downstairs. A small geology collection includes the tusk of a Straight-Tusked Elephant dredged up from the River Kennet in 1887. One piece in the small mineralogy collection particularly caught my eye – a chunk of pinkish-

19th century Chinese carved soapstone

grey carved soapstone. There were once a number of these in the museum's collections, but sadly several were disposed of in the 1960s as they were thought to be of little interest. There is also a tiny collection of Egyptian antiquities, shown in a case presented to the museum in memory of the Egyptologist, Walter Kemp.

The local archaeological collections are very good, ranging from prehistoric to Saxon. There is a particularly strong collection of Stone Age material, including implements and animal remains from the important Middle Stone Age (Mesolithic) site at Thatcham, and finely finished polished stone axes from the New Stone Age (Neolithic). One of the museum's early curators was the well-known archaeologist, H.J.E. Peake, and the collections include many items from his excavations early this century, for example that of the Saxon graveyard at East Shefford in 1912. There are some fine Bronze Age items including hoards such as that of Yattendon, in which bronze chisels, spearheads and gouges were found. This material came to light when the foundations of Yattendon Court were being dug in 1876. Another important item is the ceramic 'beaker' found at Inkpen. The so-called Beaker culture was prevalent in Britain from 2,000 BC or so, and the

Inkpen beaker is a superb example of the typical vessels of these people. A four-legged bowl or polypod is another important item, almost unique in the British Isles.

Progressing upstairs you move on to the Medieval and later periods. There are several interesting collections here. The Southby collection of pewter, mostly English and of 17th and 18th century date, includes a variety of plates, jugs and spoons, and a particularly fine pair of 17th century candlesticks. There are some fine ceramics of the 17th and 18th centuries, and a collection of watches made in Newbury – there were up to 100 clockmakers in the town between 1640 and 1840.

Newbury's past has been somewhat chequered. In the 11th century it was a flourishing town of traders, with two mills and a manor recorded in the Domesday Book. The Borough of Newbury is first recorded in the Pipe Roll of 1189. There was a castle built near the present museum in the Norman period, but no trace of it now exists. King John seized Newbury in 1200 after his properties in Normandy were confiscated. By the 15th century Newbury passed from the Earl of March to the Duke of York and the town was then drawn into the War of the Roses. The cloth trade was important to Newbury, but by the 17th cen-

tury it had declined. The town's fortunes revived in the 18th century, partly due to the trade arriving from coaches stopping on their journeys between London and Bath.

One of the most famous Newbury clothmakers was John Winchcombe, known as 'Jack of Newbury' (who died in 1519). He owned an industry with 200 looms and 1,000 employees. Cloth also comes into the tale of the Newbury Coat, which is related in the displays. On the 25th June 1811, as a result of a wager between Sir John Throckmorton and his friends, a fleece was turned into a finished coat in one day. Two sheep were sheared at 5am; the wool was prepared, spun, woven, and the cloth dyed, being ready by 4pm; the coat was then made by 6.20pm and was worn at dinner by Throckmorton that evening! It took 13 hours and 20 minutes, and there were up to 5,000 spectators. The museum has various objects relating to this feat, including a vellum certificate signed by the tailor who made the coat.

The first of the new displays on the first floor is the costume gallery. The main display of dresses (from about 1800 to the 1920s) is changed periodically. One of the most extraordinary gowns is the 'sack' dress (*c.* 1774), which follows the 18th century fashion of large 'panniers' on each hip under the fabric; at their most extreme these dresses could be six feet wide! There is

Tin-glazed earthenware charger

Printed cotton dress, c. 1837

a fine collection of baby clothes and accessories. One eyecatching display just before the costume gallery is of costume jewellery from the 18th to the 20th centuries. Professor and Mrs Hull Grundy gave items from their huge collection to some fifty museums around the country and Newbury was one of the recipients.

The Civil War display includes an audio-visual programme that graphically shows some of the battles being re-enacted. There were two battles at Newbury, in 1643 and 1644, and Donnington Castle nearby was besieged. Oxford was a Royalist centre (see the **Museum of Oxford** entry) and Newbury was a Parliamentarian centre. The battle of 1643 was fought between the army of the King (who was present at both battles) and Parliamentarian troops – some 14,000 men in all. Both battles were indecisive but finally, in 1649, Charles I was executed. The museum has a collection of Civil War objects, and those on display include helmets, weapons and a small hoard of gold coins presumably hidden by their

anxious owner at the beginning of the Civil War.

Traditional crafts and industries of West Berkshire are shown in the next gallery. These include brick and tile making, coppicing and hurdle making, and wood turning (the workshop equipment of Lailey, a turner from West Berkshire, is displayed at the **Museum of English Rural Life**). A popular local pastime is ballooning, and Newbury must be one of the few museums with two balloon baskets hanging from its rafters! There is also an audio-visual display on the history of ballooning. Revd John Bacon (1846–1904) lived in Newbury for 29 years; having made many gas balloon flights he began to experiment with burners for hot air balloons, and in 1902 patented a burner using petrol as fuel. Bacon also experimented with wireless telegraphy, and proved its success by detonating a small charge on the ground with a radio signal sent from a balloon.

A full-length window in the ballooning gallery enables the visitor to look out at what was once the wharf, and there are panels and pictures explaining what it used to be like. The Kennet and Avon canal was completed in 1810, and by 1818 about 200 boats were operating along it carrying about 174,000 tons of goods and taking 3 days, 9 hours to travel from Newbury to Bath. The coming of the railway put paid to that, and although the GWR (who bought the canal in 1852) kept it open, by 1875 long distance trading had come to an end. Many people today are interested in 'messing about in boats' so canals are coming back into use and fashion.

The museum has a ground floor temporary exhibition gallery, with five or six exhibitions mounted each year. It is hoped that the museum will be able to spread and occupy the whole Granary building in the next few years. The development of the area around the museum plus the expansion of the museum itself (with the added advantage of the proximity of the River Kennet, on which barge trips already operate) will make this a very attractive area to visit. (NH)

OLD WARDEN

The Shuttleworth Collection

Old Warden Aerodrome, Nr Biggleswade, Bedfordshire SG18 9ER
(076) 727 288
Open daily. ⬛▣   ♿**W**
♿ & ♿ must book in advance with Shop/Reception Manageress.

Old Warden lies in the heart of rural Bedfordshire, known for its market gardens on the one hand and its brickworks on the other. In the mid-1800s one Joseph Shuttleworth entered into partnership with a Nathaniel Clayton to manufacture agricultural equipment, including steam traction engines, in Lincoln. With the proceeds of his successful enterprise, Shuttleworth acquired the Old Warden Estate in 1872 and at the centre of it built a Victorian Gothic mansion. His grandson, Richard Ormond Shuttleworth, was born at Old Warden Park in 1909, just nine days before Louis Bleriot made the first crossing of the Channel by aeroplane. From an early age Richard developed an interest in mechanical things, and when he was 19 years old his love of machines attracted him to an 1898 Panhard Levassor. He was then *en route* to a creditable career in motor rallying and racing that culminated in his victory at Donnington in

1890 Panhard Levassor

1909 Bleriot XI

1935 in what was arguably the first British Grand Prix, driving an Alfa Romeo.

The Panhard, bought in 1928, was the foundation piece of what is now The Shuttleworth Collection. Along with the first aeroplane that he bought in 1932, a de Havilland Moth, and the first historic one that he collected in 1936, a 1909 Bleriot XI, the Panhard now stands at the beginning of the collection of aeroplanes, motor cars and carriages that are housed at Old Warden Aerodrome. When the Second World War broke out, Richard Shuttleworth joined the Royal Air Force Volunteer Reserve, but was tragically killed on a training flight in 1940. After the war, his mother, Dorothy, turned the Estate into The Richard Shuttleworth Remembrance Trust in memory of her son. She established the mansion as The Shuttleworth Agricultural College and put on a formal footing The Shuttleworth Collection, which opened to the public in the mid-1960s.

The aeroplanes and vehicles are displayed in seven aircraft hangars including the Workshops, Hangar 1, where some maintenance and restoration work is open to public view. This is a working collection in all senses and on the special 'flying days' in the summer

sounds of historic aircraft fill the skies above the all-grass aerodrome. Although there is plenty to see all year round in all weathers, these are the most exciting days to visit Old Warden. A small guide book recommends a route around the hangars beginning in Hangar 2, and gives a background to the collection and the Shuttleworth family. There are the original founding pieces of the collection in Hangar 2, and a display to the side of the main exhibits concentrates on airships. 'Lighter than Air', these massive contraptions are given scale by comparison with the dwarfed shape of a modern Jumbo 747.

Hangar 3 shows examples of aeroplanes in use through the First World War, although the 'lozenge' camouflage on the 1917 LVG CVI looks surprisingly modern. Photographs of the aircraft in use and information about their manufacture is mounted on boards in front of each aircraft, and uniforms, models and various aircraft parts are used as supplementary material around the hangar walls. A blank propeller in various stages of preparation shows the build-up of laminations that form the beautifully shaped finished product. The Sopwith Pup on display actually fired bullets through

the propeller, with guns that stopped firing when a blade was in the way.

In Hangar 4 there is a display of Rolls Royce engines with photographs of the aeroplanes that they powered. The Griffon MK 58, the 'ultimate in aircraft piston engines', is the biggest example on show, and these are still used by the RAF in their Shackletons. The Jupiter engine on the facing wall looks like a monstrous 'Catherine wheel', and it is easy to connect the weight of the developing engines with the increasingly sturdy aircraft in this gallery. Less string and more aerodynamic curves herald the more familiar shapes of the present day. There is a Spitfire and a Gloster Gladiator, as well as the less romantic Bowser or fuel tanker that carried petrol onto airfields.

Hangar 5, 'The Garage and Coach Room', displays horse-drawn and motor vehicles from 1860–1945. There are boneshaker bicycles and bath chairs, and a gorgeous Baby Peugeot from 1902 – and it's yellow! A very elegant Richard Brazier with a pramhood back and navy paintwork sits imperiously beside a dear little Austin 7. The Brazier in all its splendour had a maximum speed of 40 mph while the Austin reached a mighty half century! Some of the pre-1904 vehicles on display take part in the annual London to Brigton Veteran Car Run. The next area is entitled 'Extraordinary Aeroplanes', and includes a 'Flying Flea' and the Flying Machines used by

Spitfire Mk VC

Bristol Boxkite, from 'Those Magnificent Men' film

'Those Magnificent Men' in the 20th Century Fox film. Sadly, the Flying Flea, home-built and designed by a French grocer, is very unpredictable and cannot be flown. But the amazing fretwork of the 1910 Bristol Boxkite and Avro Triplane film replicas is robust enough for them to make a curtain call on flying days with the 1912 Blackburn Monoplane, the oldest genuine British aeroplane in flying condition in the world.

The De Havilland hangar celebrates the heyday of popular flying. The navy and silver of the Gypsy Moth conjures up names like Amy Johnson and images of what is known as the 'flying garden party era', which is still remembered by the 'Moth Club' in a yearly event at Woburn Abbey. 'Women of the Empire' is a two-engined aeroplane now owned by a descendant of Lady Astor, and is painted in colours that commemorate her fund-raising for ambulance aeroplanes during the Second World War.

The Shuttleworth Collection, with its extensive shop and restaurant, is adjacent to another feature of the Old Warden Estate, which predates the Shuttleworths' ownership – the Swiss Garden (administered by Bedfordshire County Council). Lord Ongley, whose family bought the land in 1695, is thought to have fashioned the garden and its grottoes, bridges and ornate Swiss summerhouse in the early 19th century. There is a chapel with a Gothic door and multicoloured glass window, and the summerhouse itself is a strange construction decorated with ornate patterns made from fir poles, fir cones and carved wood. The garden, which has developed into an arboretum of national significance, is planted with rhododendrons and shrubs that are a riot of colour at certain times of the year. Curved paths, bridges and lakes open out into vistas across the lawns, although the overall effect is of a secret place that is a joy to explore. In addition, the adjacent village of Old Warden is well worth visiting. The houses, originally built for the retainers of the estate, are overlooked by a church dating from the early 12th century that has exquisite wood carvings from Europe, including some from the private chapel of Anne of Cleves, the fourth wife of Henry VIII.

With the Victorian mansion and the Swiss Garden as a backdrop, The Shuttleworth Collection and its 1920s to '30s-style aerodrome make a visit to Old Warden an unusual and varied experience. (KH)

OLNEY

The Cowper and Newton Museum

Orchard Side, Market Place, Olney, Buckinghamshire　(0234) 711516
Closed Sundays and Mondays (except Bank Holiday Mondays); also closed mornings November to Easter. **⚑**
♿ **S**: steps into museum and down into garden.

William Cowper (pronounced 'Cooper') was born in Hertfordshire in 1731 and died in Norfolk in 1800. He achieved fame as a poet during his lifetime, although it was not until he was in middle age that he began writing poetry in earnest. He came to live in Olney in 1768, in the house that is now a museum. The museum celebrates Cowper's life and work, and also provides a window on the 18th century.

'It was a society at once narrow and cosmopolitan', which 'liked painting and politics', was 'lukewarm in religion, but scrupulous about going to

R. J. Swan, Portrait of Cowper

Church; slack about morals, strict about the proprieties . . . Outwardly so formal and so cosmopolitan, [yet] really very English, impulsive, copious, untidy, full of exceptions to the rule [and] eccentric characters.' So wrote David Cecil in *The Stricken Deer or The Life of Cowper*, 1929. The century's 'literary intelligentsia' included Gibbon, Dr Johnson and Jane Austen. The 'essential characteristic' of 18th century people, according to Cecil, 'was a disbelief in extremes. They were gregarious but not giddy, stay-at-home but not solitary. . . . You lived in order to be good.'

Cowper's mother died when he was six years old. Along with two years of bullying at the boarding school to which he was then sent, this left a lasting effect on him. He became a London lawyer but was an unhappy and unsuccessful one. Accumulated troubles in London led to Cowper's first mental breakdown. On recovering, he moved to Huntingdon and eventually lived with the Unwin family. Cowper was, by now, converted to evangelical Christianity, and converted Mary Unwin. It was through this faith that he met Rev John Newton of Olney. After Mr Unwin's death, Cowper and Mrs Unwin were persuaded by Newton to move to Olney. Mary Unwin was Cowper's lifelong companion, though they never married (this caused some gossip and rumour in Huntingdon and later in Olney).

'Orchard Side' was not the most attractive house in Olney. It was then in rather a seedy district, 'whose sordid jollities were a constant offence to Cowper.' The house was, however, near the Church. Olney is now a bustling small town set in attractive countryside, which Cowper particularly loved. The museum was established in 1900, founded by Thomas Wright and using Cowper's own 'Orchard Side', which was given to Olney by W.H. Collingridge. The first two floors have displays relating to Cowper and to Rev John Newton. There is also a small local history display, and a special feature on lace-making – a local craft industry.

The Rev John Newton was six years older than Cowper; before his conver-

Rev John Newton

sion and entry to the church, he had an adventure-filled life as a sailor working on, amongst other vessels, a slave ship. Newton encouraged Cowper to write hymns and in 1779 they published *The Olney Hymns*, one of the first hymn books published in English. Newton wrote many fine hymns himself, including 'Amazing Grace'. The museum boasts a very fine collection of books, some of which are on display; others are in the library and can be consulted by researchers, by appointment. There are several copies of *The Olney Hymns* on display, including a first edition (where 'fountain' was misspelled 'foutain' – corrected in the second edition). Cowper's hymns achieved international fame: there is even a copy of a hymn book in Japanese containing two of Cowper's hymns!

Cowper suffered a second mental breakdown in 1773, from which it took him two years to recover, largely through the devoted care of Mary Unwin. Cowper retained his Christian beliefs but became convinced of his own eventual, inevitable damnation. He threw himself into daily life and writing, and spent many hours gardening, growing plants from the new seeds that were coming from the West Indies, such as pineapple and melon. He also liked to work in the garden, setting up a writing table in the greenhouse, or in the summerhouse at the end of the garden. The latter was 'not much bigger than a sedan chair' and Cowper sometimes called it his 'Sulking Room' or the 'verse manufactory'. Do walk through the gardens to the summerhouse when you visit the museum.

Cowper was a great letter writer throughout his life, and this helped him to maintain a large circle of friends. The museum has many

Cowper's Parlour

mementoes of his greatest friends, including Lady Ann Austen. Lady Austen lived nearby for several years; she was witty, lively, and clearly infatuated with Cowper. Lady Austen helped to stave off Cowper's depression by encouraging him to write and publish more poetry. It was she who amused Cowper with the tale of a draper, John Gilpin, which Cowper then put into verse. Another poem inspired by Lady Austen was 'The Task' – the poem that first brought Cowper wide recognition and fame when it was published in 1785. 'The Task' was, in Robert Burns's opinion, 'a glorious poem'. In search of inspiration Cowper had followed Lady Austen's suggestion to write about anything – even the sofa. 'The Task' is several thousand lines long, and is a meditative poem reflecting on life. The sofa that is the subject of the first line, 'I sing the sofa,' is on display in the museum. 'The Task' was indeed a huge task: it took Cowper some three years to complete. The table on which he wrote the work is also on display in the museum.

Among other items that can be seen in the museum is a costume and textile collection. This includes Lady Austen's Court dress, worn when she was presented to King George III. There is also Cowper's bedspread, which is decorated with delicately sewn patchwork flowers, and the waistcoat that he wore when he died. The waistcoat is on display in the recently completed costume gallery.

Cowper and Mary moved in 1786 to a larger and more comfortable house in Weston, where they lived until 1795. Mary suffered several strokes and caring for her was such a strain that in 1793 a relative suggested they both move to Norfolk and stay with him. On the panel of the window shutter at Weston, just before they left for Norfolk, Cowper wrote: 'Farewell, dear scenes, for ever closed to me; Oh, for what sorrows must I now exchange ye!' Their last years were sad and so different from the life they had once enjoyed. Mary Unwin died in 1796, aged 72. In 1800 Cowper himself died, aged 69. He was buried in East Dereham, Norfolk. (NH)

OXFORD

Ashmolean Museum

Beaumont Street, Oxford OX1 2PH
(0865) 278000
Closed Sunday mornings and all day Mondays (except Bank Holiday Mondays); closed during St Giles Fair (early September) and at Christmas and Easter.
F **& W**
♦ & ♦ must book in advance through Education Service (0865) 278015; parties usually broken down into groups of 10–15, each with an individual guide. ◉ Guided tours usually Tuesdays, Fridays and Saturdays: details from Education Service (0865) 278015.

The Ashmolean is one of several museums that belong to the University of Oxford (the others being the *Museum of the History of Science*, the **Pitt Rivers Museum, The University Museum** and **The Bate Collection** of Historical Instruments). It is Britain's oldest public museum, opened in 1683 by the Duke of York (later King James II). The Ashmolean was housed at that time in the purpose-built edifice in Broad Street that now contains the *Museum of the History of Science* (a museum with fascinating collections that is well worth a visit). Its first collections were given by Elias Ashmole and consisted of curiosities or rarities (natural and man-made) from around the world. In 1692 Ashmole bequeathed additional collections that had been built up originally by John Tradescant and his son, the royal gardeners (or to give them their full title, 'Keeper of His Majesty's Gardens, Vines and Silkworms') and given to Ashmole. Some remnants of these earliest collections still exist and are displayed in the Tradescant Room. The Tradescants made trips to the New World to gather plants, and this gave them plenty of opportunity to collect curiosities too. The collection includes shells, weapons, an African drum, a Chinese rhino-horn cup, Guy Fawkes' lantern, and the robe of Powhatan (a North American Indian Chief) made from four deerskins and decorated with shells.

Camille Pissarro, Le Jardin des Tuileries, temps du pluie, *1899*

Egyptian mummy case, coffin lid and funerary equipment

Heberden Coin Room and the Cast Gallery. Displays are grouped together according to department.

The Ashmolean's huge and exceptionally fine archaeological collections began to grow rapidly in the 19th century as material from Sir Flinders Petrie's excavations in Egypt were acquired, and Sir Arthur Evans (Keeper of the Museum from 1884 to 1908) added much material from his excavations at Knossos, Crete. The Egyptian collections range from the monumental and the exquisite to the ordinary and mundane. The mundane of dynastic Egypt is fascinating, including papyrus rope that is two to three inches in diameter, and models of daily scenes of breadmaking and brewing. One object that I could not resist was a hippopotamus made of coarse red pottery: apparently hippos abounded in Egypt and models of them are common (as are models and representations of hedgehogs!).

Just beyond the Egypt galleries is the Marshall Room. If you are interested in Worcester porcelain, then this is the gallery to make a beeline for. H.R. Marshall gathered the most comprehensive collection of 18th century coloured· Worcester porcelain, which he gave to the museum in 1957.

The Medieval Room is packed with displays showing aspects of daily life in the Middle Ages, ranging from religious life to food and drink, law and order, and craftsmanship. The most famous object here is the Alfred Jewel (colour plate 7), which bears the legend: '+ *Aelfred mec heht gewyrcan*' (Alfred ordered me to be made). It is believed to have belonged to King Alfred the Great (871–899) and would have been used as the handle of an *aestel* – a rod or pointer for following the text of a manuscript.

The Eastern Art collections are as extensive as they are fine, with objects from China, Japan, Tibet, India and the world of Islam. One of the most imposing objects is the over-life-size seated Bodhisathva, the image of Avalokitesvara – the guide to souls who can help humans towards enlightenment. It was made of fig-tree wood in 13th century China and was originally in a

The original museum had an 'elaboratory' on its lowest floor, where the Duke of York and Lady Anne were shown 'some experiments to their great satisfaction'. This elaboratory became an important centre for the study of the natural sciences in the 18th century. But the museum had mixed fortunes and the collections suffered as a result. The Dodo that was in the collections became 'noisome', and today only its beak and a few rather sad fragments survive (now in the **University Museum**).

In the 19th century the museum moved to its present home, a neo-Classical building designed by C. R. Cockerell in 1845/46 to house the University's ˙growing collection of paintings and extended in the second half of the century to accommodate

other exhibits. The art collection included drawings by Michelangelo and Raphael, watercolours by Turner, Italian Renaissance bronzes and maiolica given by C. D. E. Fortnum (a major benefactor), and many Italian paintings, among them Uccello's famous masterpiece, 'Hunt in the Forest' (colour plate 6). Over the years the collection has been enriched through many gifts and bequests made to the University and allocated to the Ashmolean, among them in recent years the 'Virgin and Child' by Bellini, bequeathed by Lord Clark. The Ashmolean Museum and University Galleries, to give the museum its full title, now has some of the best collections in the world.

The museum is organised into departments of Eastern Art, Western Art, and Antiquities, and also includes the

Islamic mosque lamp from Egypt

cave temple in Shanxi. A particularly beautiful and balanced object is the enamelled and gilded Islamic mosque lamp from Egypt made in the 13th to 14th century for a mosque of Sultan Muhammed ibn Qala'un.

On the first floor are the European and Near Eastern antiquities, the Minoan material from Crete being one of the most important elements. The Cycladic figurines, such as that from Melos, are also familiar, partly because Picasso and other modern artists showed great interest in such primitive art and used similar styles in some of their work. There is a large collection of Greek pottery. One vase that caught my eye, known as the Shoemaker Vase (5th century BC), shows a shoemaker cutting a piece of leather round the foot of a young customer while his father looks on. It was quite unusual for craftsmen at work to be depicted on Greek vases but the Ashmolean has several important examples.

Part of the Ashmolean's rich and diverse collection of Western Art is displayed on the first and second floors. It ranges from early Italian, Dutch and French paintings to English 18th century pictures, one of the most extensive collections of Pre-Raphaelite

paintings and drawings, and a representative collection of French Impressionists, with paintings from virtually every member of the school. There are so many paintings on the first floor that I could exhort you not to miss! John Constable's 'Study of Clouds' is a must, as is Camille Pissaro's 'Le Jardin des Tuileries, temps de pluie' (one of an extensive collection of paintings, drawings and watercolours by the artist and his sons Felix and Lucien). There are plenty of interesting picture frames, too: don't miss those on the portrait of Elias Ashmole in the Founder's Room, and on the painting by Paolo De Matteis in the Weldon Gallery; the first is by Grinling Gibbons, and the second is an exhuberant 18th century gilded rococo frame, which is the most lavish of that period to have survived and depicts dragons, flowers and a whole host of other things.

If you time your visit to the second floor carefully, you will catch the clock on the half-landing as it strikes. One of several clocks throughout the museum,

Bodhisathva Avalokitesvara from North China

The 'Shoemaker' Attic black figure vase

all maintained in working order, it is a 'striking and musical bracket clock' in an ebonised wood and ormolu case, and was made by John Stephen Rimbault. The gallery of 18th to 20th century English paintings and bronzes is a treat; Edward Lear's 'Plains of Lombardy' and Alma-Tadema's 'Roman Garden' were just two that particularly appealed to me. There is also a small gallery of Dutch still life paintings, not just braces of pheasant but vases containing flowers of all types painted in beautiful detail (colour plate 5). Other exhibits on this floor include English and Continental glass, and French and German porcelain. Do make sure that you have plenty of energy to make it up to the second floor – it's well worth it!

There are too many riches in the museum to take in on one visit, so do make return trips. The regular guided tours are well worth joining: they focus on individual galleries or themes within the collection. Also, there is usually a 'Friend of the Ashmolean Museum's on duty, ready to give helpful tips about the museum and the work of the Friends, who help to raise money for new acquisitions. (NH)

The Bate Collection of Historical Instruments

University of Oxford Faculty of Music, St Aldates, Oxford OX1 1DB (0865) 276125

Open Monday to Friday afternoons.

: to all parts except upper gallery.

& book in advance if demonstrations or talks required: contact Curator; treasure trail, tour leaflets and instrument guides for sale.

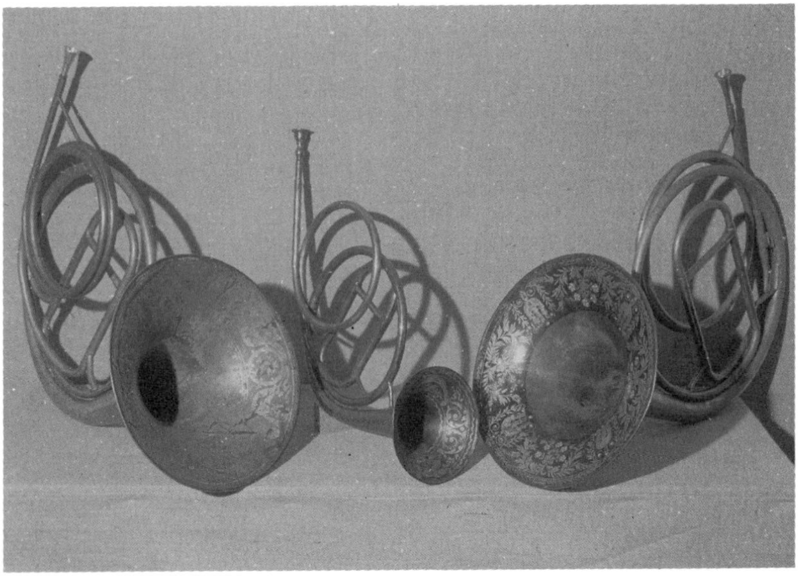

Three French horns with decorated bells

This museum boasts the most comprehensive collection in Britain of historic European woodwind, brass and percussion instruments. It also has a small collection of keyboard instruments and a complete Javanese double Gamelan.

Philip Bate, a one-time television producer and enthusiastic amateur musician, gradually acquired a large collection of historic woodwind instruments, and in 1963 generously gave this collection to Oxford University. Bate is the author of a book that is still the authoritative text on oboes, flutes, trumpets and trombones. As he has acquired more instruments, he has continued to add to the museum's collections. Important gifts have also been made by other collectors, notably Reginald Morley-Pegge, and there are instruments on loan from various sources. The Bate Collection is unique among museums of comparable importance as the instruments are intended to be used. Introductory demonstrations can be arranged for groups, and the museum also organises special weekend workshops and summer schools.

The first instrument visitors encounter on entering is the flute. Those of the baroque and classical periods had just one key and were current into the 1780s. Flutes were usually made of boxwood, but the collection includes examples made of ivory, glass, and a variety of woods. The modern flute, with its key for every finger hole, was developed by Theobald Boehm. There are a number of 'eccentric' flutes, designed by those who thought the conventional flute was difficult to hold and play. The museum's collection of clarinets also shows comprehensively the mechanical and thus musical development of the instrument from the 18th century. Early clarinets had only two keys, but more were added over the years. One of the museum's most recent and important acquisitions is an 18th century two-key clarinet, one of the two earliest clarinets in Britain.

The museum also has the oldest oboe in England, dating from around 1680 – Purcell's time. Another recent acquisition, and a most important instrument, is the Dutch oboe made by Hendrik Richters in Amsterdam around 1720. This has beautifully carved ivory mounts and is unique in a museum in Britain. The ancestor of the oboe was the shawm, of which the museum has various examples; shawms are still used in many parts of the world including the Middle East and North Africa. (For the world's greatest collection of ethnographic musical instruments, see the **Pitt Rivers Museum**, Oxford.) And no prizes for guessing which instrument Adolphe Sax invented! There are saxophones covering the soprano to bass range – the museum's B$^{\flat}$ bass saxophone by Hawkes & Son is some three feet high.

Single-reed instruments from many countries are shown together to demonstrate what a worldwide art music is. Instruments like these were used by Ancient Egyptians at least 4,000 years ago. The equipment and tools used to make a reed are displayed, showing the fine and intricate process involved in producing reeds for such instruments as bassoons.

The most important type of 'flute' for serious music from the 15th to the 18th centuries was the recorder. It is one instrument that many visitors will have been acquainted with in their childhood – in my case not very fruitfully! Trumpets, trombones, cornets and horns are also well represented. The horn was, and is, a huntsman's instrument, and was introduced into the orchestra in the late 17th century. The trumpet was an important instrument from the Middle Ages onwards. A long straight trumpet that was made for the first performance of Bach's B Minor Mass in England is on display in the museum.

The serpent is an instrument whose

name well describes its form. It was used in churches and, from the late 18th century, in military bands. As it was awkward to carry and quite fragile, a variety of new upright serpents were invented. It continued to be used in orchestras into the 1840s and in church bands until the end of the 19th century.

One of the recent acquisitions no visitor can miss is the Javanese Gamelan, given to the Faculty of Music by H.E. Sudjarwo, Minister of Forestry of the Republic of Indonesia. This gamelan has its own name, 'Kyai Madu Laras' or 'Venerable Sweet Harmony'. It consists of sixty-two individual instruments, most of them percussion instruments. They include bars, 'kettles' and gongs, and there is one string instrument and a flute. There is now an Oxford Gamelan Society, which plays the gamelan each week and holds regular beginners' sessions.

Although most of the exhibits are wind instruments, there is a small group of string and keyboard instruments, mainly displayed in the first floor gallery. Among them is a clavichord made in 1743 by Hieronymus Albrecht Haas, in Hamburg. The inside of its lid is lavishly decorated. Haas, father and son, were the greatest German clavichord makers. Another interesting group are the six surviving instruments depicted in Zoffany's portrait of 'The Sharp Family' (1779–81, on loan to the National Portrait Gallery, London, from the executors of the late Miss Olive Lloyd-Baker, from whom the instruments are also on loan). The museum also has a complete bow-maker's workshop, that of William Retford, who died in 1970. The making of bows for violinists, cellists and other string players is a skilled and precise art. Retford was the greatest English bow-maker and continued to practice his craft until he was over ninety years old.

The museum hopes to continue to develop its collections and, if the money can be raised, to extend the museum building. Among other things this would enable the gamelan to be laid out in the correct way. (NH)

Christ Church Picture Gallery

Christ Church, Canterbury Quadrangle, Oxford OX1 1DP (0865) 276172
Closed Sunday mornings. 🆂
& **S**: not accessible to wheelchairs – stairs down to the Gallery.
🚻 & 🚻 book in advance with Assistant Curator of Pictures; maximum 20 persons; guided tours can be given to groups, if arranged in advance. ☺

Christ Church Picture Gallery is tucked away and a little difficult to find, but it is one of the real gems of Oxford. The entrance among the fine College buildings is down some stone steps, and it comes as a great surprise to find this splendid, modern purpose-built gallery, which was opened by the Queen in 1968. The collections are relatively small but very fine indeed. The gallery was designed around the main collection of Old Masters, and it is sufficiently small to allow you to get to grips with the pictures and to enjoy them in peace.

The collections consist mainly of four gifts or bequests; the first of these

The Javanese Gamelan

Leonardo da Vinci, Grotesque head

The Butcher's Shop, *an early work by Annibale Carracci (1560–1609)*

was the Guise Bequest. In 1765 General Sir John Guise, who was at Christ Church as a young man, died and bequeathed his fine collection of drawings and about 300 paintings, mostly Italian and dating mainly from the High Renaissance to the mid-18th century. Some of the paintings then believed to be by Raphael, Leonardo or Correggio are now known to be by other hands, but there are at least four paintings by Annibale Carracci. One of these is the famous 'Butcher's Shop', a very large canvas that was originally owned by Charles I (bought from the collection of the Duke of Mantua) and later sold off by Cromwell. This work is particularly important because a painting of this size on a non-religious theme was a revolutionary development in 17th century Italy and marked a new move towards naturalism. The figure at the front of the picture is probably a self-portrait by Annibale, and the others may be members of his family. Some have said that Guise's military career led him to collect paintings that have somewhat gory themes, but this is a rather harsh judgement, given the quality and variety of his

collection. One very moving picture, or fragment, is the 'Lamentation of Christ' by Hugo van der Goes. This painting is unusual because its medium is tempera (pigment usually mixed with egg yolk) on linen rather than on panel. Very few of Van der Goes' works survive, and equally few works of tempera on linen have endured the rigours of the years.

There are so many paintings in the Guise Collection that need to be quietly savoured. Two others that I especially like are a stunning Tintoretto, 'The Martyrdom of St Lawrence', and 'The Deposition of Christ' by the Master of Delft (colour plate 4). The latter represents the crucifixion, burial and resurrection of Christ and is full of wonderful detail.

Another of the four main bequests is the Fox-Strangways gift (made in 1828 and 1834). The Hon W. T. H. Fox-Strangways was, like Guise, an undergraduate at Christ Church, but his particular collecting taste was for Italian primitive paintings, which he was able to indulge whilst a diplomat in Florence and elsewhere. The great majority of these pictures have reli-

gious themes, and, as with the Guise bequest, the quality of this small collection is splendid. 'Four Musical Angels' is a lovely fragment of a larger work dating to around 1340–50, while 'The Wounded Centaur' by Filippino Lippi is compelling and very different from the other pictures in this early collection. On the back of the Lippi painting is an unfinished drawing, whose subject appears to be the birth of Venus. As for the centaur, we see his family in a cave in the background, the anguished centaur himself holding a quiver full of arrows, but wounded in the foreleg by an arrow of Cupid, who can also be seen in the background. The picture is intriguing because we don't know the details of the story that has been depicted.

Van Dyck's 'The Continence of Scipio' is another masterpiece in the Christ Church collection. It was bequeathed by Lord Frederick Campbell. Van Dyck was one of Rubens' most gifted pupils – indeed a Rubens

Van Dyck, A Soldier on Horseback, *c. 1615*

Van Dyck, The Continence of Scipio, *1620–21*

The Museum of Oxford

St Aldates, Oxford OX1 1DZ
(0865) 815559
Closed Sundays and Mondays. ▪
 planned for summer 1990.
& preferably book in
advance; education room and
refreshments available for pre-
booked groups. ◉

This is Oxford's only museum about Oxford itself, providing an excellent introduction to both the city of Oxford and the University, beginning with geology and prehistory and continuing to the development of the modern industrial city. It is situated within the Victorian Town Hall on the site of the city's medieval Guild Hall.

Among the traces of early man are the Bronze Age burial mounds that lie under what is now the University Parks. Roman pottery kilns have been found around Oxford, the woods that used to exist in Headington and Cowley providing the fuel. Though there was Roman settlement in Oxford, the main settlement was to the south east at Dorchester and to the north at Wendlebury. The first known written reference to Oxford was in 912 AD; it tells of Edward the Elder turning the village into a stronghold against the advancing Danes. Oxford Castle was built near the Thames in the west of the city by Robert d'Oilly (who was given Oxford by William the Conqueror). All that remains of the castle today is the great earth mound and stone tower.

The displays chart the developing town and its growing craft industries. By the Middle Ages it was one of the largest towns in England, though it only had a population of about 6,000. The crafts included metalworking, bookbinding, leather working and stained glass work. The importance of crafts was demonstrated by the fact that the twenty or so master craftsmen and their families effectively ruled the city. The museum highlights many of these crafts.

The University gradually developed. There are references to scholars before 1200, and by 1300 Oxford was

influence seems apparent in the Scipio picture. It was painted by Van Dyck on his first visit to London; he was trying to establish a reputation in history painting, but later made his name in portrait painting. Another Van Dyck, tucked away near the temporary exhibitions gallery, is worth seeking out – the brilliant sketch 'A Soldier on Horseback', which is an almost monochrome picture of the highest quality.

In addition to the paintings, the gallery houses some 2,000 drawings, including a number by Michelangelo, Leonardo and Raphael, which form one of the most important private collections in the country. The drawings are displayed in temporary exhibitions that are well worth visiting (there is not the space to display them permanently and drawings are easily damaged by long-term exposure). Among the gallery's other collections are painted and metal icons given by C. R. Patterson, and a number of pieces of 18th century glass from the Harding Collection.

The gallery mounts temporary exhibitions on various themes every three months or so. Although many are drawn from the collections, there is an annual exhibition of the work of graduates and undergraduates. Gallery talks are organised regularly on such topics as the history of the collection, early Italian painting, and Rubens in Oxford. Another activity that has taken place annually for the last few years at Christ Church, and variously in the other Oxford museums, is the visit of the Oxmus Club, a museum club for 8–14 year olds that arranges special museum-based activities, particularly during school holidays. A recent activity at Christ Church was a day spent looking at paper – both works of art on it and how it is made, with a messy papermaking session over the road in the *Museum of Modern Art* (MOMA to its friends). The Museum of Modern Art is just a short distance from Christ Church, and is certainly a must, with its regular innovative temporary exhibitions and activities. (NH)

A caricature of Oxford Fellows by Thomas Rowlandson

still flourishing Oxford University Press established. The Civil War did not pass Oxford by. It became the royalist capital and in 1645 was besieged by General Fairfax, but the king managed to escape from Oxford in disguise and the city then surrendered.

By the 18th century the Oxford student's life had become rather more comfortable. The reconstructed student's college room of the 1770s bears this out. Increasing jollity, however, led to an increase in the number of students that failed to get degrees and to a decline in the reputation of the University. One gruesome display is the skeleton of Giles Freeman Covington, hanged for murder in 1791. His skeleton was used as a teaching aid in the anatomy school for many years!

The canals, roads and railway of the 19th century increased the pace of change in Oxford. The life of ordinary

Reconstructed Jericho district kitchen

famous throughout Europe for its scholarship and had some 1,500 students. The museum focuses on these early academic developments. Students were like apprentices; they studied with a master in one of the sixty 'halls', and learned theology, logic and rhetoric. Graduates became church leaders, lawyers and royal officials. Medieval colleges were an insignificant part of the university and had no resident students; the first to be founded were University, Balliol and Merton, in the 13th century.

Trade crafts continued to grow in importance and by the 16th century an important trade was glove making. The museum has a beautiful pair of embro-

idered gloves on display as an example of this most important craft. The City Council became increasingly important in the 16th century. Councillors were elected from among the 600 or so freemen of the town. The beautifully intricate silver mace of the mayor's sergeant on display is physical evidence of this importance.

Many of the key events of the Reformation happened in Oxford – the burning of Cranmer, Latimer and Ridley, for example. The museum also focuses on the development of printing, which began in Oxford in 1478, just one year after Caxton had printed the first book in England. By 1602 the Bodleian Library was founded and the

people there is illustrated through the reconstructed Jericho district kitchen, and the parlour display. Recalling the high days and holidays are the intricate models of funfare rides made by Neville Rainsley, and the full costume of an Oxford Morris dancer. The ups and downs of the car industry have always affected Oxford, with its huge Rover Group plant at Cowley. The last sections of the main display chart the development of industrialisation and particularly the effect of the car industry. One interesting final exhibit is a model of the Maestro assembly line. (NH)

Fanciful reconstruction of medieval Oxford by H. W. Brewer for 'The Builder', 1891

Pitt Rivers Museum

*South Parks Road, Oxford OX1 3PP
(entrance through the* **University
Museum** *in Parks Road)
(0865) 270927*
and
*The Balfour Building, 60 Banbury
Road, Oxford (0865) 274726*
Closed every morning and all day
Sunday. **F**
♿: ground floor of main museum
accessible to wheelchairs, by
arrangement, and to upper
galleries by lift; all displays in
Balfour Building accessible.
♨ & **♦** book in advance
(0865) 270928. Schools Education
Service available. ☺

The Pitt Rivers Museum houses one of
the most important ethnographic collections in the world. It has been
variously and very accurately described
as 'an Aladdin's cave of treasures' and
'a treasure house tucked away in a
hidden corner [of] Oxford, an enchanting museum that sparkles with the
cultural imagination and ingenuity of
mankind'.

The museum's founding collections
were gathered by Lieutenant-General
Augustus Henry Lane Fox Pitt Rivers
(1827–1900), better known to posterity
as General Pitt Rivers. Pitt Rivers'
early task in the army was to investigate
methods of improving the army's
firearms, and this aroused his interest
in the development of weapons, but
also of arts, crafts and industries
around the world. He gave his collection to the University in 1884 and the
museum was opened by him in 1891. A
formidable man, he became the first
Inspector of Ancient Monuments,
establishing archaeology as a scientific
discipline.

The main museum is entered
through a temporary exhibition gallery,
which has new shows about twice a
year. Turn left past the reception desk
and the aladdin's cave opens up before
you. The first cases you pass are full of
masks of all shapes and sizes, made of a
huge variety of raw materials – fibre,
bark, skin, wood and metal among
them. Exhibits are still arranged
according to Pitt Rivers' original in-
structions – by theme of object, for
example coins and items of currency
from around the world (including cow-
rie shells, leg joints of beetles, feather-
covered coils of bark and much more),
or clothing from all cultures and cli-
mates. The museum staff have been
developing the displays but have remained faithful to the 'aladdin's cave'
school of museum design!

All human cultures seem invariably
to develop ideas of spirits or gods and
of rituals to ward off bad spirits and to
placate benign ones. The museum has
a huge collection of charms, amulets
and religious statuettes of all types.
Items come not only from far off continents: there is a carved 'witch post'
from Scarborough, for example, which
formed part of the hearth of a house
and was intended to keep witches at
bay.

No visitor can fail to notice the
forty-foot-high totem pole at the far
end of the gallery. It originally stood
outside a Haida Indian Chief's house
in British Columbia and was acquired
by the museum in 1901. Among the
figures depicted are the chief, a frog, a
bear cub and a raven, the latter with a
six-foot-long beak. Several other extraordinary objects are easy to miss as
they languish in a curtained case (to
protect them from light): these are the
stunning feather cloaks worn by
Hawaiian chiefs; each of the 100,000
tufts in each cloak is made with twenty
feathers from the Oo and Liwi birds.

Man's ingenuity at making craft to
cross water, and even open sea, is
explored in the collections. The vessels

General view of the ground floor gallery of the main museum, South Parks Road

Part of the drum display in the ethno-musicology gallery

range from an Irish coracle, or 'curragh', to a Melanesian shark-fishing outrigger, and from an elaborately-carved Maori canoe to a model of a massive 18th century fighting ship with seventy guns. Among the navigation aids is a native 'sailing chart' from Micronesia. This is made with sticks to indicate the prevailing winds and tide patterns, and shells to represent islands.

Among the clothing and textiles on display is a colourful and fascinating explanation of weaving techniques. Clothes vary with climate, available raw materials and culture. There are Inuit rain capes made of walrus intestine, for example, caribou and seal-skin jackets, and also clothes of embroidered silk. You cannot deny that man is a vain creature when you look at the first-floor gallery displays of jewellery from around the world. Scores of items include hairpins and combs, ornaments for all parts of the face, and necklaces of all sorts – one rather gruesome

example is made of seeds, small birds (the *whole* bird) and a toucan. This gallery also houses the very important South Pacific material collected by Captain Cook on his second voyage in 1773–74, including feather headdresses, tools, dishes, fans and quilted cloth.

Pitt Rivers' interest in weaponry is highlighted on the second floor. The more spectacular items include Sikh war quoits (metal hoops with a sharpened outer edge), which are beautifully inlaid with gold. The worldwide variety of swords and daggers is shown through the immensely comprehensive collections. Protective clothing or armour of all types is on display: there is a suit protected with 'scales' of horn; another, from the Gilbert or Kingsmill Islands, is made from coconut fibre and is complete with a three-pronged weapon of palm wood edged with sharks' teeth. The most spectacular is the suit of armour from Japan, as worn by a Samurai warrior, including the

gloves, shoes and undergarments, and a helmet made of thirty-two metal plates riveted together (colour plate 3). This armour dates to about 1750.

The museum's first curator was Henry Balfour, and it was he who substantially developed the founding collections. For example, Pitt Rivers had collected some 300 'rather ordinary' musical instruments and Balfour expanded this to more than 5,000. Balfour had always hoped to add a new gallery to the museum, devoted entirely to music, so it is right that the 'other' Pitt Rivers Museum at 60 Banbury Road, with its major ethno-musicology gallery, should be called the Balfour Building.

The ethno-musicology gallery is tremendous. It explores the whole range of sounds that can be made by plucking, hitting, blowing, winding and rubbing. You can also hear many of the sounds on the individual headphone system that visitors can wear as they walk round. Special events are arranged around the collections – a festival of traditional music, for example, took place in the museum gardens one summer. (Those interested in music should also make a point of visiting the **Bate Collection of Historical Instruments** while in Oxford; special events are likewise held there.)

The Balfour Building also houses a display on hunter-gatherer societies past and present. 10,000 years ago the earth's whole population hunted for and gathered its food. At the time of Christ half the earth's peoples were herding and growing their food; by the 15th century only 15% or so still lived by hunting and gathering, and today only a few small pockets survive. Among today's hunter-gatherers are the San Bushmen of the Kalahari, the Inuit hunters of the Arctic and the Mbuti pygmies of the tropical forests.

One essential piece of advice when you visit the main building: don't walk round with your eyes focusing firmly in front of you. Look up, down, round and about: there are objects everywhere and you could miss some of the best bits if you don't bend, stretch and peer as you go round! (NH)

The University Museum

Parks Road, Oxford OX1 3PW
(0865) 272950
Closed every Morning and all day
Sunday. **F**
& **S**: limited access for the
disabled.
菅 & **♀** preferably book in
advance; welcome weekday
mornings with permission from the
Porter.

The University Museum is housed in a
fine neo-gothic building, which was
completed in 1860. The building's design was selected by competition and
was by all accounts deeply unpopular
with the academics of the day. The
Oxford University School of Natural
Sciences was established in the 19th
century, and the University Museum
was founded to house the collections
that had been built up since the 17th
century. It was to be the centre of
science learning rather than just a re-
pository for the collections. There
were a series of rooms leading from the
central court for the chemical, zoological and medical departments (the
names can still be seen on the door
jambs). The central court was to be the

Detail from a display of insect species

area where scientists of all disciplines
could meet. As early as 1870 the collections were outgrowing the space
available, so in the following years
some of the departments left the
museum building and only the collections remained.

The museum has four collections:
Geology, Entomology, Mineralogy and
Zoology. The most imposing exhibit is
the skeleton of the dinosaur *Iguanodon
bernissartensis* – a cast of one of a
magnificent group of *Iguanodon*
skeletons found in Bernissart, Bel-
gium, in 1877. Dinosaurs have also
been found in and around Oxford: the
local Jurassic rocks are famous for their
fossil remains. In central Oxford, for
example, a *Pteranodon* was found, in
Stonesfield a *Megalosaurus*, and in
Cumnor remains of a *Tyrannosaurus
Rex*. The finds often consist of just a
few bones, and some of the early reconstructions of what the whole animal
may have looked like, based on these
bones, are interesting as they vary a
good deal from the more accurate reconstructions we have today. The
largest-known British dinosaur is the
Cetiosaurus Oxoniensis, some specimens
from which are in the museum. This
dinosaur lived about 163 million years
ago, was over fifty feet long, and is
estimated to have weighed about ten
tons when it was alive. Another important object is an Icthyosaur – one of the
first examples that was found with
evidence of the creature's soft tissue.

The museum's collection of rocks
and minerals is extraordinary and is
one of the top three mineralogy collections in the country. Only a small
fraction of it is on display. Pillars in the
museum are made of a variety of rocks

Part of a display of minerals

from around Britain, such as Ophical-cite and Carboniferous limestone.

The museum's entomology collection runs to over three million specimens. Of the total of one million recorded species in the world, 75% are insects. Among the zoology collections is an imposing African crocodile. These crocodiles can grow to seven metres, but this specimen is a mere four metres long! There are many mounted skeletons on display, which were, and are, used in the study of zoology. One can look at the similarities and differences between those of the horse, the one-humped camel, the bison, and so on.

The museum has a few remains of the Dodo, the swan-sized flightless bird that once inhabited the island of Mauritius. Killed by sailors for food – though apparently it had tough meat that improved little with cooking – the bird was hunted to extinction by man by about 1680. A living Dodo was brought to the Netherlands and one was eventually brought to England. It was probably this bird that after its death was passed to the **Ashmolean Museum**. By 1755 the specimen was in a poor state and was to be disposed of, but a few fragments were saved and it is these that are displayed here.

The museum was the scene of the great debate on evolution between Bishop Wilberforce and Thomas Huxley in the 1860s, though the displays tell us that the 'debate' was rather less extensive and animated than history would have us believe. Among the early and influential figures in the museum's life was John Philips, a geologist who played a leading role in the building of the museum. Some of Philips's early papers are in the museum's archives, and together the collections and archives document the beginning of geology as a science.

The museum's wide-ranging and important collections are a must for those interested in the natural sciences. The dinosaurs are also abidingly popular and hold a particular fascination for children. Through the museum's main court is the entrance to the fascinating and enthralling **Pitt Rivers Museum** (see above). (NH)

READING

Blake's Lock Museum

Kenavon Drive, Reading, Berkshire
(0734) 575911 ext. 2242 (address
for correspondence: **Reading
Museum and Art Gallery**)
Closed mornings at weekends.
◼ (but ▨ likely soon).   ⚫ W
⋔ & ⋔ book in advance.

This museum is a great favourite of mine, though at the time of writing the roads in central Reading seem to be under a state of siege from roadworks, making Blake's Lock slightly tricky to find. It is on the banks of the River Kennet, not far from Reading Gaol (so hated by Oscar Wilde), and is a haven of relative peace from the hubbub of Reading town centre.

Opened in 1985, the museum concentrates on the story of Reading's waterways, trades and industries. It is housed in a building that was originally a sewage pumping station. When the Thames Water Authority was formed, the building returned to the ownership of Reading Borough Council and was used for some time as a vehicle maintenance depot. However, its fortunes changed when it was finally decided to develop the building as a museum. The displays were done on a tight budget, and are very inventive and fun.

Among the trades represented is printing, in the shape of the workshop of Parnells the Printers, who moved from Grimsby to Reading in 1900. It is fascinating to look at the trays of metal type and the Brittania hand press with the advanced technology that is applied to printing today in mind. Similarly, the Ironmongers shop window, full of household utensils, reminds the visitor how things have changed in the home, although there is a fair range of equipment that has stayed resolutely the same over the years.

The miscellany of trade adverts, posters and handbills is interesting to dwell on: at John Allright's annual sale, for example, you could buy dress material in 'good and useful colours' at $2\frac{3}{4}$d, $4\frac{3}{4}$d or $6\frac{3}{4}$d a yard. Near to this ephemera is a display of confectioner's equipment. E. V. Tull experimented with chocolate sweets in the early 1900s and became known for produc-

Some of the Huntley and Palmer biscuit tins

ing chocolate squares for early aviators. He then produced special boxes of chocolates for the troops in 1914. For the civilian sweet tooth, Tull moulded chocolate into a whole menagerie of chocolate shapes including dogs, pigs and hippos.

Reading was particularly well known for beer and biscuits, and several displays are devoted to the story of these industries. A number of the smaller Reading breweries also produced carbonated mineral water, which from 1800 or so was a popular (then medicinal) drink. Biscuits were produced locally by Huntley and Palmers: the Reading Museum Service holds the Huntley and Palmer, and Nabisco Collection of richly decorated biscuit tins and colourful advertising material. The 'Best and most Economical Sauce now before the Public' was Reading Sauce, produced by the local firm, Cocks'. The sauce achieved international fame and was a rather potent mixture of walnut and mushroom ketchup, Indian soy, chillis and garlic. Some ephemera and objects from Cocks' are displayed at Blake's Lock.

It is easy to think that health food and homoeopathic medicine are something earlier generations were unaware of; far from it! The display telling of the mineral water producers and another of a chemist shop should remove that idea. Today's brown pill bottles were preceded by small earthenware jars, the medicines being decanted from large, often highly decorative jars. The museum has a splendid, imposing example that is about two feet tall; RHUBARB is emblazoned across it in gold lettering. Rhubarb was stored in solution and used as a cure for a number of ailments. A homoeopathic medicine cabinet full of small bottles of tinctures sits next to a book on homoeopathy written by a Reading doctor, E. M. Ruddock, in 1868.

But what of the waterways? Boat building was once a familiar sight in Reading and the narrow boat is still well known today, though mostly as a leisure rather than a working craft. The narrow boat was purpose-built to fit the seven-feet-wide locks usual in the Midlands and could carry a twenty to

View of the room devoted to Pottingers, the hairdressers

thirty ton load. Another boat specially built for the stretches of river between Reading and London was the Western Barge. This was about 128 feet long and could carry up to 200 tons at a time. The museum relates the story of the waterways through objects and plenty of evocative photographs. The people who lived and worked on these barges developed a special assemblage of brightly-decorated jugs, pots and pans, and some of the stories behind their decorations are explained in the museum's displays.

The wharfs of Reading date back to the 12th century. In the 18th century Daniel (*Gulliver's Travels*) Defoe talks of Reading as a 'very large and wealthy town, handsomely built, the inhabitants rich and driving a very great trade'.

Defoe describes the transport by river of malt, timber, coal, salt, groceries and 'oyls'. All the 'handsome' buildings required materials. The displays tell us of Colliers, a local brickmaking firm that in the 18th century had sixteen kilns, one of which could hold 200,000 bricks at a time.

On leaving the main gallery you encounter masses of signs on the walls – road signs, enamel advertising signs and all sorts – exhorting you to read the *Evening Gazette*, use Newberys for your removal and storage, or to 'queue here', having halted at the major road ahead.

A whole room is devoted to Pottingers, a gents (and later also ladies) hairdressers, which opened in 1909 and finally closed in 1980. The shop interior has all the fixtures and fittings, including marble basins, cast-iron foot-rests, an early hairdryer and a fascinating revolving child's chair for particularly young customers. Gentlemen's hairdressers were also barbers, and on display are numerous cut-throat razors, with one set of seven marked for each day of the week.

Along the corridor you enter the final gallery – a temporary exhibition area covering specific aspects of Reading's past. Future exhibitions will include Reading and its railway history, and 'Yesterday's Shopping' – the early department stores of Reading. Adjacent to this area stands one of the highlights of the museum. This is a traditional gypsy caravan made by the Reading firm of Duntons nearby at Crane Wharf, around 1910. Recently restored to its original colour scheme, it is a rare feast of highly decorative carving enriched with gold leaf.

New ventures are afoot at Blakes Lock with the acquisition of two further industrial buildings, one the old turbine house set across Blakes Weir, so there should be even more to see in years to come. (NH)

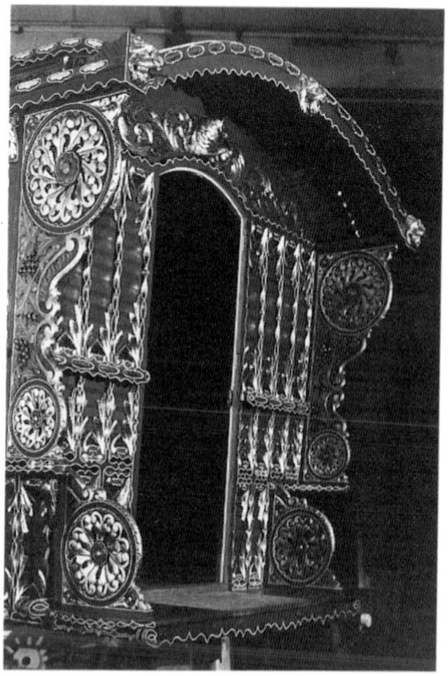

Front of a Reading gypsy caravan

Institute of Agricultural History and Museum of English Rural Life

University of Reading, Whiteknights, PO Box 229, Reading, Berkshire RG6 2AG (0734) 318660
Closed Mondays. 🚻 P
♿: all parts of museum, except Farmers Gallery, accessible by wheelchair.
🚸 & 👥 (40 maximum) by appointment; special talks can be arranged.
Archives, photograph collection and library may be consulted by appointment.

This country boasts many museums of rural life, but the Museum of English Rural Life was one of the first, and is certainly the most important. It has exceptionally fine collections dating mainly from 1750 to the present. The 1950s saw a technical revolution in farming, spearheaded by the tractor. This museum was established in 1951 to record, preserve and interpret the country's fast-changing rural heritage. Not only was the face of farming changing, but as the old tools were discarded so the crafts and industries that supported the old order went into decline (frequently terminal). The museum's rather unprepossessing building was intended as a temporary home, and the display space is not large enough to do full justice to the collections – hence the plans for a new museum development. The displays are nevertheless extremely attractive and packed with interest.

In the first gallery the tools of farming and related trades are displayed. Most of the farming hand tools in the collection are Victorian, but the design of these basic items had remained the same for hundreds, even thousands of years. In some Egyptian wall paintings, for example, there are farming tools that would easily be recognised by the Victorian farmer.

A small part of the fine basketry collection is displayed here, the baskets ranging in size from the eight-inch-long Huck Muck, used to strain home-brewed beer, to the three-foot-high Hop tally basket, used to measure the amount of hops picked. Compared with today, the pattern of Pre-War rural life was stable and slow to change. This is demonstrated by the display of the workshop tools of George Lailey (1869–1958), who was a bowl turner at Bucklebury Common near Newbury, like his father and grandfather before him. Blacksmithing, thatching, bowl turning, saddlery and wheel-wrighting were essential rural industries that provided farmers' tools and equipment; many still exist but have been reduced to the level of rural crafts.

The museum has a fine collection of smocks, which used to be to farming what boiler suits are to industry today. As with ploughs and carts, there was much regional variation in smocks, although the basic pattern and function were universal. Variety was displayed mainly in the decorative embroidery over the smocked yoke, and was as distinctive and identifiable as the sound of regional dialects is today.

The Ransomes Hall contains displays of wagons (continued outside in the courtyard), and on the development of farming in the industrial age. Wagons had their heyday in the 19th century but after the Second World

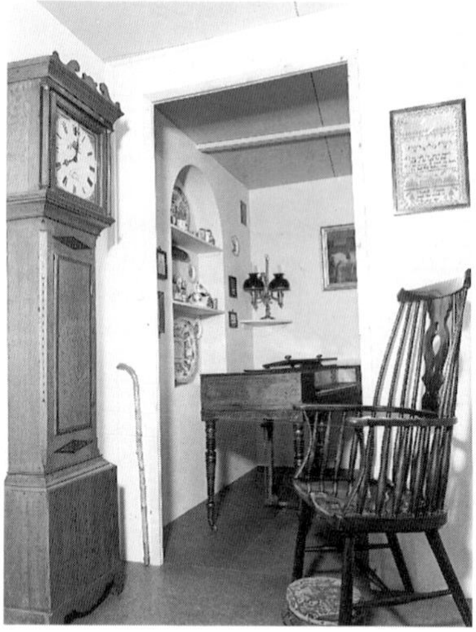

Farmhouse parlour, c. 1860

Part of the displays on Early Farming and Village Technology

Reading Museum and Art Gallery

Blagrave Street, Reading, Berkshire
RG1 1QH
(0734) 595911 ext. 2242
Closed until 1992, after which
open daily. 🇫 ▣ ♿
♿ & ♿ must book in advance.

War, with the introduction of the tractor, their importance declined rapidly. As with ploughs, wagons show great regional variation in their precise shape and decoration, although they all fall into the basic categories of box and bow wagons. A combined cart and wagon was produced by Cooke's: known as the 'Hermaphrodite' (or 'maphrodite' in Norfolk!), it effectively answered the purposes of both wagon and cart, and cost from £25 (in 1875).

Before the tractor era the horse was the main source of power on farms. H. Stephens, in his *Book of the Farm* (1844) says that 'horses which have been brought up on a farm, going through the same routine of work every year, become so well acquainted with what they have to do that, when a misunderstanding arises between them and their driver, you may safely assume that the driver is in the wrong.'! Oxen were used, but four oxen could plough only four-fifths of an acre a day compared to a full acre by a pair of horses. Steam power began to be used in farming from the 1840s, but was costly, and the machines were heavy so they could not plough the land as a tractor does today. From about 1920 it was in decline. However, steam did have a major impact on farming, 'in the establishment of railways, the influence of which has wonderfully altered the whole system of cultivation in many districts', wrote J. K. Fowler in *Recollection of Old Country Life*, 1894; 'it gave the farmer opportunities of getting a better market for his produce and cre-

ated in him a desire to advance scientifically as well as personally, and in consequence his family was better educated, his household more refined and even his costume and personal appearance improved'.

This takes us neatly upstairs to the final displays in the Farmers Gallery, which look at the social changes that were taking place in rural communities. Successful farmers were able, in the mid-19th century, to manage rather than work their farms, and to move from the traditional farmouse to a new spacious villa with parlour, drawing room and the trappings of success. In the early 19th century, farmhouses still had the traditional bakery, dairy and laundry room, which were the domain of the farmer's wife. Room settings of these all feature in the displays.

There is in fact far more to this museum that meets the eye: it has the most extensive and important rural life archive, library and photographic collection in the country. The Institute of Agricultural History was set up in 1968 to extend the research, teaching and collection work of the museum. Institute staff teach within the University and run extra-mural courses through the museum. Among the archives are the company records of some thirty agricultural engineering firms. The library holds 17,000 books and pamphlets, and the photographic archive contains over half a million images. All of these resources can be consulted by appointment. (NH)

Reading Museum and Art Gallery boasts very fine collections that include the assemblage of material from Roman Silchester (or, as it was then, *Calleva*). The museum closed in 1989 for major refurbishment and is scheduled to reopen in 1992, when it will certainly be a place well worth going out of your way to visit.

The Museum and Art Gallery was founded in 1883, and over the years many outstanding and nationally important collections have been acquired. One of the objects to be featured in the new displays will be the Bayeux Tapestry facsimile made by a group of needlewomen in Leek, Staffordshire, in 1885. This 231-ft-long embroidered 'tapestry' was based on a tracing from the Victoria and Albert Museum's watercolour copies of the original. The makers of the facsimile formed a limited company and exhi-

The Silchester eagle, Roman

bited the piece in Germany and America. However, the business venture was not as financially rewarding as they had hoped and eventually the tapestry was acquired for the museum.

The Silchester Collection is one of the jewels in Reading's museum crown. *Calleva* was first excavated in the 1860s and excavations have been continuing in recent years. The finds include building materials, personal effects, some furniture (fragments of a shale table, for example), locks and keys, large collections of fine and coarse pottery, jewellery – in fact a range that represents a cross-section of life in the Roman town. The walled town had a forum, public baths, an amphitheatre (which could seat 4,000), a temple and an inn. Silchester lies just south of Reading and is now in Hampshire, but it was the centre for the Iron Age tribe, the Atrebates, and their tribal territory extended into and beyond Berkshire.

The prehistoric archaeology collections also have some important pieces, including a rich collection of hand axes from earliest Stone Age times. The spearheads and leaf-shaped swords from the Middle Bronze Age are extremely fine; many have been recovered from the River Thames nearby.

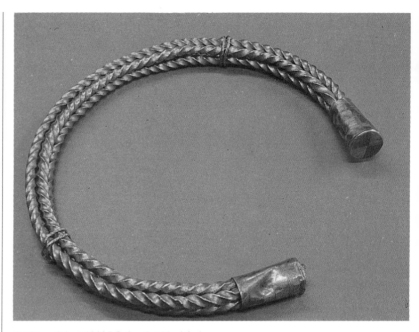

Gold torc of about 1200 BC, found at Moulsford

Romanesque capital from Reading Abbey

From the same period is a stunning gold torc found by a farmer in Moulsford (just along the river from Reading) in 1960. The torc dates to about 1200 BC and has a double-twist design.

The museum has an important collection of fine art, with over 2,000 individual works, including examples by Stanley Spencer and John Piper, as well as 19th century British pictures. Among decorative art is a fine collection of tin-glazed earthenware, European and English, and a small collection of other English, European and Oriental ceramics.

Reading Abbey will be an important feature in the new museum. The Abbey was founded in 1121, and was opened and consecrated by Thomas à Becket. Its fortunes varied: in the 13th century it was famous for its music and liturgy, but in the 14th its fortunes and finances were at a low ebb and cuts had to be made. Parliament met in the Abbey during the 15th century, to avoid the plague then raging in London. In the 16th century the Abbey exacted taxes and effectively controlled the affairs of the town. 1539 saw the dissolution of the Abbey and the execution of the abbot. This was not the end of the Abbey's involvement in Reading's history for the Abbey gateway was used as the Abbey School, one of whose pupils was Jane Austen. The architecture of the Abbey was in the Romanesque style, and the sculptured stones and capitals from the Abbey that are now in the museum form a major collection of Romanesque art.

The industrial history of the town is covered in **Blake's Lock Museum**, (like Reading Museum part of Reading Borough Council's Leisure Service), but the main museum has some fascinating social history material, including a good costume and textile collection. Another large group of objects is the Huntley and Palmer, and Nabisco Collection of biscuit tins. These are extraordinary in their range of shapes, sizes and exuberant decorations. The museum also has extensive natural history collections relating to the geological background and environment of Reading and Berkshire, which will play a significant part in the new museum displays. (NH)

SAFFRON WALDEN

Saffron Walden Museum

*Museum Street, Saffron Walden,
Essex CB10 1JL   (0799) 22492*
Open daily. ◼ for trial period.
 &␣W
⋔ & ♯ book in advance.

Saffron Walden Museum is a remarkable museum. Given the size of its collections, the range of materials, textures, colours, shapes and historical periods covered is amazing. With items of local, national and international importance, it sits like a miniature version of the Victoria and Albert Museum in north-west Essex. Particular objects, while not always associated with the town itself, are related to people – explorers and collectors, who have associations with Saffron Walden. First thoughts of a museum are recorded in 1832 and the present building was opened on 12th May 1835. The museum was then contained on the first floor. Today, the visitor has a choice of routes to take and of galleries

Viking necklace in silver, with cornelian, crystal and glass

to see. In general terms, the ground floor deals with 'local history' while upstairs the range of collections on display covers ceramics, ethnography, furniture, costume, and ancient Egypt, each having significant objects amongst them.

1988 saw the redisplay of the Great Hall, which is to the right as you enter the building. This new Archaeology Gallery brings to life the archaeology of this area of north-west Essex and orientates the visitor, giving a flavour of the area's past from the pre-historic period through to 1400. Changes in roofs and flooring give the visitor cues to changes in period, and create a lovely 'roofscape' that is best seen from the Hall's gallery. The roofs are replicas of Iron Age, Roman, Saxon and Medieval dwellings. From the gallery you will also see 'Wallace', who surveys the whole room: this was the first lion to have been born and raised in captivity (born in Edinburgh in 1816). Corn grinding, weaving and pottery stress the everyday activities of life in past time, but it is the archaeological finds that catch the eye. One feature of the displays is that 'finds' can be added as new archaeological digs takes place.

Part of an Iron Age coin hoard from the Stansted excavations in 1987 is displayed. There is Roman jewellery from local sites, and one case is devoted to objects from a Roman burial site, which includes some lovely glassware. One of the most splendid objects is a Viking necklace of two ornamented silver-gilt pendants, a silver pendant, and beads of silver, cornelian, crystal

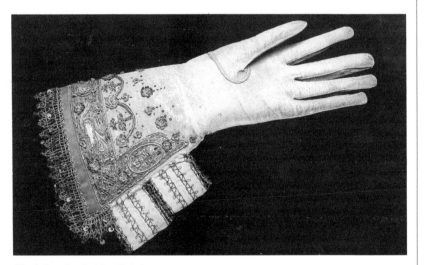

Metal-thread-embroidered kid glove associated with Mary Queen of Scots

and glass. Other excavations of skeletons from a Saxon cemetery have been re-buried in the floor of the gallery, and skilfully lit under heavy-duty glass. The Medieval section includes a remarkably preserved hat, which was found walled-up in Little Sampford church. The hat is the earliest complete example of its kind known to exist. A less charming item is the piece of skin found under a hinge at another local church in Hadstock.

The Great Hall has demonstration and activity areas, and a map that gives the geographical context of the material on display, providing a useful reference point to explore places of interest within the glorious surrounding countryside. Back in the entrance hallway of the museum building there is a Chapman and André map of Essex surveyed in 1772–74. It is easily overlooked but graphically underlines the changes that some parts of Essex have undergone since then, and as in the Great Hall refers you outward to explore further.

The local history gallery on the ground floor deals with information rather than objects, and tells the history of the town as expressed in its buildings. Building materials, techniques and designs are explained and this, together with the new Archaeol-

Oak cradle with carved decoration (dated 1723 but probably made earlier)

ogy Gallery, makes it well worthwhile beginning a visit to the town inside the museum.

Upstairs, the Ceramics Gallery includes a rare 17th century glass posset pot, designed to hold a beneficial beverage made from curdled milk with ale or wine, and with fine breadcrumbs added. It would be impossible to list all the gorgeous items you can see, but the salt glazes on the early German stoneware, the lovely blues and greens of English tin-glazed earthenware, and the grisaille panels by Cipriani, painted in 1771 for Audley End and given to the museum in the 1840s, make it worth taking time to 'stand and stare' here.

Further on, dolls, a dolls' house (a model of Clare Priory), jewellery and jigsaws compete for attention. The costume and embroidery include a lovely stumpwork casket from the late 17th century, 17th century samplers, and a rare riding habit in pristine condition from the mid-18th century. There are also some fine military helmets, including a Tarleton Cap (1820).

For many, the most stunning part of Saffron Walden Museum is its

ethnography collection. The 'Worlds of Man' gallery has displays and artefacts from Australia, North America, South America, Africa and the Pacific. There is a catalogue on sale that covers the collection, but it is the quality of the items and the wealth of documentation that makes the material so rare. The beadwork of North American Indians can be compared with South African examples of beadwork collected by travellers and missionaries in the 1830s. The hanging barkcloths and the beautiful mourning costume fashioned from strips of mother of pearl caught my eye; both from the Pacific, the mourning costume was possibly collected on Cook's third Expedition in 1776–80.

If the excitement gets too great, you can create your own musical interlude on the African xylophone given to the museum by the Prince of Wales in 1961. It is difficult to contain the breadth of this museum in a few short paragraphs. It is rather like a kaleidoscope, with different parts to catch the eye each way you turn. There is certainly something of interest for every visitor. (KH)

Lead glass lidded posset pot, c. 1685

ST ALBANS

Verulamium Museum

St Michaels, St Albans, Hertfordshire
AL3 4SW
(0727) 54659/66100 ext. 241
Open daily. ♿ (residents of St
Albans District 🅵). 🅿♿
♿ preferably book in advance.
♿ book in advance: contact
Keeper of Education (0727) 59919;
'School News' sent termly to
schools on request.

A visit to Verulamium is more than just
a museum visit. The Verulamium
Museum exhibits a collection of material that illustrates the life of one of
Britain's major Roman cities, *Verulamium*, or St Albans as it is known
today. The museum was built to house
the rich finds from the first modern
excavation of the Roman city, begun in
1930 by Dr (later Sir) Mortimer
Wheeler and his wife Tessa. Throughout the museum there are photographs
from these and later digs.

But to visit the museum alone would
be to miss the surroundings of St
Michael's village and the opportunity
of walking around the Roman remains
that are still visible and within easy
reach of the museum building. In the
park beside the museum is a Roman
hypocaust – the remains of a room
heated by hot air, which passed beneath the floor. The hypocaust has
recently been refurbished and now has
interpretative displays. The late 2nd
century mosaic floor here remains intact, as is much of the stunning Roman
theatre site, just across the main road
beyond St Michael's Churchyard.
Dressing rooms, entrances, orchestra
and stage are easily identifiable, and
from the theatre you can gaze across
fields to the boundaries of the Roman
city imagining the shops, streets and
houses that once stood there. The
place is very emotive and adds another
dimension to the objects that are on
display in the museum itself.

The museum consists of two main
galleries. In the largest, the room is
given warmth and colour by the splendid mosaics shown on the end wall.
The displays are thematic and illustrate
the development of Verulamium from
the late Iron Age to Roman times.
They contain such treasures as the two
bronze figurines that caught my attention, one depicting Venus, the other
Mercury. The lovely, lively figure of
Venus was found amidst scrap metal in
the shops that stood next to the theatre;
the Mercury group is more finely mod-
elled and was found just outside the
city boundary.

Many items on display refer to the
religious part of daily life: there are

Roman bronze statuette of Venus

ceremonial vessels, charms and talismans, some ornate, others simply severe. A Mithraic token, made from a denarius of Augustus around 17 BC, has an unusual motif on the face of Mithras rising from rocks, depicting the god's birth. It is such personal items that give a real sense of the Roman site being a busy crowded town; the tiles with animal footprints make the same point. The museum's wall paintings and mosaics are vivid reminders of the colour and style of life at the higher end of the social scale. The Lion mosaic has a lion at the centre of the design, holding a stag's head in its jaws. The marks of where a brazier once stood are still visible. Another mosaic has dolphins as its theme, and was lifted from a house that stood near to the theatre site. The Sea God floor was laid near to the hypocaust. It is as you begin to place these treasures in their context that the whole town begins to take real form and colour. The wall paintings that complement the floor decorations also enable the visitor to build a picture of life in the Roman city. On close examination, you can find Roman graffiti in the shape of a small bird and some lettering. Further help in imagining the living Roman town comes from paintings by Alan Sorrell, which reconstruct different views of Verulamium.

The smaller gallery was added in the 1960s to house the excavations of Sheppard Frere. The displays here set Mortimer Wheeler's work in an updated context. The work undertaken by Frere has become the bedrock of

Part of the reconstruction of a Roman kitchen

Part of the Sea God mosaic floor

Verulamium archaeology and Romano-British urban studies. The museum's Field Archaeology section was established in 1973, and it is important to remember the active research and conservation that backs the public displays and excellent publications. The 'recent excavations' case is a reminder of excavations still underway.

The quality of the material here in St Albans is superb: the fragile Roman glass, the soldier's helmet, ornate brooches and practical cooking utensils combine to give a rich and varied picture of the Roman occupation. In the displays that cover trades and professions, religion, and reading and writing, the similarity of some items to their modern-day counterparts is striking. The carpenters' tools in particular, have hardly altered. A mason's trowel left in the wall that the mason was working on is curious, as is the complicated lock plate in the 'Death and Burial' case. Some of the objects illustrate the finest details of everyday life – gorgeous finger rings and bow brooches, or the oyster shell that still holds the remains of red paint. Colour is again emphasised by a delicate ceiling painting that contrasts with the heavier motifs of the mosaic floors and the wall paintings. Finely painted birds and panthers' heads form a pattern of surprising lightness.

The story of the modern city since the departure of the Romans is presented at the *Museum of St Albans*, which is near the town centre. Here a series of new galleries tell the story of the city in a lively sequence of themes – the ecological background, markets, civic life, coaching and roads, the Abbey, a week in the life of the Victorian city, commuting – set out using reconstructions, graphics, sound, and the museum's rich local and social history collections. The last exhibit is a time-lapse video of a market day in 1989, taking the story up to the present and bringing the busy modern city into the gallery. The museum also houses the Salaman Collection of trade and craft tools, brought together by Raphael Salaman. Many of the tools are on display, some in the context of their use, and the Salaman Gallery is to be redisplayed during 1990. The *Museum of St Albans*, founded as the Hertfordshire County Museum in 1898, has significant natural science collections, notably in geology and entomology. Both the Salaman Collection and the natural science material can be consulted by appointment.

There is an enormous amount to see and enjoy in St Albans. Verulamium Museum gives detail and life to the rich Roman past, while in the *Museum of St Albans* visitors will find a varied and lively presentation of the past and present city. (KH)

SANDLING
Museum of Kent Rural Life

Lock Lane, Cobtree Manor Park,
Sandling, Maidstone, Kent
ME14 3AU   (0622) 763936
Open April to October (closed
Saturday and Sunday mornings,
and all day Wednesday). ▣
▣ and 2 picnic areas. ℗
&: most of museum accessible by
wheelchair (only first floor of Oast
House inaccessible) but visitors
should bear in mind that the site
is a working farm; assistance
can be given with prior notice.
⋔ welcome, at least 24 hours notice
preferred; reduced admission rate
for groups over 10.
⋔ contact Interpretation Officer for
booking form and teachers pack;
admission during winter closure
possible by prior arrangement. ◎

Located between the peaceful River
Medway and the endless traffic of the
M20, the Museum of Kent Rural Life
has the advantage of an attractive site
combined with easy access from London. The twenty-seven acre site is
devoted to explaining the changing
face of the 'Garden of England'.

Unlike many other rural life
museums, this one is not 'set' in a
particular historical period but aims to
show the evolution of the Kentish
countryside from the medieval era to
the 1950s. The development of the
Channel Tunnel is now bringing a new
wave of massive changes to the county.
But the museum staff are quick to
point out that the local landscape has
been subject to alterations in the past,
and today subtle changes are happen-
ing every year. The acreage of hop
growing is steadily declining, and traditional orchards are being replaced
with dwarf trees, which will eventually
lead to the disappearance of traditional
'blossom routes'. For both parents and
children a visit to this museum will
provide an understanding of the forces

View of the hop fields and oast houses

shaping the landscape and help in dis-
tinguishing between necessary change
and gratuitous destruction of the environment.

The Museum of Kent Rural Life
occupies part of a farm attached to
Cobtree Manor Park, whose owner left
the estate 'for the good of the people of
Maidstone and Kent'. It opened in
1984 and is in the early stages of a
twenty-year development programme.
There is already a great deal to see and
enjoy at the museum and visitors returning at intervals can expect to see
regular new additions. The displays in
the first phase concentrate on the role
of agriculture, while future plans include exhibitions on rural crafts and
industry. In a period of rapid social
change, the museum staff are intent on
recording traditional agricultural techniques as well as collecting the various
types of tools used. All the displays
have been extensively researched to
ensure a high degree of historical
accuracy. Regular craft demonstrations
also take place on most Sundays.

A visit to the museum begins at the
oast house next to the farm pond. Oast
houses were used for drying and stor-

ing hops, and their distinctive kilns,
now frequently turned into houses, are
a characteristic feature of the Kent
countryside. The museum's oast has
been extensively restored to provide an
introduction to local farming, a display
of waggons, and an excellent exhibition
of tools and equipment used in growing hops. One of the kilns has been
rebuilt for use, and every year a
weekend in September is devoted to
showing how hops were picked and
dried. Visitors are welcome to join in
and learn about the traditional
methods, which are now only used on
this farm.

Hop fields, with their regimented
rows of poles, are a distinctive but
disappearing sight in Kent as the market for British hops decreases. Next to
the oast is an area devoted to hop
growing, which shows a number of
methods of cultivation. Until the introduction of mechanisation, hop picking
was done by hand and required a large
supply of casual labour. Traditionally it
provided a paid working break in the
countryside for poor Londoners. Farmers had to provide basic accommodation, and the museum has rebuilt a row

of hop-pickers' huts, originally from a farm at Hadlow. These give a good idea of the domestic life of the migrant Londoners who went 'hoppin' in Kent.

Beyond the farmyard is a large area devoted to orchards, concentrating on the growing of apples, pears, plums and cherries. In the age of the ubiquitous Golden Delicious, most visitors will be amazed at the range and diversity of varieties originally grown in Kent. There are sixty-three types of apple and eighteen types of pears. As orchard fruit is propagated by 'budding' or 'grafting' onto rootstock, many varieties can be traced back far into the past. The orchards include varieties from medieval times to the late 19th century, among them an example of 'Coeur de Boeuf', the apple tree traditionally associated with Isaac Newton. The overall result is a unique 'growing' museum, where, as the trees mature, visitors will hopefully be able to get a taste as well as a view of the past.

Surrounding the farmhouse is an area devoted to herbs and market gardening. The former is laid out in a traditional 'knot' style. Each of the four knots contains herbs important at different periods, starting with medieval plants and continuing up to the early 20th century. Within each knot there are further divisions by use – culinary, dyeing, medicinal and aromatic. Market gardening has long been important in Kent due to the proximity of the massive London market. There are

Ploughing with Shire horses

displays of the types of vegetables grown commercially in the county between 1830 and 1910, and the area is farmed organically. Garden produce can be purchased for a real taste of history.

The rest of the site, which stretches down to the River Medway, is used to show a variety of fields. A large area is laid out to demonstrate the 18th-century system of four-field rotation. Prior to the introduction of artificial fertilisers, this method of growing a cycle of different crops ensured that the soil retained its fertility. The permanent pasture has been sown with a mixture of grasses, clovers, vetches and herbs to resemble a field of about 1900. The museum keeps a small selection of livestock. The Romney Marsh sheep, renowned for their heavy even fleece, and Sussex cattle, traditionally kept for beef, are particularly interesting. Visitors will also find chickens, ducks and geese wandering around the farm.

A further reminder of the massive changes in the countryside is a hay meadow that has been replanted with over eighty grasses and wild flowers to recreate artifically a sight common fifty years ago. Visitors wandering further afield can explore an area of woodland maintained by coppicing, or the riverside wharf, which is a reminder of the Medway's importance as a transportation link. There is also a site used for the demonstration of local crafts, and a working sawbench restored by the Friends.

The Museum of Kent Rural Life successfully combines enjoyment with education, and maintains a high level of historical accuracy. The site is always changing, and a visit can range from a couple of hours to a short break from the M20 when travelling to the Channel ports. Different sections appeal to a range of ages and interests, although parents should remember that farming equipment can be dangerous and small children should be supervised. For those wanting to explore further there is a nature trail at Cobtree Manor, or you can follow the river towpath from the museum site to the centre of Maidstone. (GM)

SLOUGH

Slough Museum

23 Bath Road, Slough, Berkshire SL1 3UF   (0753) 26422
Open afternoons Wednesdays to Sundays. 🅵 🅿 ♿
♿ & ⚥ welcome, advance notice preferred; visits outside normal opening hours can sometimes be arranged with advance notice: contact Curator.

The idea of a museum for Slough was nurtured by a group of local people, who in 1983 established the Slough Museum Trust. Thanks to the enthusiasm and dogged persistence of this group and the museum's first curator, the ambition for a Slough Museum was realised in 1986. The museum began by mounting a temporary exhibition about life in Slough during the 1930s, and has continued to mount temporary exhibitions on major local themes. Through these exhibitions the museum has begun to develop a permanent collection. Due to lack of space, collecting was less active in the first three years than had originally been hoped, but the museum has recently been able to set up its first long-term exhibition on the history of Slough.

It is perhaps easy to forget that Slough has a history before the 1920s. Yet Upton Court, a large house close to the centre of Slough, dates to the 13th century and most probably started life as a medieval manor house. At Cippenham, to the west of Slough, there was a deer park and palace at which Richard, Earl of Cornwall and son of King John, is thought to have stayed during his honeymoon in 1231. There is also the Montem mound, a strange mound of unknown antiquity that is situated just behind the museum. Some believe it to be the remains of a 'motte and bailey' from a Norman castle, but this theory remains untested; in its later years it was used by the boys from nearby **Eton College**

Scale model of Herschel's 40ft telescope

as the venue for a strange 'Salt' cere-mony (discontinued following crowd violence in 1844). In 1985 fragments of Saxon pottery were found near the mound and the site is now scheduled as an ancient monument.

One of the Slough residents who had a profound national and interna-tional impact was Sir William Hers-chel. Born in Hanover in 1738, Hers-chel came to Slough in 1786. He began his career in music, but his interest in astronomy grew and he began building larger and more powerful telescopes. The museum has a scale model of his largest, 40ft telescope, which graphi-cally shows what a feat its building was. Herschel was methodical in his observation and in 1781 was rewarded with the discovery of a new object, first thought to be a comet but later recog-nised as a previously unknown planet, later named Uranus. Herschel's dis-covery brought him fame, which cul-minated in his appointment as 'King's Astronomer' to King George III. It was thanks to this royal patronage that he moved to Slough, in order to be closer to Windsor. Herschel's discoveries continued, and he was the first to realise that what he observed through his telescope had happened in the past, as light takes time to travel across the vast distances of space. He is buried in St Laurence's Church, Upton, Slough.

Another famous Slough resident was James Elliman. The museum's new display features his contribution to the nation's health – Elliman's Embroca-tion. In 1847 James Elliman Senior began selling a new product that cured the strained muscles of both animals and humans. Among those who attested to the efficacy of the embroca-tion was Victorina, 'the strongest lady in the world'. The embrocation was made from an unlikely mixture of in-gredients – eggs, vinegar and turpen-tine. James Elliman Junior took over his father's business and marketed the product. The museum has several col-ourful original advertisements for Elli-man's Embrocation. The Ellimans were great local benefactors; among their gifts were twenty-six acres of recreational land for the people of Slough (still in use as the Salt Hill playing fields – James Elliman did not want the area to be named after him), a fire engine, a fire station, and land for a drill hall for the Slough Company of Volunteers. A lead box containing pap-ers and objects of the day for the interest of future generations was buried in the foundations of the fire station. It was dug up when the fire station was demolished in 1972 and is now a part of the museum's collection.

The coming of the railway had a great impact on Slough. The railway was the brainchild of Isambard King-dom Brunel, who was the Great West-ern Railway's Engineer. The section of railway that ran through Slough was opened on 4th June 1838. It was the first stretch to be opened of the Great Western Railway's new route to Bris-tol. Slough quickly seized upon the advantages of improved communica-tion offered by the railway and soon grew in size as a result.

One of the most important custom-ers of the railway from the 1920s was the Slough Trading Estate. The Slough Trading Company was formed in 1920 on land that during the First World War had been used by the Ministry of Defence as a Vehicle De-pot for broken-down military vehicles. The Slough Trading Company bought the land – nicknamed locally 'the Dump' – and the vehicles on it, re-paired and sold the vehicles, and then let as factory space the buildings that were left behind. In 1926 the company changed its name to Slough Estates Limited. It was one of the first trading estates in the world and led to a period of rapid growth for Slough, drawing in people to the area from all over the country, attracted by the new jobs

An advertisement for Elliman's Embrocation

SOUTHEND-ON-SEA

Beecroft Art Gallery

Station Road, Westcliff, Southend-on-Sea, Essex SS0 7RA
(0702) 347418
Open daily. 🅵 ▣
& S: wheelchair access to ground floor only.
♟ & ♟ book in advance.

The Beecroft Art Gallery was opened in 1953 as a temporary home for Walter Beecroft's personal collection and for the municipal collection of works of art. The Gallery now has some 2,000 works in its permanent collection, including pictures by Constable, Turner, Rowlandson, Norman Hepple, Lear, David Cox, Ruskin Spear, Edward Seago and Ken Howard. Between 12 and 22 temporary exhibitions are held each year, drawn from the Beecroft's collection or other sources. Every summer the annual 'open' show attracts 1,000 entries from artists who live and work in Essex.

Walter Beecroft was inspired to provide a focus for art in the area. This regional centre was to be based on his own collection of mostly European paintings, particularly 16th and 17th

available. The Trading Estate had its own internal railway, which linked up with the main line to London and Bristol, enabling it to transport goods. Special trains were also laid on to transport the estate's workers to and from work.

Close to the Trading Estate was the site of the Slough Social Centre, one of the first workers' social centres, which was opened in 1937. The museum has a growing archive of photographs, among which are many charting the history and life of the Community Centre. Among the activities available were swimming, football, chess and even elocution.

Slough was less badly hit by the recession of the 1930s than many towns. It was a time when new homes were built that had bathrooms and electric lighting, and when the radio and gramophone became domestic attractions. This was also the 'golden age' of the cinema: Slough Museum made a record of the Granada cinema's interior before it closed in 1987.

The museum has a growing sound and photographic archive that can be consulted by appointment, and is also increasingly using video to record local sights and sounds before they change or disappear. The oral history archives are particularly compelling – hearing people's stories in their own words so that history speaks across the years and generations. The museum has also done much innovative work with local GCSE students, some appropriately enough from the Sir William Herschel Grammar School, and stages regular temporary exhibitions and events. The latter included an artist in residence project in 1986.

John Betjeman had few good words for the town of Slough: 'Come friendly bombs and fall on Slough/It isn't fit for humans now.' Yet the museum's work and its attractive displays belie this image of the town. Slough Museum's early years have not been entirely easy, but it has achieved much so far and has the potential to develop well over the years. (NH)

Jacob Epstein, Marchese Casati

G. W. Heda, Still Life with Herring, *late 17th century*

tions change frequently. The first floor rooms are full of light, with glorious views over the Thames estuary. They contain changing exhibitions that cover professional and amateur works in all media from ceramics and sculpture to photography or oils. One of the top floor rooms includes Epstein's sculpture of Marchese Casati, a beautiful example of the artist's sensitivity and skill. On a recent visit, alongside Epstein's work, were tapestries that had won the adult and school entries in a competition commemorating Domesday, spectacular examples of combining art with craft. Coffee is served in one of the first floor rooms, giving the visitor a chance to sit and look at the view or to contemplate the works of art.

Another first floor area is given over to showing a selection of work by the eighty volunteer stewards of the Gallery. This emphasises the personal quality that the building and its displays encourage. A sprayed plastic sculpture, 'The Dancers' by G. A. Holman, stands in one of the Beecroft's corridors. Its sweeping sharp lines step straight out of the early 1930s and one almost expects to turn round and find a maid carrying a breakfast tray down the stairs!

In the modern addition to the building there is a topographical section, an extension of the Thorpe-Smith bequest of topographical works. 'Had-

century Dutch and Italian. Another benefactor, Sydney Thorpe-Smith, added a collection of local topographical works. From this mixed background the gallery now collects contemporary British art with special reference to the county of Essex.

The gallery itself has a particular flavour. Previously the Warwick Hotel, the Beecroft still maintains the genteel air of a mid-1920s boarding house. The Warwick was advertised as 'well furnished with personal supervision', which in a sense still applies. Special guests are still served tea in a service with an artist's palette and 'Beecroft Art Gallery' printed on the cup and saucer, which was a private order in the 1950s. Frank Salisbury's 'The Bridal Train', which hangs on the upper landing, is a painting that epitomises this atmosphere. A striking portrait hangs opposite: the mixed media 'Portrait of a Lady' is by Warren Baldwin and was exhibited in the Royal Academy sum-

mer exhibition of 1985. It is full of soft greys and thoughtfulness.

In a complicated building there is no clear order to the galleries and exhibi-

Frank O. Salisbury, The Bridal Train, *c. 1930*

C. C. Coventry, The Royal Terrace, Southend, *1807*

STEVENAGE

Stevenage Museum

St George's Way, Stevenage,
Hertfordshire SG1 1XX
(0438) 354292
Closed Sundays. ⬛ ♿ W
⛪ & ♦♦ book in advance: contact
Education Officer.

Stevenage Museum serves the 'new town' and the villages that surround it. The museum itself is in a slightly bizarre setting, amidst the concrete walkways of the first traffic-free shopping centre, and housed in the undercroft of a church. It is a friendly and informative museum, whose great strength lies in its interpretation of 20th-century change. The permanent displays emphasise the history of the New Town development, and extensive photographic and oral history archives add depth to the collections of artefacts. People's memories are recorded by the museum staff as archive material and to enliven displays, particularly those relating to subjects within 'living memory'.

Stevenage was essentially a town on a great road, set in the chalk bedrock valley lying between the Chilterns and the East Anglian heights. The Saxon settlement of Stithenaece moved away from its church nearer to the old Roman road that became the Great North Road; this shift of settlement is described in maps and relief models.

leigh Castle' by Henry Bright (1840) is very pretty, but almost entirely fictional. A recent acquisition of the same subject by George Shadler (*c.* 1860) is a much truer representation of the marshland and actual setting of the monument. 'The Royal Terrace' by C. C. Coventry (1807) shows a Southend that is difficult to imagine today: the Royal Terrace stands proudly at the top of the cliffs in the picture, overlooking a pierless estuary. There is a lovely pencil sketch by a Benfleet architect in the same room, 'Brown's Barn'; the soft medium suits the recording of a ramshackle barn, long since disappeared, in a then remote and somewhat forgotten part of Essex.

Another room contains a selection of prints, available for loan on the print loan scheme – another reminder of people's involvement in this particularly personal art gallery. A bust of John Betjeman sits in the hallway. It was commissioned from John Doubleday in 1986 by the Borough Council, financed by public subscription. Echoes of Betjeman's poetry are easy to imagine in the Beecroft. The Gallery is a great mixture of experiences, none of which would normally be associated with Southend-on-Sea.

But the Beecroft is not the only surprise in Southend. *Southchurch Hall*

is a medieval Manor House standing in moated gardens. It is restored as a medieval open hall with period settings, and with an interpretation gallery showing the history of the site and secular life in medieval times. At the opposite end of the town – and of medieval life – is *Prittlewell Priory*, a former Cluniac monastery which has displays that concentrate on the religious aspects of living and particularly of communication. From illustrated manuscript to EKCO wireless and pocket television, the links may not always be obvious. 'Communication' is interpreted broadly. EKCO radio was a local business, E. K. Cole Ltd., and the museum service has an extensive collection. There are also natural history displays, which link with the working beehives at both Southchurch and Prittlewell. At Prittlewell there is a full-scale observation hive where a real colony can be seen at work.

The *Central Museum* houses the main collection and reserves of the museum service, and holds a programme of temporary exhibitions. There is no reason why Southend shouldn't have a contemporary art gallery, a medieval Manor House, a Cluniac monastery, extensive permanent collections and beehives; but it does all come as a lovely surprise! (KH)

Muntjac deer

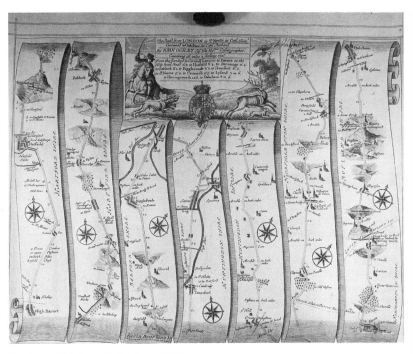

Road map, High Barnet to Oakeham, 1675

Part of the hoard of 2,579 Roman silver coins found at Stevenage in 1986

work in 1961 traces of an Anglo-Saxon hut were discovered in Broadwater. Finds from this and other excavations are on display, including a hoard of Tudor silver coins from Little Wymondley. A hoard of Roman silver coins, however, is the museum's real treasure. No bigger than 5p pieces, the coins range from AD 193–263. They represent ten to twenty years of one person's savings, and tell us much about propaganda, manufacture, gods and goddesses, and methods of exchange in the Roman Empire. The most important coin amongst the hoard belonged to the reign of Emperor Pacatian, who reigned for a few months in AD 249 before being murdered by his army. This is the only coin of its type found in England.

Stevenage today is the home of modern science-based industries, such as ICL computers and British Aerospace. At the museum you can trace the town's origins as a small farming community that served drovers and travellers, explored in diagrams, models, maps and artefacts. Thirty-two miles from London, Stevenage made an ideal stop for changing horses, and the coaching age brought wealth to the town, which is reflected in the buildings along the High Street. Samuel Pepys once stayed at the Swan posting house (now the Registry Office). There was a lull in prosperity during the 19th century with the arrival of the railway, for with less passing trade there was little development. A small cameo setting of a Victorian sitting room introduces the domestic accent of the 20th century exhibitions.

One small display concentrates on a Nathan Hodgson, 'Machinist and Inventor', who repaired and made domestic machinery in Stevenage. One of his inventions, the 'Gem Knife Cleaner', is displayed alongside a printing stamp used in its advertisement. Further reference to local personalities is made through photographs and texts. Henry Trigg was a wealthy grocer who saw bodysnatchers at work one evening, on his way home from the Black Swan in Hitchin. Mr Trigg decided there and then to have his earthly remains committed to the west end of

Further aerial photographs and maps are also used later in the displays about more recent history. One prominent aspect of the local landscape dates back to the Roman period: the Six Hills are

Roman barrows that lie to the west of the present London Road, south of Lytton Way and east of the original line of the Roman road, now a cycle track.

During New Town construction

Sitting Room of 1950s show house, Stevenage New Town

his barn, in the roof beams. He died in 1724 and, safe from thieves, his coffin still remains in the roof of his barn, now within the property 37 High Street, owned by the National Westminster Bank. This story, like many other subjects relating the life of Stevenage, is covered in an excellent series of publications on sale at the museum shop. E. M. Forster, the theatrical designer Edward Craig and Charles Dickens all have connections with Stevenage. Dickens set up a home for poverty-stricken artists here in 1865, in liaison with the writer and eccentric Bulwer Lytton, who lived nearby at **Knebworth**.

It is the modern town development, however, that dominates Stevenage and the museum's contemporary collecting and recording. Photographs and quotations from a speech delivered by Lewis Silkin, Minister of Town and Country Planning in Stevenage in 1946, herald the beginnings of the New Town dream. His tyres were let down and sand put in his petrol tank by less visionary locals! Essential services, transport systems, churches, schools and landscaping are shown as integral parts of the planners' scheme. The Development Corporation worked towards today's Stevenage until its services were gradually taken over by the Borough Council. The turret clock of the Corporation's headquarters at Aston House is on display at the museum. A 1950s room setting in the museum's new displays is based on the real home of a family who moved to Stevenage New Town in 1957. The furniture and furnishings were given complete to the museum's collection and now lend atmosphere and understanding to an important part of the town's history.

Natural history displays encompass fossils and local geology. The products of local chalk and gravel pits lead on to the local brickmaking industry. Animal life is represented by local animals, which include the Muntjak – a small deer particular to parts of Hertfordshire and Buckinghamshire – and live fish in the aquarium. There is plenty more to see besides. The museum holds six temporary exhibitions a year on a wide variety of topics, and has an excellent range of publications and postcards. Modern Stevenage may not have immediate appeal, but the museum gives a lively insight into what lies behind the roundabouts and dual carriageways that tend to swamp other impressions of the town. With its accent on modern history, the museum makes connections between the past and present that are of interest beyond the local boundaries, and stresses that history is about people. (KH)

TRING

Zoological Museum

Akeman Street, Tring, Hertfordshire HP23 6AP (044) 282 4181

Open daily. E

S: wheelchair access to ground floor only.

preferably book in advance.

book in advance; pre-booked F.

The Zoological Museum at Tring was begun by Lionel Walker, second Baron Rothschild. Today it retains much of the character and atmosphere of a private 19th century collection, with its original cases, wrought-iron balconies and parquet flooring. In his will, Lord Rothschild bequeathed the collections at Tring to the Trustees of the British Museum, on condition that the museum became an annexe of The Natural History Museum; the present buildings now include The Natural History Museum's sub-department of Ornithology. Tring has become a major centre for bird research, with laboratories, research scientists, special storage facilities, over a million bird skins, a million eggs, and several thousand skeletons and preserved birds. The museum also houses a vast library based on Lord Rothschild's original library of some 30,000 books.

The displays are still based on a selection of the finest specimens collected by Lord Rothschild, and range from mammals to reptiles, insects, birds and fish. The galleries are dimly-lit to preserve the colouring of the specimens on display, and very delicate collections, such as butterflies, moths and insects, are kept in shuttered cases, which the visitor may open to view. The museum's famous 'dressed fleas', made in 1905, are in one such case. Dressing fleas was a curious pastime originating in Mexico.

The galleries are numbered, with lists of the animal types on display at each gallery entrance. Gallery 1 ranges through birds, apes, bears and gorillas, lions, monkeys, tigers and wolves. The

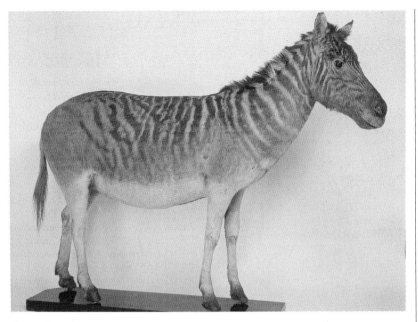

Quagga (now extinct)

mighty polar bear stands opposite a display of tiny humming birds; sleepy snowy owls gaze at the equally sleepy-eyed lemurs, and the museum's popular gorilla waves menacingly at a group of startled penguins. In this gallery in particular it is difficult not to put characters behind the still expressions and to read stories into the juxtapositions of the animals. On another level, of course, the displays hold information about different species and habitats, information that is backed up by the colourful guide book.

The classification of species, a system introduced by the Swedish naturalist Linnaeus in the 18th century, produces some interesting names amongst the tropical birds with 'family' names such as *Pittidae* and *Cotingidae*, which seem as exotic as some of the plumage. The incredible feathers of the Paradise Flycatcher; the blue and gold tail of the Oscillated Turkey from Central America, or the vivid reds of the Vermillion Flycatcher defy description, and would seem unreal if painted or photographed. Here, you are able to wonder at the colours and textures in reality.

On the first floor, Gallery 2, or the Rothschild Room, tells the story of Tring Museum from its beginnings as two cottages built by Lord Rothschild – one for his books and collections, the other for the caretaker. A large building, built behind the cottages to house the mounted specimens, was the beginning of the Zoological Museum. The caretakers, curators and librarians at Tring are detailed, as is the vast Rothschild family tree, looking not unlike the evolution charts in the galler-

Komodo Dragon

ies! A book on sale in the bookshop, *Dear Lord Rothschild* (written by Miriam Rothschild, a natural historian in her own right) enlarges the story of Tring and the Rothschild family. Outside the Rothschild Room is a specially designed case with a collection of gorgeous humming birds. In the dim light their feathers seem fluorescent.

Gallery 3 moves on to crocodiles, fish, insects and large mammals. Here the celebrated dressed fleas take their place amongst dragonflies, stick insects, bugs and beetles. A case of crustacea is dominated by the Giant Spider Crab from the North Atlantic coastline. There are starfish that look like sweets, and extraordinary sponges like the Venus Flower Basket Sponges. In the central area sharks and camels, elephants and rhinoceroses vye for attention.

In Gallery 4, the visitor is seemingly surrounded by zebras, although one zebra-like specimen is actually a Quagga. Now long extinct, the last example of this strange creature died in Amsterdam Zoo in 1883. The Quagga is part of the odd-toed, hoofed mammal group that also includes horses, rhinos and tapirs. The graceful gazelles and impalas in the next gallery are even-toed, but it is their eyes that I found hard to ignore. Often lying with heads at floor level the specimens gaze mournfully at passers-by. Antelopes, sea-lions and curly-horned wild sheep give way to bats, snakes, lizards and tortoises in this large L-shaped room, the heavy armour plating of scaly anteaters contrasting with the outrageous colours of the Cassowarys from New Guinea. The gallery also contains the museum's unique display of domestic dogs. These are not part of the original Rothschild collection but are drawn from specimens held by The Natural History Museum in London. They range in date from 1834 to the present day, and include a Russian lapdog only some eight inches long, and the noble Great Dane and St Bernard. The Irish Wolfhound, used by Irish medieval kings in hunting wolves, shares with the Great Dane title of tallest living breed. The Dalmation arrived in Britain during the 18th century from India, via Dalmatia, and became popular as a guard dog to accompany carriages.

By the time you reach the walrus, there is a certain relief in knowing that the 'family', *Odobenidae*, contains only the walrus. Tring is a remarkable museum – both in itself and in its collections. It is a manageable size and has proved enormously popular with generations of children and adults alike. The shop is a recent addition and holds an extensive range of posters, both educational and ornamental, along with models, trails, kits, books and jewellery. Much of Tring's appeal is that it retains a sense of belonging to another age. Its continuity of collections and scholarship begun by Lord Rothschild make it a unique place to visit. (KH)

Moa

WALTHAM ABBEY

Epping Forest District Museum

39/41 Sun Street, Waltham Abbey, Essex EN9 1EL   (0992) 716882
Closed mornings and all day Wednesdays and Thursdays (except for party bookings). 🄵 ▣
⟨ **S**: wheelchair access to ground floor only.
🚻 & 🚹 must book in advance: contact Assistant Curator (Administration). ☼

Waltham Abbey sits between the M25, the River Lea and Epping Forest. In past centuries, the forest lands surrounding this historic market town were known as Waltham Forest and were dominated by the Abbey of Waltham. The Epping Forest District Museum stands in Sun Street, a few hundred yards away from the Abbey

Church, one of a cluster of historic buildings and sites that form the town's conservation area. The museum is housed in numbers 39 and 41 Sun Street, next to the town's library. The displays and temporary exhibitions reflect the character and history of the town and of the Epping Forest District from the Stone Age to the 20th century. The museum is bright and friendly, maintaining high standards of display, furnishings, shop goods and even coffee! It has a rare mixture of style and warmth.

The ground floor of no. 41 was offered as a local museum to the Waltham Abbey Historical Society in 1975 and was run and staffed on a voluntary basis. In 1981, nos. 39 and 41 were combined and converted to the District Museum with full-time professional staff. The conversion has revealed many of the ancient timbers, recreating in part the original layout. A model of no. 41 as first built around 1520 is on display, part of a small exhibition focusing on the building's history that includes photographs, and personal belongings found during the conversion.

Bronze mural commissioned by Demetrios Demetriou

Purbeck marble head of a Knight

The museum is entered from Sun Street. Its front door forms part of an impressive bronze mural commissioned by a local taverna owner, Demetrios Demetriou, and sculpted by Philip Jackson, which features the crowning of King Harold, who is believed to have been in Waltham in 1066. The entrance leads into the well-stocked museum shop. Here the coffee percolator sets an atmosphere, as do the bright modern furnishings. These sit surprisingly well throughout the building in a blend of old and new. The beautiful handwritten labels continue the thoughtful mixture with clear lines and great style.

The museum's most important purchase in recent years is the Purbeck Marble head of a Knight, dating from the last quarter of the 13th century (ill. on cover). It was part of a tomb effigy in the Abbey, but was stolen. When it reappeared after export to the Metropolitan Museum in New York, a long legal debate ensued; the head finally returned to Waltham in 1986. It now sits, specially lit and protected, in the large ground floor room of the museum. Here, too, the Town Mead hoard is displayed – a collection of smith's tools found in 1967 and dating from the Iron Age and Early Roman

period. Other Roman artefacts from the area come from a Roman farmstead at Sewardstone, south of Waltham Abbey. Clear drawings and graphics accompany the objects throughout these displays and are particularly effective in describing Saxon settlements. There is a skeleton and a few small finds from this period, which include a lovely silver-gilt pin, so delicate against the rough sherds and bones that are the normal finds from Saxon sites. A door leads from this room to the attractive formal herb and flower garden, somewhat unexpected in the street setting.

The other, smaller room on the ground floor is lined with the most glorious oak panelling, carved for the Abbot of Waltham during the reign of Henry VIII. The Tudor rose is used as a motif, as is the pomegranate, symbol of Henry's queen at the time, Catherine of Aragon. Another image in the carving is known locally as the 'Abbey Tabby'; this strange creature, a cross between a cat and a court jester, has been adopted as the museum's logo. The richness of the panelling gives a good indication of the wealth and influence of the Abbots of Waltham. One such Abbot's bones lie on display alongside inventories and maps. A thumb ring of a polished agate stone set in gilt over silver adds a human dimension to the story of this powerful monastic settlement, as does the curious bronze beer tap with a twin animal-head decoration. The Abbot had a seat in Parliament, was subject only to the Pope and the King, and, as Lord of the Manor of Waltham, held markets and fairs; even today, Waltham holds two markets a week. The Abbey was the last of the monasteries to be dissolved by Henry VIII in 1540, and with its loss (only part of the church now survives, as the parish church) the town's prosperity declined.

The small-scale industries and

Part of the oak panelling carved for the Abbot of Waltham during Henry VIII's reign

trades of the 20th century are the subject of displays at the foot of the stairs and in the main gallery on the first floor. The story of the local Walsham family, who started trading as confectioners in the market in 1904, is told in photographs and advertising material. Their first premises were in the market square; later they moved to 26 Sun Street where one Tommy Holmes was employed as 'sugar boiler' to make confectionery, using some of the moulds and rollers on display. The first-floor gallery concentrates on different trades associated with local agriculture: tools and contemporary photographs of blacksmiths, farm workers and machinery are displayed on practical yet effective white picket fences lining the walls.

On the second floor are two temporary exhibition galleries. The museum stages an impressive programme of temporary exhibitions (some twelve to fifteen a year) covering a wide range of topics from the purely historical to the fine and decorative arts, crafts, photography, costume and textiles. There is something for every interest and taste. One of the major exhibitions is the annual Artists in Essex Exhibition and Competition, open to artists living and/ or working in the historic county of Essex. Through purchases from this exhibition, the museum is building up a unique collection of contemporary art.

The museum also runs innovative educational and outreach programmes, the latter taking the work of the museum to parts where museums do not usually reach! Activities include a major community festival in May each year when the museum, in cooperation with local community groups, organises the 'Waltham Abbey Time Machine', a celebration of local history including a massive procession, performances, street theatre, exhibitions, concerts and a firework display, all on the theme of local history. There are also regular events, demonstrations, workshops, oral history sessions, and museum 'fun days' for children. The museum combines the virtues of a traditional museum with modern initiative, energy and style. (KH)

WANTAGE

Vale and Downland Museum Centre

The Old Surgery, Church Street, Wantage, Oxfordshire OX12 8BL (02357) 66838
Closed Sunday mornings and Mondays. 🄵 ▣ 🅿 🄴W
🚻 & ♥ book in advance: contact Museum Education Service at County Museum, Woodstock (0993) 811456

The Vale and Downland Museum Centre is a lively bustling place, which plays an important role in the local community. The museum is part of the Oxfordshire County Museum Service and is operated jointly with a museum trust. The displays themselves are broadly chronological, and trace the development of the local landscape and the gradual impact of people on that landscape.

Some 135–65 million years ago, seas washed over what is now the Vale of the White Horse: hence the layer of chalk, made up of the shells of countless sea creatures compacted over time. Many millions of years after the sea

came the ice – in the last two million years Britain was several times under thick ice sheets. Evidence of people first appears in the form of axeheads and other tools from the Paleolithic period, from sites such as one at Turner's Court near Henley. In the Neolithic (the period of the first settlements and the beginning of farming) there was extensive trading across large distances. Two such trade routes in the Wantage area were the Ridgeway, linking the coast and the river Thames, and the Thames itself. These routes were marked by henge monuments (such as at **Dorchester**) and causewayed enclosures such as at Radley.

In the Bronze Age, farmers moved from one seasonal pasture to another and their graves, or barrows, were often located near Neolithic sacred places. Part of an Iron Age hut is reconstructed in the displays, putting such objects as pots and loom weights into context. The Vale of the White Horse was named after the horse cut into the chalk downland at Uffington. In the 13th century this, one of the oldest figures cut into the chalk, was described as the second-best marvel in England (second only to Stonehenge). If you go to see the White Horse you could also pop into the *Tom Brown's School Museum* in Uffington village.

The arrival of the Romans quickly

A Berkshire wagon of about 1914

Reconstruction of a farm kitchen

had an impact on lowland Britain as it soon fell to the invaders, and natives were encouraged to leave their fortified hilltop encampments and live in towns and settlements in valleys. Coins, ornaments and pottery survive as evidence of the Roman occupation. After the Romans departed the Anglo-Saxons settled around their deserted towns and farmsteads in the Vale. Saxon finds on display here include pottery, a disc brooch and the central part (or boss) of a shield. By the Middle Ages the Vale was prosperous and had a growing population.

Final displays about the Vale as a whole look at agriculture and the country estates. An attractive display is one depicting aspects of farming life around 1900. A boy aged about seven then might work as a plough boy, and another job for children was to wave a castanet-like object that scared the birds away from crops. The meadows in the west of the Vale were ideal for cattle farming and pig rearing – Faringdon and Wantage were noted for their bacon markets.

The displays move back in time to tell the story of Wantage itself. The town has a varied and interesting history. It was probably the birthplace of King Alfred the Great (he of the burned cakes). After a battle with the

Vikings, Alfred laid siege to Chippenham and forced the Danes to leave Wessex. It was then that Alfred declared himself the first ever 'King of the English'.

In a very restricted space the displays relate some of the more recent history of Wantage, for example the story of the Ormond family. John Ormond, having moved to Wantage in

1784, married a local woman and they had nine children. The museum's collections include an excellent archive of papers relating to the family in the time of John and of succeeding generations. Some of the local shops of the past 100 years or so are featured, among them Hughes, the shoe shop. Transport is also covered, and exhibits include the Wantage Tram model (*c.* 1923): 'A curious fact has come to pass/Between an engine and an ass/The Wantage Tram all steam and smoke/Was beat by Arthur Hitchcock's moke.'

Adjoining the back of the museum is the reconstructed 18th century Hunt's barn from East Hendred. In it are displayed a variety of wagons and farm machines, including a Berkshire Wagon from Sutton Courtenay.

One of the memorable features of this museum is its splendid food, so you can rest and take refreshments before going up to the temporary exhibition gallery or into the kitchen display, which illustrates what a local farm kitchen would have been like at the turn of the century. Apart from the temporary exhibitions, there are also regular treats like the W.I. cake stall on Friday mornings. This is an enjoyable museum that feeds both body and soul! (NH)

Old photograph of Hughes of Wantage's van in the shape of a shoe

WATFORD

Watford Museum

194 High Street, Watford,
Hertfordshire WD1 2HG
(0923) 32297

Closed Sundays. **F P**

W: wheelchair access to ground
floor via ramp at rear of museum
(press door bell); access to first
floor by lift.

& book in advance; evening
group tours available for a fee.

Watford Museum is located in a fine
18th century building close to the town
centre. The house was built in 1775
and stood in front of the now-
demolished Benskins Brewery. Inside,
objects as varied as Iron Age spearheads and Elton John's suit tell the
story of Watford town from pre-history
to the present day.

The entrance area is bright and inviting, and picks up most of the main
themes in Watford's history. A bar to
the right refers to the significance of
brewing in the town's wealth, as well as
to the museum building itself – the
family mansion and then offices to
Benskins Brewery. Bottles and containers add context, as do the notices
and prints from the *Brewers Journal* of
1902. A lovely three-quarter length
portrait of 'A Lady in Grey' by Hubert
von Herkomer (1849–1914) heralds
the museum's collection of fine art,
while printing presses refer to the other
major industry in the town. Watford is
the home of Odham's Press, as well as
Watford United, whose most famous
Chairman, Elton John, commissioned
a suit in the team's colours from Ebony
Designers in 1984. This can be seen
on the first floor.

The printing section is dominated by
the heavily ornamented Columbian
Press of 1822, but the reconstructed
section of a compositor's desk creates a
more evocative atmosphere of the
workplace. Large black and white
photographs of a compositor at work,
added to the array of typefaces, gives a
good indication of the complexity be-

Bar in the Brewing display

hind the printed word. The different
processes used and the various materials involved in printing are covered in
the displays with sections on relief,
lithography, intaglio, the gravure cylinder, even ink-making. Video films on
the theme are shown on request, including a pre-World War II film about
Sun Printers of Watford, and the story
of the *Evening Echo*, a past local paper.

From printing, the exhibitions lead
into a plush red area where photographs, costumes and programmes
illustrate public entertainment. Watford at war comes next. Mementoes
kept by the people of Watford include
one of the boxes of chocolate sent by
Queen Victoria in 1900 to soldiers
fighting the Boer War in South Africa,
still uneaten. Such personal touches
give the displays a poignancy that is
heightened by the eye-witness
accounts included in the accompanying
text and by photographs taken of war
damage in Watford. A map shows the
position and type of the bombs that fell
here during the Blitz, when some 300
houses were destroyed.

This gallery leads the visitor upstairs
to the first floor, where the displays
concentrate on local history from prehistoric times to the development of
the modern town. There is an explanation of the geology of the area, and of
the layers of soil and information
usually uncovered in archaeological
digs. The displays that follow show
items uncovered at various sites around
Watford. They are bright and informative, with a mixture of drawings and
text, and objects displayed in well-lit
sunken cases that give the effect of
viewing the objects as if they were in
the ground. The Bronze Age hoard is
particularly spectacular, with the dense
dark colour of the axe and spear heads
contrasting starkly with their bright
surroundings. In the finds from the two
Roman sites at Hamper Mill and
Netherwylde, a native British villa site
and a more wealthy Roman villa, one is
able to compare two very different
lifestyles in Roman Britain.

The next section changes pace
again, recording the great influence of
the Abbey of St Albans on the area and

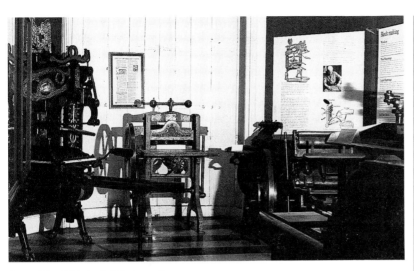

Some of the exhibits in the Printing section

how that influence was altered during the Peasants Revolt of 1381. We learn that 14th century Watford had two fairs granted by Edward III, while Watford's market, granted in the reign of Henry I, gained enough public popularity to be the origin of a local saying, 'I'd rather be hanged in Watford than

die a natural death in Bushey'! Agriculture was of prime importance in the 15th century (as it remained until the 19th). Displays on working the land lead from the 15th into the 16th and 17th centuries, where new building and the techniques of timber farming are explored. A wall painting with the coat of arms of James I was found under layers of plaster at 137 High Street, and photographs in the displays show how other features of 17th century building have been revealed, either through fires or demolition. The Cassiobury Estate, once the home of the Earls of Essex, has a section to itself, which includes J. M. W. Turner's painting of the mansion's west front. The Victorian section is a wonderful jumble of wallpaper patterns, colour cut-outs and textiles. Further displays include boneshakers, prams, transport systems and workhouses. Don't miss the maths test cards and school cap, which really conjure up 'school'.

The largest trophy in the English Football League, the Sheriff of London's Charity Shield, was presented to the football world by Thomas Dewar in 1897 and sits proudly in the final gallery. Alongside, there is coverage of Watford United's history from its beginnings in 1870 as the Hertfordshire Rangers through to its most illustrious Chairman, Elton John.

The Picture Gallery displays a selection of the museum's fine art collection, which ranges from 17th century Dutch paintings to modern pieces by local artists. The temporary exhibition gallery mounts a series of changing exhibitions. Some of the sculpture owned by the museum is housed on the landing. A case of work by Jacob Epstein complements the more angular pieces by Ronald Pope, a Derbyshire engineer-turned-artist who uses a wide variety of materials to express themes of life. A final treat is in store as you descend the stairs: 17th century landscapes by Gaspard Poussin, Salvator Rosa and Jacob van Ruisdael. This is a museum with style and pace that offers plenty of fascinating things to see as well as giving the visitor a colourful insight into what made Watford. (KH)

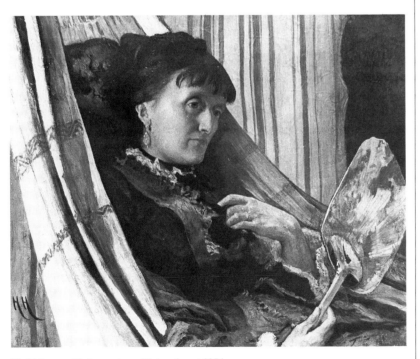

Sir Hubert von Herkomer, Anna Weise, *August 1876*

WEYBRIDGE

Brooklands Museum

The Clubhouse, Brooklands Road,
Weybridge, Surrey KT13 0QN
(0932) 857381
Currently only open to organised
groups on a restricted basis:
⚏ & ⚏ must book in advance. The
first phase of the site will open to
the public in Spring 1991: please
'phone to check details. ▤ ▣
⚏ W

In 1991 what promises to be Surrey's
largest and most popular museum will
open at Brooklands, near Weybridge. It
will be the culmination of over ten
years of hard work by many groups and
individuals to ensure the preservation
of this key site in the history of British
motor racing and aviation. Brooklands
will be unusual in many ways, not least
in that it will be devoted solely to the
history of the 20th century.

Many visitors to the site today find it
strange to discover a massive factory
complex nestling in the middle of the
Surrey stockbroker belt. However, at
the turn of the century much of the
area was still open countryside, scattered with large houses set in extensive
grounds. In 1906 Hugh Locke King,
the owner of one such estate, decided
to build Brooklands, a great oval banked motor racing circuit. It was a typi-
cally British individualistic idea, but it
was to become an outstanding success.
The track was the first of its kind in the
world and was to become not only the
home of British motor racing until
1939 but also the birthplace of the
British aviation industry. 'Brooklands'
was to become synonymous with
speed, excitement and powerful engines.

With the closure of the British
Aerospace factory at Brooklands in
1988, the entire area of the racing
circuit and airfield is currently being
redeveloped. But thirty acres at the
northern end of the site have been
saved for the museum, and various
important structures elsewhere will be
preserved or moved.

When Brooklands opened as a race
track on 17th June 1907 cars were still
relatively primitive. The site saw the
rapid advance in their performance and
was used to test many of the technical
developments that were to revolutio-
nise driving. The lap record of 143.44
mph for the 2¾ mile circuit was established by John Cobb in his Napier-
Railton in 1935, by which time speeds
were far higher than those for which
the banking had been designed and
there was little margin for safety. Such
have been the recent advances in car
technology that this record could easily
be matched today by several types of
sports cars with their radios playing. In
the early days there were no established rules for motor racing and the
pioneers simply copied horse racing.
Drivers were identified by jockeys'
silks and were 'handicapped', with the
cars being checked on a weighbridge in
the clubhouse.

The calm air conditions inside the
banked track made the site immediately attractive to the pioneers of British
aviation, many of whom were to establish production facilities in south-west
London. In 1908 A. V. Roe achieved
his first successful hop flight at Brooklands – the first flight by a Briton in a
British-built plane. Aviation subsequently boomed, and soon several
companies, including Vickers, Bristol
and Sopwith, were using Brooklands to
test, and often eventually build, their
planes. The site also became an important training centre and half the pilots
in the country who qualified before
1914, including Mrs Hilda Hewlett,
Britain's first female pilot (1911 –
No. 122) learnt to fly there. From
1914–20 the site was taken over by the
Royal Flying Corps, and Brooklands
became Britain's largest aircraft manufacturing centre during the First World
War. Output included the Vickers FB5
Gunbus – the first aircraft specifically
designed with a machine gun.

Brooklands' heyday was in the 1920s
and '30s, when it became an important
and fashionable social centre with the
slogan 'The right crowd and no crowd-
ing'. Along with Hendon Aerodrome,
Brooklands became the place for
young men to take their girlfriends on
Saturdays and Bank Holidays, to enjoy
the races, the flying displays or simply
lying in the sun. The location on a
wealthy gentleman's country estate always helped preserve a special sort of
atmosphere. Alongside the racing and
entertainment, however, much serious
work took place, and the maiden flight
of the Hurricane fighter at Brooklands
on 6th November 1935 is a reminder

Brooklands Motor Track and Flying Ground

Postcard showing the Clubhouse exterior, 1907

Press photo of John Cobb racing at Brooklands in his Sunbeam 4 litre V12 Tiger, 1934

of the importance of the site for the defence of Britain a few years later.

With the outbreak of the Second World War the race track closed for good and the entire site was taken over by Vickers for aircraft manufacture. Large manufacturing sheds were built on the track, and over 2,500 Wellington bombers and many other planes were built. After the war the site was retained by Vickers and a series of famous aircraft, including the Viking, Varsity, Viscount, Vanguard, VC10 and BAC 1-11, were developed and built there. Weybridge also made major contributions to international col-

laborative schemes, notably on Concorde, the Jaguar and the Tornado. Manufacturing finally ceased at Brooklands in 1987 after more than 8,000, mainly large, aircraft had emerged from the site, as well as a mass of ideas and trained personnel.

Clearly, with such a complex history, the museum section of the site includes a variety of buildings designed for a range of purposes. Fortunately the original 1907 Clubhouse survives and has recently been restored by Gallaher Ltd. In addition, a large section of the banked track has been cleared of undergrowth and is being conserved.

When the museum opens fully in 1991 visitors will be able to take a journey back in time to the motoring and aviation villages of the 1920s next to the original finishing straight. The focal point will be the restored Clubhouse, which will recapture the social scene of the period with restored room settings and displays about racing. In the paddock next to the Clubhouse a range of buildings will include displays about the 'Heroes of the Track', among them S. F. Edge, Parry Thomas, Malcolm Campbell, Whitney Straight and John Cobb. Close by is an evocative courtyard of original wooden buildings used as workshops and tuning sheds. These include the famous Dunlop Mac's tyre depot, and there will be a major display on Frazer Nash.

The museum already owns a great deal of material relating to the story of aviation at Brooklands, some items being very large. The collection will be housed in a former aircraft assembly hall, and includes the Sultan of Oman's VC10 as well as replicas of early 'planes such as the Sopwith Camel and the Roe 1 Biplane. Perhaps the most remarkable survival is the Wellington bomber, 'R for Robert', recovered from the bottom of Loch Ness in 1985. This is the only operational Wellington to survive from over 11,000 that were produced, and it is currently being restored at Brooklands. The museum also owns several other 'planes with local connections, which will be restored and displayed as resources allow. Associated buildings include the world's first flight ticket office of 1911, and the impressive stratosphere testing chamber designed by Sir Barnes Wallis in 1945–46.

Many other aspects of the story of Brooklands will be explored, including its role as a centre for motorcycle and cycle racing. A visit will not only offer a chance to discover a fascinating site and story, but will be a remarkable reminder of how the massive industries of today were based on the pioneering spirit, enthusiasm and bravery of a few individuals. For those who cannot wait until 1991, the museum is currently open on a restricted basis to organised groups. (GM)

The Sultan of Oman's VC10

WINDSOR

Household Cavalry Museum

Combermere Barracks, St Leonards Road, Windsor, Berkshire SL4 3DN (0753) 868222 ext. 203
Closed lunchtimes, and all day Saturday and Sunday. ⃞ ⃞
⃞ & ⃞ book in advance: contact Curator.

People the world over recognise the Household Cavalry when they provide the Queen's Life Guard at Whitehall or the Sovereign's Escort on state occasions. The Household Cavalry also operates in the field, and has seen active service ranging from Tangiers (1661) to the Falklands War (1982). The museum reflects all aspects of the Household Cavalry's history; it is rich in objects relating to ceremonial and state occasions, as well as field operations The museum collections were built up from 1952, and in 1964 the Duke of Wellington opened the present museum inside the main gate of Combermere Barracks. The barracks are located south of central Windsor and parking is in nearby streets – but *don't* let that put you off: the museum is

Modern helmet, Peninsular helmet, cocked hat, and officers swords

definitely worthy of several hours absorbed browsing.

The Household Cavalry is today composed of The Life Guards and The Blues and Royals. The Life Guards is the senior regiment of the British Army and was originally formed in 1660. King Charles II fled into exile in France after the Battle of Worcester (1651) and with him went cavalier noblemen who in 1660 were formed, and paid, as the regular mounted bodyguard to the King. The Blues had their

origin in Hesilrigs Ironside Regiment, raised in 1650 and taken into Charles II's service after the Restoration. The 1st Royal Dragoons were raised in 1661 as a Troop of Heavy Cavalry for the defence of Tangiers. The Royal Horse Guards and 1st Royal Dragoons were amalgamated to form The Blues and Royals in 1969. The Queen is the Colonel-in-Chief of each regiment.

The Colonels of each regiment are appointed by Her Majesty the Queen, and also hold the title of Gold Stick (an office created by Charles I). The Queen passes all orders to the regiment through the Gold Stick. The Gold Stick carried by General Earl Cathcart, Colonel of the 2nd Life Guards 1797–1843, is on display in the museum.

The Household Cavalry dress today includes a helmet and plumes, and a cuirass (breastplate). The present style of helmet was introduced in 1842 by Prince Albert (hence known as the Albert helmet). Officers' headwear until 1812 was the two-pointed cocked hat. The high bearskin hat was introduced by George IV; its design has changed slightly over the years. The museum has the bearskin worn by Captain John Trotter from 1825–36, which has Grenadier badges on the front and back and a large white feath-

Waterloo helmet, service dress coatee and medals of Col Sir Robert Chambre-Hill of The Blues

Detail from a set of drawings made by John Sandeman, Royal Dragoons, in the Crimea, 1854

er curled over the top. Polished metal cuirasses have been worn since the coronation of George IV in 1821, and have changed little since then. Earlier cuirasses were made of blackened steel; those worn in the Jacobite wars of 1690–97 weighed over 35 lbs!

Ceremonial uniform was not just worn by the men. The horses wore shabraques – types of blanket. These range from simple sheepskin to highly decorated models for officers' horses. Officers' ceremonial shabraques are extremely expensive (even before 1914 each one cost £500). The museum has a fine collection, including one of the oldest surviving rank-and-file shabraques of the Royals, dating to 1716. It was not until 1816 that the colour of the horses (black) was laid down; until then officers had bought their own charger, saddles and other equipment.

At the Battle of Waterloo the Household Cavalry routed a corps of French Cuirassiers that was threatening the retiring British infantry. One display, entirely devoted to the Waterloo campaign, contains perhaps the oddest item – a cork leg. This leg was worn by the 1st Marquess of Anglesey after the original was struck by a cannonball at Waterloo and amputated with a saw. His widow donated the replacement to the museum on his death. John Edwards (then aged 15) was the trumpeter of the 1st Life Guards at Waterloo and his bugle is also on display. Trumpeters were non-fighting soldiers and carried a sword with a broken-off blade to symbolise

this. From the 17th century on they were selected if they had 'an acceptable manner, the ability to carry messages and to parley with the enemy'. Edwards, who blew the order to 'charge' at Waterloo, served in the 1st Life Guards until 1841, aged 41.

Trumpets and drums had special cloth banners, many examples of which are on display. An early, and very rare, drum banner of 1760 is displayed; it was worn over the bronze kettle-drums used at that time. In 1831 William IV gave a pair of silver kettle-drums to the 1st and 2nd Life Guards. Those of the 2nd Life Guards are displayed in the museum and are used on some ceremonial occasions. They are very ornate and impressive objects.

Impressive, too, is the range of highly decorated fabric Standards and Guidons. Standards were carried into battle, and there have been many different patterns or designs over the years: the Blues had five patterns from 1751 and the museum has examples of each, the oldest dating to 1760.

The museum's most recent acquisitions relate to the Falklands War of 1982. Three days after the invasion, troops from The Blues and Royals left for the Falkland Islands on the P&O liner 'Canberra'. They provided fire support during many assaults en route to Port Stanley, and their role was described as 'one of the success stories' leading to the British victory. One of the items brought back was an Argentine army vehicle, now on display outside the museum. (NH)

WITNEY

Cogges Manor Farm Museum

Church Lane, Cogges, Witney, Oxfordshire OX8 6LA
(0993) 772602
Open April to end of October, Tuesdays to Fridays and weekend afternoons. 🅂 ▣ ℗
& **ST**: wheelchair access difficult to some parts.
👪 & 👫 book in advance. ◎

The Cogges Manor Farm Museum complex is a wonderful and evocative range of buildings reflecting some 600 years of occupation and changing farming practices. Its importance is affirmed by the fact that it is a scheduled Ancient Monument. The farm was acquired by the County Council in 1974 for use as a museum of farming and the countryside.

The Bayeux Tapestry has a representation of the first Lord of Cogges. He is shown as a mounted knight organising the plundering of Hastings, and above his likeness are the words *'Hic est Wadard'* – here is Wadard. Wadard controlled Cogges for a relatively short time; by about 1100 another Norman family, the Arsics, were in charge. They lasted a bit longer: in their 150 years at Cogges they built a moated enclosure and a house near the banks of the River Windrush; they also founded a priory. By 1242 the Manor of Cogges was granted to the De Grey family. The hall-house built for Walter de Grey in the mid-13th century still partly survives in the present Manor House (which is due to be restored during the early 1990s – only the ground floor is open at present). The priory founded by the Arsics continued; it was an alien priory, so called because it was effectively run by Fecamp Abbey. The medieval village of Cogges is no longer visible, except for some humps and bumps in the ground indicating where peasant houses used to stand.

Education work outside Cogges Manor farmhouse

setting in the Oxfordshire countryside. Eventually there will be a variety of audio-visual programmes to suit different audiences. In addition, the small barn will be used for evening activities, such as courses, lectures and demonstrations. The larger barn will also open in 1990 and in the future will contain displays that will interpret the social history of the countryside and the science of agriculture.

Cogges has long been known for the variety of special demonstrations and activities mounted throughout the season. The daily and seasonal cycle at work on the farm and in the Manor House form the basis of the demonstration programme at Cogges. Milking and feeding time are popular farming events with visitors; there are also regular demonstrations of cooking. On a cool bright summer or autumn day there is nothing nicer than going into the Cogges kitchen with the cooking range providing a glowing warmth, and with plenty of delicious cooking smells to savour! Other demonstrations relate to the nature and fabric of Cogges itself. A restoration workshop and an archaeological dig are part of the 1990 programme.

There are also history and nature trails to enjoy. The history trail, which can be followed from a leaflet and from information panels, enables visitors to see the site of the deserted medieval village, the medieval priory church (still used today) and the moats.

One of the dairies has been adapted to house a visitor centre, shop and restaurant. The farmyard is stocked with pigs, sheep, horses and many chickens, and there are cattle in the adjacent meadows. These represent some of the types of livestock that the Edwardian Mawle family would have owned. The orchard is also stocked with old varieties of fruit tree, many rarely seen today. This theme continues in the walled garden, with old vegetable varieties growing alongside modern ones.

There is already plenty to enjoy at Cogges, and as the years progress more of the site will be opened up or interpreted, so repeat visits will be worthwhile. (NH)

The estate passed from one owner to another, and in the 18th century was bought by Lord Harcourt. By this time there was 'The manor house and the two great barns and the stables and outhouses, yard, orchard and appurtenances'. Lord Harcourt let the farm to tenants, among them Mr Moreland, who was not a farmer but a teacher and ran a school there. The Hollis family leased the farm, three generations of the family living and working there for the next century. The Mawle family rented Cogges Manor Farm from 1877, also for nearly 100 years. During that time the Mawle family actually purchased the Manor Farm from the Harcourt Estate, and in 1974 it was Ted Mawle who sold it to Oxfordshire County Council.

In 1988 a Development Project for the museum began. Over a five-year period the 25-acre site will be developed to form a unique centre for the understanding of the countryside's past and present use.

One of the first phases is to restore two large 18th-century barns. The smaller of the two will be open to the public for the 1990 season and will contain an audio-visual display to introduce the visitor to the site and its

WOODSTOCK

Oxfordshire County Museum

Fletcher's House, Park Street, Woodstock, Oxfordshire OX7 1SN
(0993) 811456
Closed Sunday mornings; closed Mondays October to April. 🅵 🖭
&: wheelchair access to ground floor only.
🏛 & 🍴 preferably book in advance; guided tours by arrangement. ◉ County Museum Education Service based here

The Oxfordshire County Museums Service has its headquarters in Woodstock and the museum here tells the story of the county as a whole, rather than that of Woodstock itself. The museum displays are arranged chronologically starting with the development of the landscape. During the early 1990s significant changes will be made; the present displays are now fifteen years old and were arranged before some of the outpost museums, such as at **Wantage** and **Banbury**, were developed to their present extent.

One of the most eye-catching parts of the prehistoric displays in the museum is the section from the Neolithic long barrow at Ascott-under-Wychwood. This barrow was important because of its completeness, and one of the two pairs of cists, or large 'boxes' of huge stone slabs, which provided areas for burial within the barrow, is rebuilt in the museum. The barrow contained the remains of fifty individuals. Other examples of prehistoric burials are several Bronze Age ones with charred bones in ceramic pots.

Generally the best surviving monuments of the Iron Age are hillforts, of which there are a number in Oxfordshire, such as at **Dorchester** and Blewbury. The displays illustrate something of the life in these and other Iron Age settlements.

Reconstructed section of Neolithic long barrow at Ascott-under-Wychwood

Objects from the time of the Roman occupation include Roman amphorae, brooches, rings, and even tools used by a Roman woman to apply her make-up. A hoard of coins found in Great Tew, which was hidden in about 270 AD, is also on display. Oxfordshire had some important potteries in the Roman period; part of a kiln from the potteries at Headington, dating to about 240 AD, is reconstructed here (at its peak Headington had up to six kilns in action). There are examples of various types of pottery available for visitors to handle, so that you can feel the different textures of the finer wares and the grit-encrusted mortars for grinding grain.

Moving on – and upstairs – to the coming of the Saxons in 410 AD, there is a reconstructed grave from the Saxon Berinsfield cemetery, which con-

16th century wall painting from Thame

of its kind and was to be extended to all counties in England, but was abandoned after the completion of Oxfordshire and Staffordshire. All aspects of natural phenomena are covered – 'Of Planets', 'Of Brutes', 'Of Arts', 'Of the Earth'; Dr Plot was nothing if not comprehensive.

The effect of the Enclosure Acts on the local landscape and agricultural practice during the late 18th and 19th centuries is examined in the displays. Increasing mechanisation of agriculture brought new and often less easy working practices. Jobs were lost, and the new machines were seen by workers as part of a conspiracy between the landowners; Oxfordshire saw some violent Luddite opposition to the new machines.

Some of the important crafts and industries of the 19th and early 20th centuries are highlighted, including glove making and cut-steel jewellery making in Woodstock itself. Towns grew as new industries developed. In Chipping Norton, Witney and **Banbury** new textile mills offered much new employment, while the Morris car company turned Oxford from a market and university town into an important industrial centre. The landscape of the county today, after some sixty centuries of human activity, is almost totally man made and is increasingly dominated by the claims of housing, transport and industry.

The County Museum offers more than just displays. There are regular temporary exhibitions and events; and the public can consult the Sites and Monuments and Biological Records by appointment, as well as some of the special collections stored here, such as the Packer Collection, an archive of tens of thousands of glass-plate negatives from a photographer's in Chipping Norton.

A day in Woodstock is always pleasant and rewarding. The day's activities could combine a visit to the museum with lunch in one of the excellent local hostelries and a visit to Blenheim Palace, with its opulent interior decorations and the wonderful park landscaped by Capability Brown. (NH)

tained over 100 burials. Some of the grave goods on display include jewellery – brooches and beads – and a shield boss, which lies in the reconstructed grave at the side of the mortal remains of a man aged 30–35, who was around 5ft 7ins tall. Another important Saxon find was grave F67 in a Saxon cemetery in Shrivenham. This appears to have been the grave of a member of the local Saxon elite, judging by the fine grave goods, which include a belt and buckle made of tinned bronze, perhaps imported from the continent.

During the Middle Ages the Oxfordshire landscape was very different from what we see today, since medieval forests covered a wide band of the county. Virtually all the churches in Oxfordshire are medieval in origin, or are on the site of a medieval church. Some such churches no longer exist; *Wallingford*, for example (a Thames-side town with its own small independent museum, which is worth visiting), had fourteen churches in the Middle Ages.

After the Dissolution much church land passed into private hands, and in the 16th and 17th centuries there was a great burst of building activity in the county. A popular feature in some houses of the period was monochrome wall and/or ceiling painting. The museum has a particularly fine example from a timber-framed house in

Thame. It was common for such paintings to have a central text: in this example it is from the Bible, Romans 11 v.33–36. These 16th and 17th century buildings were increasingly comfortable. Vessels of pottery and leather were used, but other household containers were increasingly of glass. Pewter and brass vessels were also used more widely.

In 1677 Dr Robert Plot's *Natural History of Oxfordshire* was published. It was the first detailed scientific survey

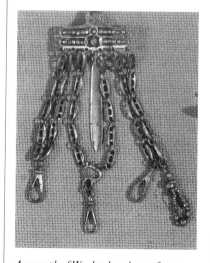

An example of Woodstock steel manufacture

Museums in the Home Counties

Museums shown in **bold** are described fully in the main text of this volume.

BEDFORDSHIRE

BEDFORD

Bedford Museum

The Cecil Higgins Art Gallery and Museum

DUNSTABLE

Dunstable Museum
Dunstable Library, Vernon Place, Dunstable
(Beds Dunstable) 863289
Local history displays.

ELSTOW

Elstow Moot Hall

LUTON

Luton Museum and Art Gallery
Wardown House, Wardown Park, Luton, Bedfordshire
LU2 7HA   (0582) 36941/2
Natural history, archaeology, social history, decorative art, and Beds. & Herts. Regimental Collection.

Stockwood Craft Museum and Gardens

OLD WARDEN

The Shuttleworth Collection

BERKSHIRE

CLEWER

Clewer Museum of Local History
Clewer Church, Clewer, Nr Eton, Berkshire   (07535) 65185
An enchanting local history collection gathered and cared for by Rev Denis Shaw.

COOKHAM-ON-THAMES

Stanley Spencer Gallery

ETON

Eton College Collections

NEWBURY

Newbury District Museum

MAIDENHEAD

Royal Borough Collection
Royal Borough of Windsor and Maidenhead, Town Hall, St Ives Road, Maidenhead, Berkshire
At present much material from the collection is on view in the 'Royalty and Empire' exhibition at Windsor station; the reserve collection can be viewed by appointment with the Hon. Curator.

READING

Blakes Lock Museum

Cole Museum of Zoology
Department of Geology, Reading University, Whiteknights Park, Reading, Berkshire RG6 2AJ
(0734) 875123
Natural history themes shown in small but interesting displays, including some live specimens such as green tree frogs!

Institute of Agricultural History and Museum of English Rural Life

Reading Museum and Art Gallery

Ure Museum of Greek Archaeology
Faculty of Letters, Reading University, Whiteknights Park, Reading, Berkshire RG6 2AA
(0734) 85123 ext. 7939
Fine collection of Classical pottery, the fourth most important in the country, built up by Professor and Mrs Ure; also some Egyptian material.

SANDHURST

Royal Military Academy Sandhurst Collection
Royal Military Academy, Sandhurst, Camberley, Surrey GU15 4PQ
(0276) 63344 ext. 489
Actually in Berkshire despite the postal address; houses collections relating to the Academy's history and a splendid loan collection from the National Army Museum. *By appointment only*.

SLOUGH

Slough Museum

SULHAMPSTEAD

Thames Valley Police Museum
Training Centre, Sulhampstead, Berkshire   (0734) 585111 ext. 3013
Collections showing the history of the Thames Valley Police, including displays on some notable cases such as the Great Train Robbery.

WINDSOR

Berkshire Yeomanry Museum
T.A. Centre, Bolton Road, Windsor, Berkshire SL4 3JG   (0753) 860600
The history of the regiment from 1794.
By appointment only.

Household Cavalry Museum

Royal Mews
Windsor Castle, Windsor, Berkshire
(0753) 868286

Exhibition of gifts presented to the
Queen, plus the royal carriages.

BUCKINGHAMSHIRE

AMERSHAM

Amersham Museum
49 High Street, Amersham,
Buckinghamshire

The museum is being relocated to this
small 15th century hall house and is
due to re-open during 1990.

AYLESBURY

Buckinghamshire County Museum

BUCKINGHAM

Claydon House
Middle Claydon, Nr Buckingham,
Buckinghamshire MK18 2EY
(0296) 73349

18th century house run by National
Trust with splendid rococo
staterooms and a museum with
collections relating to Florence
Nightingale and the Verney family.

CHALFONT ST GILES

Chiltern Open Air Museum

HIGH WYCOMBE

Wycombe Local History and Chair Museum

MILTON KEYNES

Stacey Hill Collection of Industry and Rural Life

Stacey Hill Farm, Southon Way,
Wolverton, Milton Keynes,
Buckinghamshire MK12 5EJ
(0908) 316222

A large collection of domestic and
agricultural items from North Bucks.

OLNEY

Cowper and Newton Museum

PITSTONE

Pitstone Green Farm Museum
Pitstone Green, Pitstone,
Buckinghamshire
(0296) 668223

An extraordinarily varied, large and
important collection relating to local
rural and craft history.

ESSEX

BASILDON

Basildon Heritage Centre
Wat Tyler Country Park, Pitsea,
Basildon, Essex SS16 4UW
(0268) 550088

Rural life displays illustrating domestic
and working life around Basildon since
the late 14th century. *First phase
scheduled to open summer 1991.*

National Motorboat Museum

BRAINTREE

Braintree Museum
Town Hall Centre, Market Square,
Braintree, Essex CM7 6YG
(0376) 43140

Varied collection from the district
including objects associated with the
Courtauld family.

BURNHAM-ON-CROUCH

Burnham-on-Crouch Museum
Providence, Burnham-on-Crouch,
Essex   (0621) 782670

Local history museum that interprets
the history of Burnham.

CANVEY ISLAND

Dutch Cottage Museum
Canvey Island, Essex
(0268) 794005

Tiny 17th-century cottage housing
local history museum.

CHAPPEL and WAKES COLNE

East Anglian Railway Museum
Chappel and Wakes Colne Station,
Colchester, Essex CO6 2DS
(0206) 242524

19th and 20th-century railway
buildings, engines and railway
memorabilia.

CHELMSFORD

Chelmsford and Essex Museum and
Essex Regiment Museum

COLCHESTER

Colchester Castle Museum

Hollytrees Museum

The Minories Art Gallery
74 High Street, Colchester, Essex
CO1 1UE   (0206) 577067

Art collections and temporary
exhibitions.

Natural History Museum
All Saint's Church, High Street,
Colchester, Essex CO1 1DN
(0206) 712481/2

Natural history and geology of Essex.

Social History Museum
Holy Trinity Church, Trinity Street,
Colchester, Essex CO1 1JN
(0206) 712481/2
Rural life and crafts.

Tymperleys Clock Museum

DEDHAM

The Sir Alfred Munnings Art
Museum
Castle House, Dedham, Colchester,
Essex CO7 6AZ   (0206) 322127
The house and work of Sir Alfred
Munnings.

FINCHINGFIELD

Finchingfield Guildhall and Museum
Finchingfield, Essex   (0371) 810504
Local history museum housed in 15th-
century Guildhall.

GRAYS

Thurrock Local History Museum
Central Complex, Orsett Road, Grays,
Essex RM17 5DX   (0375) 383325
Extensive displays of archaeology, and
social, agricultural and industrial
history.

GREAT BARDFIELD

Great Bardfield Cottage Museum
Great Bardfield, Essex
An ancient charity cottage with displays
of farm and domestic equipment.

HALSTEAD

Brewery Chapel Museum
Adams Court, Halstead, Essex
(0787) 237586
Local history exhibition centre in a
Victorian chapel.

HARLOW

Harlow Museum
Passmores House, Third Avenue,
Harlow, Essex CM18 6YL
(0279) 446422
Georgian manor house with local
history and archaeology displays,
including important Roman and
medieval collections; regularly
changing temporary exhibitions.

**Mark Hall Cycle Museum
and Gardens**

MALDON

Maldon Museum
High Street, Maldon, Essex
(0621) 52439
Displays of local history with changing
exhibitions.

SAFFRON WALDEN

Fry Art Gallery
Saffron Walden, Essex
Collection of works by artists who have
lived or worked in north Essex during
the 20th century.

Saffron Walden Museum

SOUTHEND-ON-SEA

Beecroft Art Gallery

Central Museum
Victoria Avenue, Southend-on-Sea,
Essex SS2 6EW   (0702) 330214
Extensive displays covering all aspects
of the town's history, plus changing
exhibitions.

Prittlewell Priory
Priory Park, Victoria Avenue,
Southend-on-Sea, Essex
(0702) 342878
12th-century monastery with wide-
ranging displays, from early books to
20th century radios and
communication equipment.

Southchurch Hall
Southchurch Hall Close,
Southchurch, Southend-on-Sea, Essex
(0702) 67671
14th-century timber-framed manor
house with Tudor additions;
reconstructions and displays on
medieval life.

TILBURY

Riverside Museum
Tilbury Leisure Centre, Anchorfields,
Civic Square, Tilbury, Essex
(03752) 856886/7
Displays telling the story of shipping,
Tilbury docks and life in the riverside
community.

WALTHAM ABBEY

**Epping Forest District
Museum**

WALTON-ON-THE-NAZE

The Old Lifeboat House
East Terrace, Walton-on-the-Naze,
Essex   (02556) 77087
Local agricultural and maritime history
housed in former lifeboat house.

WEST MERSEA

Mersea Island Museum
West Mersea, Essex   (0206) 383301
Small museum with displays covering
local natural and maritime history.

WIVENHOE

Nottage Institute
Wivenhoe, Essex
Educational institute with displays of
local boatbuilding in progress.

HERTFORDSHIRE

ASHWELL

Ashwell Village Museum
Swan Street, Ashwell, Baldock,
Hertfordshire SG7 5NY

Housed in a timber-framed building;
displays cover village life from the
Stone Age to present day.

BISHOP'S STORTFORD

Bishop's Stortford & District Local
History Museum
Cemetery Lodge, Apton Road,
Bishop's Stortford, Hertfordshire
(0279) 7225577

Local archaeological and history
displays.

Rhodes Memorial Museum and
Commonwealth Centre
South Road, Bishop's Stortford,
Hertfordshire   (0279) 51746

Birthplace of Cecil Rhodes, containing
material relating to his life and career.

HATFIELD

**Mill Green Museum and
Mill**

HERTFORD

Hertford Museum

HITCHIN

Hitchin Museum and Art Gallery
Paynes Park, Hitchin, Hertfordshire
SG5 1EQ   (0462) 34476

Extensive displays on the development
of Hitchin including costume and
natural history; also the Herts.
Yeomanry Trust.

HODDESDON

Lowewood Museum
High Street, Hoddesdon,
Hertfordshire   (0992) 445596

Displays relating to the archaeology
and local history of Hoddeson and
Cheshunt.

KNEBWORTH

Knebworth House

LETCHWORTH

**First Garden City Heritage
Museum**

Letchworth Museum

LONDON COLNEY

Mosquito Aircraft Museum
Salisbury Hall, London Colney,
Hertfordshire   (0727) 22051

Many De Havilland aircraft including
the prototype 'Mosquito' built in 1940.

ROYSTON

Royston and District Museum
Lower King Street, Royston,
Hertfordshire SG8 5AL
(0763) 242587

Begun by the Royston and District
Local History Society, the museum
displays themes that relate to the
history of the town and its
surroundings.

ST ALBANS

Museum of St Albans
(formerly City Museum)
Hatfield Road, St Albans,
Hertfordshire AL1 3RR
(0727) 56679/66100 ext. 2927

Story of the modern city since the
departure of the Romans, using
reconstructions, sound, video and
objects.

Verulamium Museum

STEVENAGE

Stevenage Museum

TRING

Zoological Museum

WARE

Ware Museum
The Priory Lodge, High Street, Ware,
Hertfordshire   (0920) 67869

Social history, industry and
archaeology displays telling the 'Story
of Ware'.

WATFORD

Watford Museum

KENT

ASHFORD

Ashford Local History Museum
Central Library, Church Road,
Ashford, Kent   (0233) 20649

History of Ashford and the
immediate area concentrating on
everyday life in the last 150 years.

Intelligence Corps Museum
Templer Barracks, Ashford, Kent
TN23 3HH   (0233) 25251 ext. 208

The history of military intelligence and
the Intelligence Corps from the reign
of Elizabeth I to the present day.

BIRCHINGTON

**The Powell-Cotton Museum
and Quex House**

BROADSTAIRS

Dickens House Museum
2 Victoria Parade, Broadstairs, Kent
(0843) 62853

Devoted to Dickens' connections with
Broadstairs; the house of Mary Strong,
on whom Dickens based the character
of Betsy Trotwood.

CANTERBURY

Canterbury Heritage Time-Walk Museum

Royal Museum and Art Gallery
High Street, Canterbury, Kent
CT1 2JE   (0227) 452747

Exhibitions on local history, decorative arts; regular programme of temporary art exhibitions; also houses the Museum of the East Kent Regiment (The 'Buffs').

CHATHAM

The Historic Dockyard, Chatham

Royal Engineers Museum

CRANBROOK

Local History Museum
Cranbrook, Kent   (0580) 713497

Small local history exhibition and Boyd Alexander collection of birds.

DARTFORD

Dartford Museum
Market Street, Dartford, Kent
DA1 1EU   (0322) 343555

Displays on the human and natural history of the area. Exhibits include the fine glass 'Darenth Bowl' (*c.* AD 450), an extremely rare discovery from the Dark Ages, and a replica of the skull fragments of Swanscombe Man (in fact a woman), the oldest human remains yet found in Britain.

DEAL

Deal Archaeological Collection
Deal Library, Broad Street, Deal,
Kent CT14 6ER   (0304) 374726

New display of local archaeological material of all periods.

Maritime and Local History Museum
22 St George's Road, Deal, Kent
CT14 6BA   (0304) 362896

Original boats, ship models, figureheads and much other material relating to Deal's local history, particularly its maritime connections.

Time-Ball Tower
Victoria Parade, Deal, Kent
(0304) 360897/201066

Semaphore signalling station built in 1821 as part of an anti-smuggling campaign; in 1854 a time-ball was added, which still works every day at 1300. Displays cover the history of maritime communication; also a small collection of local watercolours.

DOVER

Dover Museum
Ladywell, Dover, Kent CT16 1DQ
(0304) 201066

Displays on local and natural history which will shortly move to a new museum being constructed as part of a major heritage centre in Market Square. Museum presently located below the Maison Dieu, restored in the 19th century to form a court and Dover's gaol; cells now open to the public and include displays on crime and punishment. The museum also runs the unique 'Grand Shaft' staircase built in 1809 during the Napoleonic War to connect Dover with the fortifications on the Western Heights.

Dover Transport Museum
Connaught Pumping Station,
Connaught Road, Dover, Kent

History of local land, sea and air transport; exhibits include an 1878 Fox-Walter locomotive, 1890 Folkestone cliff lift car and a Worthington Simpson triple expansion steam pumping engine, currently under restoration.

'All the Queen's Men'
Regimental Museum of the Queen's
Regiment
Dover Castle, Dover, Kent

Military museum (administered by English Heritage) exhibiting the history of the county regiments of Kent, Surrey, Sussex and Middlesex, which were amalgamated in 1966 to form the Queen's Regiment.

Roman Painted House
New Street, Dover, Kent
(0304) 203279

Part of a Roman house found during excavations in the 1970s and now displayed along with associated finds including extensive areas of fine painted wall plaster.

FAVERSHAM

Belmont House and Harris Clock
Collection
Belmont, Nr Throwley, Faversham,
Kent   (079) 589 202

Historic house with important clock collection; worth a special journey.

Fleur de Lis Heritage Centre
13 Preston Street, Faversham, Kent
ME13 8NS   (0795) 534542

Housed in a fine 16th-century building; audio-visual and museum displays explain the history of the town, which has a wealth of historic buildings.

FOLKESTONE

Folkestone Museum
Central Library and Museum, Grace
Hill, Folkestone, Kent CT20 1HD
(0303) 57583

Local and natural history including displays of fossils, birds, archaeology, coins, paintings, prints and drawings.

GOUDHURST

Finchcocks Living Museum of Music

GRAVESEND

Gravesham Museum
High Street, Gravesend, Kent
(0474) 23159

Archaeological finds from the local Roman site at Springhead and a wide range of interesting objects illustrating the history and growth of Gravesend in the last 200 years.

HAWKINGE

Kent Battle of Britain Museum
Aerodrome Road, Hawkinge Airfield, Nr Folkestone, Kent   (0303) 893140

Devoted to the Battle of Britain in 1940. Housed in the original RAF buildings on the airfield that was only minutes from the Luftwaffe bases in the Pas-de-Calais and subsequently subject to repeated attacks. The museum has the largest and most comprehensive collection of aircraft remains recovered from excavation sites in south-east England. There are also extensive collections of RAF and Luftwaffe uniforms, insignia and equipment.

HERNE BAY

Herne Bay Museum
Herne Bay Library, High Street, Herne Bay, Kent   (02273) 4869

Small museum which has recently been redisplayed; tells the story of Herne Bay.

HYTHE

Hythe Local History Room
Oaklands, Stade Street, Hythe, Kent
(0303) 66152

Small local history museum illustrating the importance of this ancient borough.

MARGATE

Margate Museum
Market Square, Margate, Kent

Local history museum displayed in the old police station and court building.

The Tudor House and Museum
King Street, Margate, Kent
(0843) 225511 ext. 317

Early 16th-century timber-framed farmhouse which is one of the oldest buildings in Margate.

MAIDSTONE

Maidstone Museum and Art Gallery

Tyrwhitt-Drake Museum of Carriages

RAMSGATE

Ramsgate Museum
Ramsgate Library, Guildford Lawn, Ramsgate, Kent   (0843) 593532

Museum telling the history of Ramsgate.

Royal Air Force Manston Spitfire Memorial Pavilion
RAF Manston, Nr Ramsgate, Kent
(0843) 89351 ext. 323

Spitfire Mk XVI (TB 752), Gloster Javelin and English Electric Canberra PR3, as well as exhibits illustrating the importance of the airfield in the Second World War; the only front-line Battle of Britain airfield still in use.

ROCHESTER

Guildhall Museum
High Street, Rochester, Kent
ME1 1QU   (0634) 48717

Housed in the fine 17th-century Guildhall. Displays largely show the development of the town and include archaeology, arms and armour, costume and social history material as well as civic regalia.

SANDLING

Museum of Kent Rural Life

SANDWICH

The Precinct Toy Collection
38 Harnet Street, Sandwich, Kent

Collection of dolls houses and toys dating from the last 150 years.

Sandwich Town Museum
Guildhall, Sandwich, Kent
(0304) 617197

History of the town and its immediate locality.

SEVENOAKS

Sevenoaks Museum
Sevenoaks Library, Buckhurst Lane, Sevenoaks, Kent   (0732) 452384

New display showing the history of Sevenoaks and illustrating many aspects of everyday life in the past.

SITTINGBOURNE

Court Hall Museum
The High Street, Milton Regis, Kent
(0795) 22162

Local archaeology and history housed in a 15th-century timber-framed court house.

Dolphin Yard Sailing Barge Museum
Crown Quay Lane, Sittingbourne, Kent   (0622) 62531

Traditional large building and repair yard with display of models, paintings and photographs relating to sailing barges. Housed in the old sail loft. Small collection of barge-building tools.

TENTERDEN

Smallhythe Place
Smallhythe, Nr Tenterden, Kent

Half-timbered 16th-century house now maintained by the National Trust; home of the actress Ellen Terry for many years and contains a small collection of memorabilia connected with her career and the contemporary theatre world.

Tenterden and District Museum
Station Road, Tenterden, Kent
TN30 6HN   (05806) 3605

Small local history museum showing
the history of the town and the rural
life of the surrounding area. Special
collection of material relating to
English and Welsh light railways.

TUNBRIDGE WELLS

Tunbridge Wells Museum and Art
Gallery
Civic Centre, Mount Pleasant,
Tunbridge Wells, Kent TN1 1RS
(0892) 26121 ext. 171

Social history of the area;
comprehensive collection of wooden
Tunbridge Ware. Regular programme
of changing exhibitions.

WHITSTABLE

Whitstable Museum
Oxford Street, Whitstable, Kent
(0227) 452747

New museum in the Old Foresters'
Hall telling the story of this fishing
port.

WYE

Wye College Agricultural Museum
Wye College, Wye, Ashford, Kent
TN25 5AH   (0233) 812401

Extensive collection of mostly 19th and
early 20th century agricultural
equipment housed in a fine 14th-
century barn.

OXFORDSHIRE

ABINGDON

Abingdon Museum
The County Hall, Abingdon,
Oxfordshire   (0235) 23703

Displays illustrating the local history
and archaeology of the town and
environs.

BANBURY

Banbury Museum

BLOXHAM

Bloxham Village Museum
The Court House, Bloxham,
Oxfordshire   (0295) 720283

An ancient and beautiful village whose
history is reflected by the museum,
housed in the court house still
belonging to the Bloxham Foeffees.

BURFORD

Tolsey Museum
The High Street, Burford, Oxfordshire
(0367) 81294

Collections illustrating the social and
industrial history of this magnificent
Cotswold town.

CHARLBURY

Charlbury Museum
Market Street, Charlbury,
Oxfordshire   (0608) 810203

A small museum focusing on the
traditional crafts and industries of
Charlbury.

CHIPPING NORTON

Chipping Norton Museum
New Street, Chipping Norton,
Oxfordshire   (0608) 2754/3779

Displays on local history and local
industries including Bliss Tweed Mill.

CLAYDON

Granary Museum
Butlin Farm, Claydon, Oxfordshire
(0295) 89258

Displays on the homes, farms and
craftsmen's workshops of North
Oxfordshire.

COMBE

Combe Mill
Blenheim Sawmills, Combe,
Oxfordshire   (0867) 52652

Mid-19th century sawmill with
working steam beam engine and
working blacksmith's forge.

DIDCOT

Didcot Railway Centre

DORCHESTER-ON-THAMES

Dorchester Abbey Museum

EAST HENDRED

Champs Chapel Museum
Chapel Square, East Hendred,
Oxfordshire   (0235) 833312

Displays of local history material
housed in an interesting 15th century
chapel.

HENLEY-ON-THAMES

Fawley Court Historic
House and Museum

LONG WITTENHAM

Pendon Museum of Miniature
Landscape and Transport
Long Wittenham, Oxfordshire
(0867) 307365

Enchanting museum of miniature
landscapes including working trains of
the 1930s set in the wilds of Dartmoor.

OXFORD

Ashmolean Museum

The Bate Collection of
Historical Instruments

British Telecom Museum
35 Speedwell Street, Oxford
(0865) 246601

Equipment illustrating the history and
development of telecommunications.
By appointment only.

Cathedral Treasury
Christ Church, Oxford
(0865) 276154

An exhibition of the plate belonging to the cathedral.

Christ Church Picture Gallery

Museum of the History of Science
Old Ashmolean Building, Broad Street, Oxford
(0865) 277280

Housed in the oldest public museum building in the country with highly important and comprehensive collections illustrating the development of the sciences.

Museum of Modern Art
30 Pembroke Street, Oxford
(0865) 815559

Collection of modern photographs, posters, prints etc.; main displays are temporary exhibitions of 20th century art and design, with films, lectures, workshops and performances.

The Museum of Oxford

Oxfordshire and Buckinghamshire Light Infantry Regimental Museum
T.A. Centre, Slade Park, Headington, Oxford
(0865) 778479

Militaria of the county regiment of Oxfordshire and Buckinghamshire.

Pitt Rivers Museum

The University Museum

UFFINGTON

Tom Brown's School Museum
Broad Street, Uffington, Oxfordshire
(0367) 82635

Life and works of Thomas Hughes, author of *Tom Brown's Schooldays*, plus social history collections from the area.

WALLINGFORD

Bensen Veteran Cycle Museum
61 Brook Street, Benson, Wallingford, Oxfordshire   (0491) 38414

A fine collection of some 450 veteran cycles dating from 1818 to 1930.

Wallingford Museum
Flint House, High Street, Wallingford, Oxfordshire
(0491) 35065

History of the town, which once boasted a castle and 14 churches; temporary exhibitions.

WANTAGE

Vale and Dowland Museum Centre

WITNEY

Cogges Manor Farm Museum

WOODSTOCK

Oxfordshire County Museum

SURREY

BAGSHOT

Museum of the Royal Army Chaplain's Department
Bagshot Park, Bagshot, Surrey GU19 5PL   (0276) 71717 ext. 45

History of religious personnel in the British army.

CAMBERLEY

Surrey Heath Museum
Surrey Heath House, Knoll Road, Camberley, Surrey   (0276) 65222

Newly-opened exhibition showing the local history of the area and the heathland habitat.

Royal Military Academy Sandhurst Collection
See Berkshire

CATERHAM

Easy Surrey Museum
1 Stafford Road, Caterham, Surrey
(0883) 40275

Small history museum with changing displays on local topics of interest.

CHERTSEY

Chertsey Museum
The Cedars, 33 Windsor Street, Chertsey, Surrey KT16 8AT
(09328) 65764

Local history museum housed in an attractive 18th century house. Objects relating to the archaeology and history of north-west Surrey; also fine costume collection.

CLANDON

Queen's Royal Surrey Regiment Museum
Clandon Park, West Clandon, Nr Guildford, Surrey

Exhibits connected with the history of Surrey's two infantry regiments, displayed in a National Trust house.

COBHAM

London Bus Preservation Trust
Redhill Road, Nr Cobham, Surrey
(0932) 64078

An independent trust's collection of London buses, complementing the London Transport collection in Covent Garden. Buses dating from the 1930s to the present day in various stages of restoration.

COMPTON

The Watts Gallery

DORKING

Dorking and District Museum

The Old Foundry, West Street, Dorking, Surrey (0306) 883429

Small local museum with exhibits relating to the history and geology of the area.

EGHAM

Egham Museum

Literary Institute, High Street, Egham, Surrey TW20 9EW (0784) 32689

Objects, pictures, maps and documents relating to the history of Egham, particularly in the 19th century.

Royal Holloway and Bedford New College Picture Collection

Royal Holloway and Bedford New College, Egham Hill, Egham, Surrey TW20 0EX (0784) 34455

Superb and nationally-significant collection of 79 paintings donated to the College by its founder, Thomas Holloway, in the 1880s. The College buildings, based on the French château at Chambord, are dramatic and well worth seeing. The collection of 79 paintings was purchased over a very short period and is an extraordinary reflection of Victorian taste. Amongst the more interesting works are Frith's 'The Railway Station', Millais' 'The Princes in the Tower', Landseer's 'God proposes. Man disposes', Holl's 'Newgate: committed for trial' and Long's 'Babylonian Marriage Market'. *By appointment only.*

EWELL

Bourne Hall Museum

Spring Street, Ewell, Surrey KT17 1UF (01) 393 9573

Human and natural history of the area; small art gallery.

FARNHAM

Farnham Museum

FRIMLEY

Royal Army Ordnance Corps Museum

Deepcut, Nr Frimley, Surrey (0252) 24431 Blackdown, ext. 5515

Military museum showing history of Corps from its beginnings to the present day.

GODALMING

Godalming Museum

109a High Street, Godalming, Surrey (0483) 426510

History of Godalming from prehistoric to modern times. Garden in the style of Gertrude Jekyll, who lived in the area.

GUILDFORD

Guildford House Gallery

155 High Street, Guildford, Surrey GU1 3AJ (0483) 503406

Housed in an interesting 17th-century building with fine plaster ceilings. Regular changing exhibitions of regional and national interest with periodic showing of the permanent collection.

Guildford Museum

Women's Royal Army Corps Museum

HASLEMERE

Haslemere Educational Museum

LEATHERHEAD

Leatherhead Museum of Local History

Hampton Cottage, 64 Church Street, Leatherhead, Surrey (0372) 58722

Small museum devoted to local history of the area and housed in a 17th-century timber-framed cottage.

REIGATE

Reigate Priory Museum

Bill Street, Reigate, Surrey RH2 7RL

School museum; the Priory is a 750-year old, Grade 1 listed building. *Restricted opening.*

SHERE

Shere Museum

The Malt House, Shere, Surrey (048) 641 3245

Small museum devoted to the local history of the area and exhibiting mainly Victorian and later objects.

STAINES

Spelthorne Museum

Adjacent to the Old Town Hall, Market Square, Staines, Surrey (0784) 61804

Small museum showing local archaeology and history material.

TILFORD

Old Kiln Museum

Tilford, Nr Farnham, Surrey (025) 125 2300

Extensive collection of objects connected with village and rural life in the 19th and early 20th centuries.

WEYBRIDGE

Brooklands Museum

Weybridge Museum

Weybridge Library, Church Street, Weybridge, Surrey KT13 8DE (0932) 843573

Local history, archaeology, natural history, painting, prints, drawings and costume.

WONERSH

British Red Cross Archives and Historical Exhibition

Barnett Hill, Wonersh, Nr Guildford, Surrey GU5 0RF (0483) 898595

Small display of photographs and objects illustrating the history of the Red Cross movement from 1863. Includes VAO uniforms and memorabilia from the First World War.

B E D F O R D S H I R E

- **Olney**
- **Bedford**
- **Elstow**
- **Old Warden**

Claydon

Banbury

Bloxham

○ Milton Keynes

Ashwell ○   Roys

○ Buckingham

B U C K I N G H A M S H I R E

Letchworth ●

Hitchin ○

○ Chipping Norton

Stevenage

Dunstable ○

● **Luton**   ● **Knebworth**

Charlbury ○

H E R T F O R D S

Combe ○   **Woodstock**

Pitstone ○

○ Burford

Aylesbury ●

Hertford ●

Witney

● **Tring**

Hatfield

○ **Oxford**

St Albans ● ●

Hoddesd

O X F O R D S H I R E

London Colney ○

Abingdon ○

Amersham ○

Watford

Long Wittenham ○   ● **Dorchester-on-Thames**

Chalfont St Giles

Uffington ○

Didcot

High Wycombe

○ Wallingford

Wantage   ○ East Hendred

Cookham-on-Thames

G R E A T E R

Henley-on-Thames ●

○ Maidenhead

L O N D O N

Clewer ○   ● **Eton**

Windsor

B E R K S H I R E   ● **Reading**

Staines ○

Egham ○

Newbury ●

○ Sulhampstead

Bagshot ○   ○ Chertsey

Sandhurst

Weybridge

○ Camberley

Cobham ○   ○ Ewell

○ Frimley

Leatherhead ○

Clandon ○

Caterhan

Towns in which museums
in this guide are located

Guildford ●

Dorking ○   ○ Reigate

Farnham

Compton   ○ Shere

S U R R E Y

● Museums described

○ Wonersh

○ Tilford   Godalming

○ Museums listed only
(excluding town names
already among museums
described)

Haslemere

Index of Museum Names

Index of Subjects

Printed in the United Kingdom for HMSO
Dd. 291112 C50 7/90 3735